The Decorative Work of Robert Adam

OSTERLEY PARK, Middlesex

THE DECORATIVE WORK OF

ROBERT ADAM

DAMIE STILLMAN
Ph.D.

LONDON/ALEC TIRANTI/1966

TO
MY WIFE

PRINTED BY LAWRENCE BROS. (Weston-super-Mare) LTD., WESTON-SUPER-MARE
BOUND BY C. & H. T. EVANS LTD., CROYDON

MADE AND PRINTED IN THE UNITED KINGDOM

CONTENTS

PHOTOGRAPH CREDITS

The following drawings are reproduced by courtesy of the Trustees of Sir John Soane's Museum (photographs of which, excepting Figs. 132 and 133, are by R. B. Fleming & Co. Ltd.): Figs. g, h, l, 8–12, 25, 30, 34, 40, 42, 45, 50, 51, 54–58, 60, 72, 73, 83, 87–89, 93, 99, 103–106, 109, 112, 115–117, 119, 128, 129, 132–134, 136–138, 141, 142, 146, 148–158, 160–162, 165, 168–170.

I am indebted to the following for their courtesy in connexion with other illustrations: Capt. Charles Adam, Figs. 166, 167; B. T. Batsford, Figs. 15, 20, 22, 24, 65; British Museum, Fig. 78; B.T.H.A. Photo Library, Fig. 62; Copper Union Museum, Fig. f; Courtauld Institute of Art, Figs. 38, 39, 82, 107, 110, 111, 159; Derbyshire Countryside Ltd., Fig. 21; Fototeca di Architettura e Topografia dell'Italia Antica, Rome, Figs. 77, 143; Gabinetto Fotografico Nazionale, Figs. 71, 74; Greater London Council, Figs. 33, 80; Lord Jersey, Figs. 26, 28; Metropolitan Museum of Art, Figs. 31, 97, 121; Musée du Louvre, Cabinet des Dessins, Fig. 173; National Buildings Record, Figs. 13–16, 18–20, 22–24, 26, 28, 52, 65, 91, 102, 122, 130, 132, 133; The Hon. Robin Neville (photo: Ministry of Public Building and Works), Figs. i, 126; Philadelphia Museum of Art, Fig. 135; Royal Institute of British Architects, Fig. 76; Scottish National Buildings Record, Figs. 2, 3, 6, 7, 94, 114; Bertram Unné, Figs. 32, 35, 59, 140; University Library, Warsaw, Fig. 79; Victoria and Albert Museum, Figs. 27, 29, 36, 43, 44, 46, 75, 92, 95, 96; Warburg Institute, Figs. 84, 85, 86, 144; F. R. Yerbury, O.B.E., Figs. 14, 16, 18, 19.

The remaining photographs are by the author.

PREFACE AND ACKNOWLEDGEMENTS

The decorative work of Robert Adam was the most significant as well as the most exciting facet of his career, as a result both of circumstances and of his own innate predilections. It is with this aspect of his work that this book is concerned. Attention is focused here on the general interior decorative treatment, the walls, chimney-pieces, ceilings, floors, and decorative accessories. Though mentioned peripherally, exteriors and plans are beyond the scope of this study; and furniture, with the exception of such large pieces as organs, wall cabinets, and bookcases, has similarly been excluded. Within these limits, however, I have tried to trace the development of Adam's decorative style, its sources, and the role of the multitude of collaborators in the creation and execution of that style.

During the research for this study, I have benefited from the help and kindness of many people. My deepest thanks go to Professor Rudolf Wittkower and to Sir John Summerson, both of whom gave freely of their time to advise and encourage me as well as to discuss with me problems and tentative solutions as I worked on this subject. To the scholars who shared with me their unpublished research, I also express my sincere appreciation: Mr. Geoffrey Beard, Mr. Edward Croft-Murray, Mr. John Fleming, and Professor Thomas J. McCormick.

I am grateful to Columbia University for the award of a University Fellowship in 1959–60 which made possible my research in Europe and to the Faculty Grants Committee of Oakland University for generous financial assistance toward the purchase of photographs for this volume.

To the owners of Adam houses and to their estate agents who greatly facilitated my research, I am indeed thankful. Many of them not only allowed me to take photographs all through their houses and to examine documents and drawings, but also gave generously of their time.

I am indebted also to the many librarians and curators who assisted me in my research. I cannot mention all of them, but I should like specifically to express my thanks to the following: Miss Dorothy Stroud of Sir John Soane's Museum whose assistance during the months that I spent there and in the years since has been invaluable; Mr. John Harris, Mrs. Prunella Fraser, and Mr. James Palmes of the Royal Institute of British Architects; Mr. Cecil Farthing and the staff of the National Buildings Record; Mr. Adolf Placzek and the staff of Avery Library, Columbia University; Dr. C. T. McInnes and Mr. W. Anderson of the Historical Records Dept., Register House, Edinburgh; Miss Catherine Cruft of the Scottish National Buildings Record; Mr. Keith K. Andrews of the National Gallery of Scotland; Major T. Ingram, Archivist of Nostell Priory; Mr. F. G. Emmison and Miss Nancy Briggs of the Essex Record Office; Mr. E. J. Davis and Mr. A. G. Veysey of the Buckingham County Record Office; and various members of the staffs of the Metropolitan Museum of Art and the Victoria and Albert Museum.

For assistance with photography and in the obtaining of photographs, I am indebted to Mr. Ron Shirk; Messrs. R. B. Fleming & Co. Ltd; and Miss M. Elinor Betts.

Finally, I should like to thank my wife for her constant encouragement, for her reading of my manuscript and her many suggestions for improvement, and for her readiness at all times to read a section or to discuss with me the myriad problems that arose in the writing of this work.

CHAPTER ONE

INTRODUCTION

In 1792, the year of Robert Adam's death, Thomas Malton published a book entitled *A Picturesque Tour Through the Cities of London and Westminster*. In this work, he effectively described the contribution of Robert and James Adam to English architecture and decoration:

> To their researches among the vestiges of antiquity, we are indebted for many improvements in ornamental architecture; and for the introduction of a style of decoration, unrivalled for elegance and gaiety; which, in spite of the innovations of fashion, will prevail so long as good taste exists in the nation.[1]

By the end of his career, Robert Adam, with the help of his younger brother James and a host of craftsmen and office assistants, had indeed succeeded in bringing about a significant change in the planning, decoration, and furnishing of English houses. Although acknowledged by Malton and others in 1792, the change was already apparent by the middle of the 1760's. Within only a few years of his return from Italy in 1758, Adam had evolved a style that was to dominate English architecture during a substantial part of the last half of the eighteenth century. His style was an important manifestation of international Neo-classicism, and in England Adam was among its most influential practitioners.

Born and trained in Scotland, Robert Adam undertook a Grand Tour from 1754 to 1758, and this Italian sojourn was both the decisive event of his life and the catalyst of his style. When he left Edinburgh in the autumn of 1754, Adam fully intended to return to live and practice there, but within a half-year of his arrival in Rome he had changed his mind and broadened his horizons. London was to be his arena. With his characteristic attention to the main chance, Adam lost no time in establishing his office in London in 1758 and in making himself known to the nobility and gentry. Very soon, his services were in great demand, and by 1760 he had already acquired a number of his most famous commissions. Three years later he could write of his extensive work all over England, 'which I am with difficulty able to get managed with Honour to myself & Satisfaction to my Employers.'[2] His practice had expanded by the middle of the 1760's into one of the most important in England.

Until his death in 1792, Adam remained a powerful force in English architecture. A new group of architects emerged in the 1770's and '80's to claim a portion of the patronage and fame that Adam had shared in the 1760's only with Chambers and, to a lesser extent, Stuart. Yet, Adam's activity in the year before his death still included, in the words of his obituary notice, '8 great public works, beside 25 private buildings, so various in their style, and so beautiful in their composition, that they have been allowed, by the best judges, sufficient of themselves to establish his fame unrivaled as an artist.'[3]

The fame that was heaped upon Adam was something that he and his brother James did not shirk. With uncommon candour, they took credit for having 'brought about in this country, a kind of revolution in the whole system of this useful and elegant art.'[4] This 'kind of revolution' was the Adam brothers' term for the introduction of Neo-classicism into English architecture, the anglicizing of the spirit and details of ancient art. The result was antiquity selected, rearranged, flattened, and made both more decorative and more elegant by an eighteenth-century master. It was classical art tempered by Robert Adam's Scottish training, by his acquaintance with Burlingtonian Palladianism in England, by what he saw in Italy, and by the ideas that permeated mid-eighteenth-century Europe. To a substantial extent, the Adams were justified in their claim.

The exact nature of their contribution was also indicated by the Adams, and in this, too, they were merely stating the truth, unencumbered by the requisites of modesty. They cited as their innovations 'a remarkable improvement . . . in the form, convenience, arrangement, and relief of apartments; a greater movement and variety, in the outside composition, and in the decoration of the inside, an almost total change.'[5] Of these three major areas, exterior architectural treatment, as they themselves realized, was the least significant, though it was none the less influential. This is partially due to Adam's relatively smaller number of commissions for completely new buildings. By the time of his appearance in London at the end of the 1750's, the spate of great country house building that had characterized the Burlingtonian era was largely at an end.[6] While Adam did erect some structures from the ground up, his primary activity was the redecoration of older houses and the completion of works already under construction.

In the exteriors that he designed, Adam was neither so adventurous nor so revolutionary as his own statements might indicate. His façade compositions were largely dependent on Burlingtonian precedents, though, as with all of Adam's work, made both more attenuated and more elegant. To the end of his life, Adam retained the staccato-like emphasis on centre and ends that had characterized such major Palladian structures as Holkham or the Horse Guards, and his later *b* exterior designs (Register House, Edinburgh, 1770–92; or Gosford House, *c*1790) show relatively little advance over his early ones (*e.g.*, first proposal for Osterley, *a* 1761; projected south front at Kedleston). This 'staccato' quality is related to the concept of movement, which the Adams cited as one of their contributions, a

2

concept they defined as 'the rise and fall, the advance and recess, with other diversity of form, in the different parts of a building, so as to add greatly to the picturesqueness of the composition.'[7]

Figure a. Proposed South Front for Kedleston Hall, Derbyshire, *c*1760–61. From Colen Campbell, *Vitruvius Britannicus*, ed. J. Woolfe and J. Gandon, Vol. IV (1767), Pl. 45.

Also derived from Burlingtonian architecture was Adam's devotion to the Palladian motif within a relieving arch, a virtual insignia of his exterior designs. On the other hand, such new themes as sculptured plaques, columned-screened entrances, and attenuated orders, as well as the much freer use of the orders altogether, indicate the influence of Adam's Grand Tour on his exterior designs. The coupling of Ionic capitals with a Doric entablature (*e.g.*, Society of Arts) effectively demonstrates his freedom from rules. These innovations and the tendency toward elongation and delicacy in exterior treatments were influential aspects of the 'Adam Style,' yet planning and decoration were far more significant.

The Adam brothers were interested in the problems of planning almost from the start of their careers. Sketches by James in a volume of 1755 and the multitude of sketch plans drawn in Rome by Robert[8] evince a concern with room shapes and arrangements that was to blossom in England in the early 1760's. A fascination with the form and disposition of rooms is seen in the circular, oval, and octagonal spaces and their placement as well as in the transformation of rectangular or square rooms into far more exciting areas by means of screens of columns and the introduction of apses. Robert Adam's study of antique *thermae*, of their interpretation by the Burlingtonians, and of the room shapes and *enfilade* of French eighteenth-century architecture led to a remarkable proliferation of unusual shapes and interesting relationships between the rooms. Perhaps the best illustration of

a, b, c

c

3

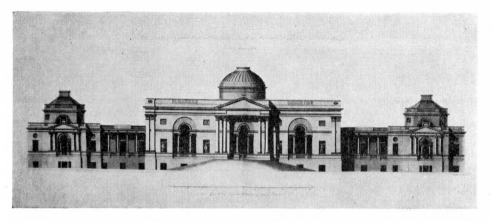

Figure b. West Front of Gosford House, East Lothian, *c*1790. From George Richardson, *New Vitruvius Britannicus*, Vol. I (1802), Pls. 49–50.

d his finesse in planning is seen as early as 1761 in his design for Syon. Here, within a sixteenth-century shell with varying floor levels, Adam designed a succession of impressive (and sumptuous) rooms. Adam's subsequent career was marked by a continued delight in inventive and unusual plans, as displayed adroitly in such town house designs of the 1770's as Derby House, Grosvenor
e Square.

Within an exciting progression of spaces, Adam introduced the decorative work that is the central aspect of his style, the crux of his 'kind of revolution.' Robert and James felt, as Robert's would-be biographer John Clerk of Eldin wrote:

> that their art must ever remain extremely deficient, untill they should be able to supply some new & undiscovered resources for the internal decoration of private apartments, by introducing elegance, gayity, & variety, instead of that dull & elaborate floridity, which universally prevailed in the buildings of this Island, till the time of Mr Adam's return from abroad.[9]

Even here, of course, Robert did not break completely with the style of his predecessors. Rather, he retained parts of it, combining these with various innovations to produce a synthesis characterized certainly by 'elegance, gayity, & variety.' This interior style is truly his hall-mark, the facet of his work evoked by the label 'Adam Style.' It is the Adam chimney-piece or Adam ceiling, Adam wall decoration or Adam carpet, as well as Adam furniture, that is most frequently noted as the principal characteristic of his art. This was partially, as we have seen, a matter of circumstances but partially also a matter of Adam's own disposition.

While Adam had relatively fewer commissions for totally new structures, even in cases where he built anew, the exterior designing was generally of lesser

Plate IV.

Elevation of the House of the Society for the Encouragement of Arts, Manufactures & Commerce, situated in John Street, Adelphi.

Elevation de la Maison de la Societé pour l'Encouragement des Arts, des Manufactures, et du Commerce, situeé dans la Rue de Jean, aux Adelphi.

ARTS AND COMMERCE PROMOTED.

Figure c. Façade of Society of Arts, Adelphi, London, *c*1772. From *The Works in Architecture of Robert and James Adam*, Vol. I (1773), Part iv, Pl. 4.

consequence than his interior work. This is especially noticeable in the succession of London residences of the 1770's, for in the most famous houses, such as those for Lady Home or Sir Watkin Williams-Wynn, Adam lavished the greatest attention on the interior, rather than the façade. And the most challenging of all of his works were those, typified by Syon or Osterley, where Adam was called upon to remodel and redecorate older houses.

48–52, 84–87
38, 39, 159

14–19, 62
27–29, 46, 75

If Adam was compelled to concentrate on interior decoration, he was, despite his longing for 'the grand,'[10] not unsympathetic to his task. The specific innovations claimed by the Adams emphasize their interior treatment—a great diversity of ceilings, friezes, and decorated pilasters coupled with a mixture of grotesque stuccoes, painted ornaments, and rinceaux.[11] And Adam's attention to all the facets of decoration in a number of his projects—including such minor elements 160–165 as door knobs, escutcheons, fire grates, candlesticks, and silver plate—surely indicates his addiction to decoration. It is indeed his decorative work that is the most imposing aspect of his *oeuvre*.

*   *   *

For his career as an architect and designer, Robert Adam had prepared himself well, and he did not intend to fail. The twenty-nine year old figure who thrust himself onto the London architectural scene in January 1758 was neither a novice nor a student. He had been a practicing architect for at least six years and had absorbed the atmosphere and inspiration of Italy. Born in Kirkcaldy, Fifeshire, in 1728, he was the second son of William Adam, the leading Scottish architect of his day. Robert attended the high school in Edinburgh and in 1743 matriculated at Edinburgh University.[12] Like his older brother John, Robert was trained by his father and towards the end of William Adam's career assisted him in his architectural work. After the father's death in 1748, the two elder brothers continued their father's architectural works and his commissions under contract for the Board of Ordnance and private individuals; they put into execution plans previously devised by William Adam; and they engaged in new projects of their own. It was this experience at building, as well as designing, in Scotland in the six years before his departure for Italy in 1754 that laid the basis for Robert's practice and his style after his establishment in London. Despite the enormous influence of the Italian sojourn, the early years in Scotland formed an enduring aspect of the Adam manner. The impact of Italy and of Neo-classicism not on a 2 blank slate but upon an architect trained in William Adam's robust manner and influenced by the lighter, English Rococo spirit of the late 1740's and early 1750's produced the style of Robert Adam.

This new and lighter style of decoration was the principal innovation of the Adam brothers in the years immediately following their father's death. In the

6

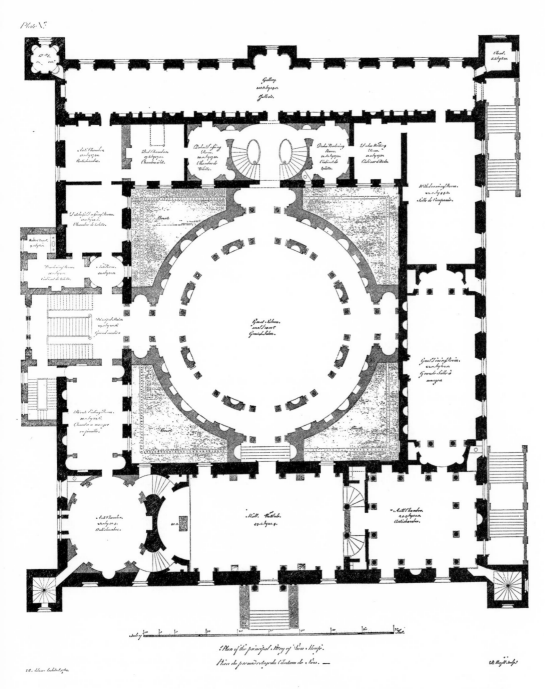

Plate V.

Figure d. Plan of the Principal Floor of Syon House, Middlesex, *c*1760–61. From *The Works in Architecture of Robert and James Adam*, Vol. I (1773), Part i, Pl. 5.

7

main project at hand, the completion of Hopetoun House, and in their own commissions of the mid-1750's, especially Dumfries House (1754–60) and the west wing of Arniston (begun *c*1754), John and Robert, and later James as well, introduced Rococo cartouches, loosely-flowing foliage friezes, a variety of chimney-pieces, and, on the whole, a greater delicacy. Despite the generally Rococo nature of the decorations, the seeds of Robert's later development can already be seen in these Scottish works of the 1750's.

At Hopetoun, the Adam brothers' most important decorative activity was concentrated in the present Yellow and Red Drawing Rooms. The Yellow Drawing Room with its foliage and floral frieze, modillioned cornice, and cove punctuated by magnificent Rococo cartouches in the corners was probably begun in the earlier part of the 1750's, though its exact date is not known. Work on the Red Drawing Room, started by the middle of the decade, was completed, except for the red damask wall covering, in 1760.[13] The frieze, cove, and ceiling again illustrate the Rococo influence evident in the cartouches of the first room, while in the ceiling flat there appear touches of *Chinoiserie*. These elements, combined with the ceiling division, the raised guilloche-decorated mouldings, the modillioned cornice, and the caryatid chimney-piece, create an effect very much on a par with English decoration in the early and mid-1750's.

The chimney-piece with stiles composed of female figures was the forerunner of a series of such pieces that adorn Robert's early houses in England. Carved by Michael Rysbrack, it was already under way by 18 November 1756, when the sculptor listed it among his current projects. In addition to his written description of the Hopetoun chimney-piece, there are two Rysbrack drawings that are related to it. On the other hand, Robert Adam's responsibility for some share in the design of this piece is suggested by two letters that he wrote from Rome in the spring and summer of 1755, for he there commented upon a chimney-piece sketch with some alterations that he had sent to Lord Hopetoun. While it cannot definitely be determined if the Red Drawing Room chimney-piece is the one to which Adam referred, the very classical frieze of griffins and candlesticks possibly indicates the classicizing 'alteration' inspired by Rome. The interrelationship of Adam and Rysbrack in this work is further complicated by their probable collaboration on a similar piece at Hatchlands, Adam's first important English commission, and by the occurrence of this type of chimney-piece, though without the classical detail of the Hopetoun example, in English work of the second quarter of the century.[14]

As at Hopetoun, the chimney-pieces designed for Dumfries House and Arniston were also to serve Adam in London as well as in Scotland. The chimney-piece with both front- and side-facing console stiles in the drawing room at Dumfries and the Ionic colonnette stiles, corner urns, and decorative tablet of the drawing room piece at Arniston both reappear in Adam's English works.

Figure e. Plan of the Parlour Floor of Derby House, Grosvenor Sq., London, 1773. From *The Works in Architecture of Robert and James Adam*, Vol. II (1778), Part i, Pl. 1.

3–6 The same stylistic similarity between these three major Scottish works of the Adam brothers can also be seen in other aspects of their decoration. The modillioned cornices, the loose foliage friezes, and the lively decoration in medium relief are found in all three works; while the wide cove with Rococo decoration and the raised mouldings ornamented with guilloches in the Red Drawing Room at 6 Hopetoun are likewise features of the drawing room at Arniston. Equally Rococo 7 is the ceiling of that room with its birds amidst C-scrolls and S-scrolls of foliage.

Despite the rush of activity caused by the various works of the young Adam brothers, Robert was able to make a trip to England in 1749–50, and this was probably a strong impetus for the more Rococo style that characterized Adam decoration of the 1750's. Four years after his first visit to London, Robert stopped there briefly again, but this time he was on his way to Italy. Among his principal artistic tastes as he began his Grand Tour were the softened Rococo manner, the Palladianism of Burlington and Kent, and the playful, unarchaeological type of 166–167 Gothic then popular. These tastes and traditions persisted, but they were overlaid by a world of new ideas and designs. The Adam style was born in Italy from the interplay of these various forces.

Robert's journey took him through Brussels, Paris, and the south of France to Genoa and from there to Pisa and Florence, before his arrival in Rome on 24 February 1755. Along the way he met many people of importance and social position, attended a good many operas, saw the Roman ruins of Provence, and sketched some of the sights. But he also made in Florence the most important acquaintance of his Italian sojourn—and perhaps of his entire career. That individual was Charles-Louis Clérisseau, and no better description of his importance to Adam can be found than the letter Robert wrote home on 19 February 1755:

> I found out Clerisseau, A Nathaniel in whom tho' there is no guile, Yet there is the utmost knowledge of Architecture of perspective & of Designing & Colouring I ever Saw, or had any Conception of; He rais'd my Ideas, He created emulation & fire in my Breast. I wish'd above all things to learn his manner, to have him with me at Rome, to Study close with him & to purchase of his works. what I wish'd for I obtain'd; He took a liking to me, He ingag'd in doing what drawings I pleas'd. He engag'd to go with me to Rome & if it suited my Conveniency wou'd Stay in the Same House with me, wou'd Serve me as an Antiquarian, wou'd teach me perspective & Drawing, wou'd give me Copys of all his Studys of the Antique Basrelievos & other ornaments, in Short he sets out the day after me in order to be at my Command as Soon as I arrive at Rome, And I shall furnish him a Chamber & pay his [meals?], And think it is one of the luckyest circumstances cou'd have happen'd.[15]

Clérisseau (1722–1820), a French architect and delineator of ruins, had won a *Prix de Rome,* had studied at the French Academy in Rome, was acquainted with the young French architects in the forefront of the new movement, and was *au courant* with the ideas of the newly developing Neo-classicism. In addition, as

Adam wrote eight months later, 'he has all these Knacks, so necessary to us Architects.'[16] The relationship between the two men was complex, for while Clérisseau instructed Adam in the drawing of ruins and in the study of antiquities, he also executed commissions for Adam. It was certainly not an employer-employee situation, but neither was it a master-pupil one. The full impact on Robert's style of his journey to Italy was a direct result of the Adam-Clérisseau interchange.

From Clérisseau's teaching and that of Laurent Pécheux (1729–1821), his master of anatomical drawing, Adam learned a good deal that would be useful to him. It was a vigorous course of instruction, but he worked eagerly. He sketched daily with Clérisseau, and he examined ancient ruins and Renaissance palaces. He began assembling an impressive store of study materials—architectural fragments and casts, professional drawings of decoration, and drawings executed by the draftsmen whom he employed. He became imbued with a sense of the grand, was caught up in the archaeological excitement of the day, and was introduced to the advanced theories of Laugier and Winckelmann. These influences, conveyed to him by the aesthetic climate of Rome, by Clérisseau, and by Piranesi, were to alter substantially his architectural taste. Through Clérisseau and Pécheux Adam met Mengs and almost certainly Winckelmann, and in Piranesi he knew the foremost exponent of the archaeological fervour characteristic of Neo-classicism. Though Adam somewhat distrusted Piranesi and reacted rather strongly to the Italian engraver's personality, he considered Piranesi to be the only Italian of the time 'to breath the Antient Air.'[17]

At the same time as Adam was learning to draw in a new way and studying ancient, Renaissance, and Baroque buildings and especially their decoration, he was also cultivating certain English nobles. All of this was part of a concerted effort to prepare himself for a London career, and his two years in Rome were filled with both artistic and social activities. In addition, he saw the remains of Herculaneum and the other ancient sites in the vicinity of Naples—Pozzuoli, Baia, and Cumae. Finally, in May 1757, fully supplied with drawings, sketches, architectural fragments, and two draftsmen, Adam, accompanied still by Clérisseau, left Rome on the start of his return journey. After stops in Florence, Bologna, and Venice, Adam and his entourage went to Spalato (Split) to measure and draw the ruins of Diocletian's Palace. During their six-week stay (22 July– 28 August 1757), Clérisseau did perspective sketches; the two draftsmen made measured drawings; and Adam presumably supervised, sketched and studied the ruins.

Adam's visit to Spalato, or Spalatro as he called it, was ostensibly based on his desire to study the remains of a great domestic building of the Romans, regardless of its late date (*circa* A.D.300). Though he may have been sincerely interested in Roman domestic architecture, the choice of Spalato was probably determined for more pragmatic reasons—its accessibility and the fact that it had not been previously investigated. Adam had wanted to visit Calabria, Sicily, and Greece, but did not have the time.[18] Spalato seems to have been the substitute, with the results sumptuously published in 1764 as the *Ruins of the Palace of the Emperor Diocletian at Spalatro in Dalmatia*. By then it was an anti-climax, as far as its original purpose was concerned, for Robert Adam no longer needed a 'puff' to spread his name. By 1764 he was already among the busiest architects of the day.

After making arrangements in Venice for the engraving of the plates, Adam and his group went on to Vicenza, where Adam and Clérisseau parted company. Adam with his two draftsmen went north to Germany, and Clérisseau returned to Venice to supervise the engraving of the *Spalatro* plates while awaiting the arrival of James Adam, whom he was also to accompany throughout Italy. Robert travelled through Germany and the Low Countries, finally reaching London on 17 January 1758. And there he began immediately to set himself up as an architect of distinction. He attracted clients, and before the year was out he was already at work on several commissions. In these and in the commissions of the succeeding years he introduced a new style combining the fruits of his Italian tour with his Scottish training. This new style is to be seen earliest and most completely in his decorative work.

Figure f. Design for a Lamp, *c*1755. Cooper Union Museum, New York.

CHAPTER TWO

ADAM'S DECORATIVE WORK

ITS CHARACTER AND COMPONENTS

If the Adam style of decoration was born in Italy during Robert's Grand Tour, it matured very rapidly in the brisker climate of his first years in London. Within two years of his return from Italy, Adam had not only established his practice but also set the keynote for his style. And by the middle of the 1760's, after only seven years in the capital, he had expanded that practice into one of the leading ones in England and had developed the diverse elements of his style into a unified whole. His earliest designs in England present a virtually undigested mixture of ideas and motifs, a mélange of elements from his career in Scotland and his studies and observations in Italy. Very quickly, however, Adam refined his style, eliminating certain features and modifying others. He pruned the excesses and the robustness, flattened most of his relief, and suppressed the ambiguities in such a way as to produce a style completely devoid of tension, an elegant and linear style. It was a style characterized by novelty and variety, theme and infinite variation.

Despite the rapid maturating of the Adam style and its subsequent development in the direction of increased delicacy, attenuation, and refinement, its basis was firmly laid in the early years of Adam's London career. The first two years in London, the 'first flash of Character,' as Robert described it in advance,[19] is thus an extremely significant period, for it demonstrates in capsule form Adam's ties to tradition and his innovations. The inheritances from his Scottish manner are very much in evidence in Adam's [11] earliest identifiable domestic work, an addition to Thistleworth House for General Humphrey Bland in 1758–59, though they are also to be found in an unexecuted [10] design for the remodelling of Castle Ashby and in his first major project, the [12] decoration of Hatchlands (both of 1759). While the general heaviness of the three designs is the most striking difference from his later works, these projects include specific interior architectural features of a more conservative nature. The modillioned cornices, tabernacle frames, overmantels (including one with a broken pediment), door cornices on brackets, and chimney-pieces all hark back to the Adam brothers' work in Scotland. Robert himself was aware that the Thistleworth

15

drawing room was by no means in the true antique style, but he blamed this failing on his inability 'to get English workmen who will leave their angly Stiff Sharp manner.' Still, he added, 'As they know no better in England they cannot be so vext as I am myself nay perhaps they like it better than they wou'd in t[he] other manner.'[20]

11, 115

The difficulties with workmen and his own training in Scotland did not prevent Adam from introducing into his early designs a number of elements of the new Neo-classicism. Plaques inspired by ancient reliefs; arabesque foliage; and such motifs as anthemia, urns, and griffins indicate, even at Thistleworth, Adam's new allegiance. This is further emphasized in the designs for the re-decorated hall at Castle Ashby and the dining room at Hatchlands, where the most impressive features are the grotesque panels. Although filled with thick and fairly simple forms, these unexecuted panels represent one of the most important innovations of the Adam style, with the grotesque decorations here already demonstrating the illogical mixture of elements that characterizes the far more intricate examples of his mature work. In addition to the grotesques, such other Italianate features as ruin scenes, niches, screens of columns under an arch, and various classical plaques are included in these wall elevations. The ceilings at Hatchlands similarly illustrate the combination of traditional and new elements, of inheritances and innovations.

9, 10, 12

117, 118

In the next five years or so, the first half of the 1760's, Adam pulled together these disparate elements into a coherent and elegant style. It is this style that characterizes the beginning of his great series of country houses, as well as the first of his London works. At Shardeloes (c1761–64),[21] Kedleston Hall (1760–68), Croome Court (1760–66), Syon House (c1760–69), Bowood (1761–c1770), Mersham-le-Hatch (1761–72), and Audley End (1762–67), as well as other country seats, can be seen substantial amounts of decorative work that Adam designed prior to 1766. The most important town house begun during this period was Lansdowne House (begun c1761, though decorations date mainly from the mid-1760's), but there were other less grandoise designs. Together these various projects demonstrate the swift maturing of the Adam manner. In them we can witness the smoothing out of the heavy architectural elements and the lightening of the plaster decoration, the subordinating of many obviously Palladian features and the refining and classicizing of others. The antique inspiration is more pronounced, and the designs become suave and assured. As the style develops, one is less conscious of the mixture of elements; it is the overall effect of refine-ment and elegance that triumphs.

13–25

Adam's rapid development during the first half of the 1760's can be seen very effectively by comparing two of the rooms at Syon House, the hall designed in 1761 and the gallery designed at least by 1763 though not quite completed in 1767. Even considering the difference in character and scale of the two rooms—the large two-storey entrance hall and the interminably long gallery—the change

14

15

16

in Adam's style in two years is enormous. The protruding half-columns, bold architectural decoration, and powerful ceiling in high relief in the hall have given way in the gallery to attenuated pilasters with painted arabesque ornamentation, low-relief stucco decoration on the walls, and a ceiling that is flat, linear, and complex.

Having achieved a mature style by the mid-1760's, Adam further consolidated and refined it during the last half of that decade and the first year or two of the next. Many of the decorative projects begun in the earlier part of the 1760's reached the finishing stage in the mid- or late-sixties, and there were many new undertakings of importance. The later rooms at Bowood and Kedleston were paralleled by such other country house interiors as those of Harewood House (designs dated mainly 1765–71, but with some as late as 1777), Kenwood (1764–73, with later work), the earlier rooms at Osterley Park (begun 1766), Nostell Priory (begun 1766), Newby Hall (begun c1767), and Saltram House (1768–71). In London, too, a number of town houses began to testify to the new style and to Adam's success. Among them were the major rooms at Lansdowne House and the newer commissions at Coventry House (Piccadilly, 1765–67), General Burgoyne's (Hertford Street, 1769–71), Northumberland House (begun 1770), and the first and greatest of the Adam speculative schemes, the Adelphi (1768–75). It was a period of intense activity and of increasingly flat and elegant designs.

27–36
80, 81
128–140

The major interior architectural features tend to be less pronounced and more subsidiary to the overall decorative effect. The chimney-pieces are more elaborate and not as ponderous, though types developed in the Scottish practice or in the first years in England are still much in use, if somewhat less vigorous. Ceilings become more complex and much flatter, while small delicate classical motifs appear all over—in ceilings and friezes, chimney-pieces and panels. Colour, which Adam had begun to exploit in his earlier projects, now assumes the crucial role that it was to maintain to the end of his career.

The library of Kenwood (1767–69) epitomizes Adam's style during this period. Using a tunnel-vaulted ceiling, which he considered the most impressive type, and a pair of apses set off from the central area by screens of columns, Adam created a magnificent room in which all of the parts are subordinated to the whole. Here Adam effectively demonstrated his ability to take aspects of ancient art—the shape of the ceiling, its division into small decorative panels, the screened apses, and much of the detailed decoration—and make of them interiors aptly suited to life in late eighteenth-century England.

33

Despite its basically flat decoration, the Kenwood library is by no means a purely linear exercise. Adam's movement in that direction, however, characterizes his work of the 1770's. To Horace Walpole, who had once been an admirer of the Adam style, this period of Adam's work was 'all gingerbread, filigraine, and fan-painting';[22] but it was also the era of his most elegant and linear manner. During the decade from the early 1770's to the early 1780's, Adam achieved an amazing synthesis, combining certain Burlingtonian inheritances with a wide range of more classical influences and subjecting the whole to a process of refinement and linearization. In some ways Adam erred on the side of delicacy and over-elaboration, as Walpole's criticism suggests, but in general the decoration is so flat and elegant that one is hardly conscious of the minutiae, which are completely subservient to the overall effect.

This style is seen at its best in such town houses as Sir Watkin Williams-Wynn's (20 St. James's Square, 1772–74), Derby House (Grosvenor Square, 1773–74), Apsley House (Hyde Park Corner, 1774–75), Home House (20 Portman Square, 1775–77), Sir Abraham Hume's (17 Hill Street, 1778–79), and Cumberland House (Pall Mall, 1780–81, 1785). Yet, it also pervades the large number of country commissions upon which Adam was then engaged. The later rooms at Osterley are highly characteristic of Adam's manner of the 1770's, and the same is true of those at Nostell Priory. Among the new projects were Headfort House (Ireland, *c*1770–73), Moccas Court (1775–81), Wormleybury (1777–79), and Culzean Castle (*c*1777–91).

The difference between Adam's decorative work of the seventies and that of the late sixties can be emphasized by juxtaposing the music room at Home House with the library at Kenwood. The delicate linear elegance and the extreme attenuation of the later room with its exquisite decoration make it a perfect foil to the more substantial elegance of the Kenwood library. Typical, too, of the direction of Adam's development in the 1770's is his most striking innovation of the decade, the 'Etruscan' room. In the only fully preserved example, that at Osterley, and in the drawings for the others, the refinement and the almost rarified classicism of Adam's most linear style are readily apparent.

Also symptomatic of Adam's development during this decade are the introduction of chimney-pieces with broad, flat, and complex stiles and the increasing complexity of the tripartite ceilings. These tendencies continue into the very early years of the 1780's in such rooms as the great dining room at Cumberland House or the library and drawing room at Byram, where the Adam manner of the 1770's is preserved and, if anything, heightened.

In the period from about 1781 to 1789, Adam was engaged on far fewer projects, due partially to a decline in 'the national ardour for the fine arts,' caused by the American War of Independence.[23] But in the spate of activity during the last three or four years before his death in 1792, the elegant, linear manner typical of Adam's style at its zenith is still present. During these years Adam tends at times to combine delicate and complex sections with a relatively sparser wall treatment, as in some of the rooms at Newliston (*c*1789–92), though in his most impressive domestic projects, such as the designs for Archerfield (*c*1790–91), we see the characteristic elegance, refinement, and elaboration. Grotesque panels, attenuated pilasters with exquisite decoration, classical plaques, and complex ceiling designs are all present in the Archerfield designs. Yet even here, there is

18

that most telling indication of the traditional influences on the Adam style, the Palladian motif within a relieving arch.

Across a span of thirty-five years, Adam greatly modified his early manner, adding some new elements and reducing certain ties to his predecessors. But despite the lapse of time and the increased delicacy and linearization, Adam's late works remain a highly developed version of his 'first flash' in England. He had introduced a new style, and he remained true to it, perfecting, refining, and elaborating it, but never deserting it. Although this can be seen by looking at his work as a whole, it is even more evident when one examines the various aspects of Adam's interior decoration in some detail.

WALL DECORATION

Adam's treatment of wall decoration—from the pronounced architectural character of his earliest designs to the two-dimensional elegance of the 1770's and later—furnishes perhaps the most succinct summary of the development of the Adam style. In Robert's first designs for interiors in England—Thistleworth, Castle Ashby, and Hatchlands—the relatively heavy architectural decoration and numerous projecting forms vied with such Neo-classical elements as niches, alcoves, and a variety of friezes and decorative panels. The more *avant-garde* features tend to become more significant as the 1760's advance, whereas the more conservative architectural ones receive less and less attention, though they survive, at least in modified form, for a good part of Adam's career.[24]

9–12

The tendency toward flatness and away from more conventional interior wall treatments is especially noticeable in Adam's use of the classical orders. The architectonic character of General Bland's drawing room, for example, soon gives way to a less orthodox use of the orders, as in the dining room at Syon (*c*1761–63), where the only columns are in the screens across the alcoves and in the overmantel. There are friezes and bands but no full entablatures, and the chimney-piece and overmantel are the sole projections from the wall. Again, the contrast between the hall and gallery at Syon demonstrates Adam's strong movement toward two-dimensionality and a less traditional employment of the orders. Columns with heavy entablatures are replaced by pilasters whose very supporting character is destroyed by decorative panels inserted in place of the usual shaft. The Syon gallery is an excellent example of Adam's retention of interior architectural features in a modified, flatter, and more subdued role. There are pilasters and tabernacle frames, but they are flat and subsidiary to the general wall treatment, completely different from such earlier efforts as that at General Bland's.

11
18

14, 15

19

By the late 1760's, the flat, attenuated, and decorative use of the orders is quite common in Adam's work. The hall at Osterley, like that at Syon, includes orders, alcoves, and classical statuary; but the aim is refinement and the effect

27, 14

19

33 quite different. Even the library at Kenwood, despite its size and magnificence and its screens of columns, is characterized by a basically flat decorative treatment. This becomes more emphatic and the interiors even less architectonic in the 1770's, when such projects as Home House demonstrate extremely attenuated pilasters **52** and delicate wall decoration (music room), pilasters with refined arabesque panels **51** (rear parlour), or vertical arabesque panels replacing pilasters altogether (second **60** drawing room). The same is true as late as 1790, when Archerfield exhibits similar flat and, on the whole, non-architectural interior decoration.

There are, of course, pronounced architectural features that appear in later Adam rooms, such as the Palladian motif and Doric frieze in the designs for the **93** library at Archerfield, but they are part of the overall two-dimensional decorative treatment, not the prominent accents of the early interiors. Certain types of rooms tend generally to have a more architectural quality. This is especially true of the entrance halls, where Adam often employed an ornamented kind of Doric order with fluted columns, enriched capitals and bases, and decorations in the metopes. This form of decoration Adam had specifically singled out for halls in his famous letter to Lord Kames of 1763;[25] and examples of its use are quite numerous, **14, 27, 35** including Syon and Mersham in a heavier fashion, Osterley and Newby in a more refined treatment.

Just as Adam expressed his ideas on the Doric, as well as the other orders, in both the letter to Lord Kames and in his actual decoration, so, too, he frequently demonstrated in a variety of ways his relative independence in regard to this time-**c** honoured subject. He felt free to combine an Ionic capital with a Doric frieze, or **65, 33** to employ obscure antique capitals, or even to design his own order if he thought it desirable. But these departures from Burlingtonian practice and theory are also manifestations of his general de-emphasis of the whole question of the orders. Adam's non-architectonic treatment eliminated the need for full entablatures and often for the columns or pilasters themselves. Even when used, the orders might be applied only to door frames, chimney-pieces, or bookcases. As a result, the importance of the orders in earlier periods gave way to other features, though at times the articulation of the wall by means of pilasters or the demarcation of space by screens of columns commands attention in an Adam interior. Increasingly significant as the decorative role of the orders decreased were friezes and panels—and their decoration.

72 While the number of different friezes and decorative borders employed by Adam is enormous, they are mainly variations on a few basic types—straight running patterns, a simple alternation of two motifs, compositional repeats, and alternating compositional repeats. Within these general categories, the variety is astounding, with the friezes ranging from simple Doric triglyph-and-metope bands to complex repetitions of intricate motifs. As might be expected, the complexity, but also the flatness and delicacy, increases with time. In the early friezes, simple **120, 131** running patterns predominate, with Greek key, guilloche, and Vitruvian scroll

20

exceedingly common. The loosely-flowing foliage frieze of Robert's Scottish practice also is seen in early works after his return from Italy, but this straggly variety was largely superseded by rinceau scrolls, at first fairly loose, though in an organized pattern. Later, these become more luxuriant scrolls of foliage, frequently employed in connexion with other motifs. In this same fashion, other early friezes become crisper, more delicate, and more intricate. Smaller and more delicate motifs, as, for example, wreathed heads or geometric shapes, begin to assume a greater importance in Adam's straight running patterns after the early period, though the common ones continue to be extensively used.

In friezes composed of alternating motifs, such Neo-classical forms as swags, urns, griffins, sphinxes, putti, and anthemia abound. Though encountered not infrequently, friezes of swags, either alone or in combination with other motifs, are not nearly so ubiquitous in Adam's work as is usually supposed. Probably more typical is the anthemion frieze, the many variations of which exemplify the complexity of Adam's style and the fertility of his imagination. Animals face-to-face or back-to-back are among the most common motifs in the friezes with compositional repeats. Beginning with the addorsed griffins in the cove of General Bland's drawing room, this type can be traced through various combinations of griffins, sphinxes, altars, urns, and putti.

The most elaborate of Adam's friezes are those that combine different compositional repeats. Although occasionally used in the earlier years, as in the putti confronting a lyre alternating with urns in rinceau (the saloon at Kedleston), such involved arrangements are much more frequent in the period after 1765. Increasingly complex frieze compositions, as well as a more intricate use of the simple varieties, mark Adam's maturity and later career. A few new motifs were introduced after the mid-1760's, but the general tendency is toward an adaptation or intermingling of the elements used in the earlier years in London.

The motifs and even many of the patterns found in Adam's friezes also occupy an important place in his decorative panels. Designed to hold inset paintings or decorations in bas-relief, these panels featuring classical scenes, grotesques, trophies, and the myriad motifs common also to friezes were instrumental in the creation of Adam's new concept of interior decoration. The plasterwork plaques, generally executed by Joseph Rose, were very early a part of the finished decoration; but relatively few of the painted panels, though designed as early as 1759, were completed until after the mid-1760's, when painters such as Antonio Zucchi were available and when the great projects had advanced to the finishing stage.[26] In these panels, the influence of Adam's Grand Tour is immediately evident.

His Italian drawings frequently included the kinds of subject panels that are common in his interiors. The long sculptured plaque containing a narrative frieze or decorative motifs, almost a hall-mark of his drawings, is found early and often in his English houses in both bas-relief and grisaille. Ruin scenes, in which Adam

3, 4, 6

18
57

68, 44

31, 32, 72

62, 65, 70
101, 105, 111

g, 73

24
33, 55

8

18, 20

21

himself revelled in Italy, were planned for a large number of houses, beginning with Hatchlands and Castle Ashby, but were mainly executed from the mid-sixties on.[27]

10, 12
29, 30, 32

Similarly of Italian inspiration are the grotesque panels, both painted and in plaster, that are perhaps Adam's most significant single contribution to English interior decoration. Again, this innovation had been indicated in the drawings for Hatchlands and Castle Ashby, where the panels are rather simple with thick foliage. Adam moved quickly toward a more delicate, more refined, and flatter treatment, as in his earliest executed grotesque panels, those in the dining room at Shardeloes (c1761–64). The delicate graceful flow of the arabesque here almost obscures the lack of logic in placing the rectangular plaque and other extraneous objects in the middle of the natural foliage. Although all of the parts are classical, the combination is completely un-antique, evoking instead a purely eighteenth-century spirit.

9, 12

13

The panels in the dining room at Osterley (c1766–68) represent Adam's mature grotesques. Here, refined elegance and flat surface decoration have triumphed over logic, and Adam is in complete control of the diffused elements he first utilized only a few years earlier. Variation and further refinement mark the later examples of this type of decoration.

75

82, 57

Related to the larger grotesque panels and equally significant are grotesque and arabesque pilaster panels. In the form of arabesque scrolls rising from a plant or of involved drops of trophies, foliage, and the like, both visible in the gallery at Syon, this kind of decoration first appears toward the end of the pre-1765 period. After that it is a very frequent feature of Adam's interiors, emphasizing the refined, delicate, and non-architectonic quality of Adam's Neo-classical decoration.

19

43, 54

The full-length trophy panel is another type with which Adam adorned his walls. It is especially to be found in ante-rooms (e.g., Syon) and halls, as at Osterley and Newby. Smaller trophy plaques and medallions, however, are far more common.

16

27, 35

Aside from the large subject, grotesque, and trophy panels, most of Adam's panel decoration was on a small scale. Placed around the walls and in the ceilings, these panels were generally filled with bas-reliefs of single objects or symmetrical groupings. Swags, urns, anthemia, rinceau, and the confronting griffins and sphinxes are among the various motifs that enliven the panels, imparting a Neo-classical character to Adam's interiors.

Of all of Adam's wall treatments, perhaps the most unusual and most distinctive is his 'Etruscan' decoration. With its special character conveyed by the total ensemble rather than by any single element such as panels or chimney-piece, the 'Etruscan' room is in some ways the epitome of Adam's Neo-classicism. Although at least eight rooms were designed by Adam in this style, all in the 1770's and early 1780's, only one—that at Osterley (1775–77)—survives in virtually intact condition, complete even with chairs designed *en suite*.[28] Characteristic of

45, 46, 56

46

22

Adam's work of the 1770's, the Etruscan Room at Osterley is flat, elegant, linear, and thoroughly eighteenth century.

WALL FURNITURE

In planning his wall decoration, Adam considered such interior architectural elements as doorways, niches, alcoves, and chimney-pieces, as well as such decorative features as friezes and panels. In certain cases, however, he added an additional ingredient—large pieces of furniture that by their very nature tend to dominate wall elevations. Adam's movable furniture is outside the scope of this volume, being the subject of a book of its own;[29] but such objects as bookcases, organs, and wall cabinets were so integrally a part of the wall treatment that they deserve mention here. Although sometimes actually built into the walls, these pieces are more often movable in a technical sense, even if in reality they were seldom or never moved.

Of the large case pieces of this kind, the organs are perhaps the most interesting, for while few in number, they are spread through much of Adam's career. Among his early designs in England, for example, were the two versions of the organ for Kedleston, and in them we see Adam's typical early style. Highly **88** architectural with boldly carved caryatids, they are filled with heavy decoration. By the mid-'70's, in the organ for Home House, Adam had become infinitely more **87** chaste and elegant. Thin, attenuated pilasters have replaced the caryatids, and the decoration is as delicate and refined as everything else by Adam at the height of his career. The Cumberland House organ of 1781 continues this trend. There are **89** less linear organ designs in the 1770's—for 20 St. James's Square and for Great Saxham—but even here restraint and refinement are very evident. Large cabinets and cupboards, also relatively sparse in the Adam *oeuvre*, exhibit a similar development—from the architectonic design and heavy classical decoration of a clothes press for Lord Coventry (1764) to a more delicately detailed cabinet with very thin pilasters designed for Lansdowne House six years later.[30]

Far more numerous are bookcases, which likewise follow the same pattern of development. There are dark architectural pieces with relatively thick decoration (Croome, 1761–64), as well as bookcases with attenuated pilasters, delicate **90** decoration, and a very subdued architectural character (Archerfield, *c*1790–91). **93** In between are pedimented and Ionic-pilastered libraries at Osterley, Nostell, and **91, 92** Mellerstain (all between 1766 and the mid-1770's), where the low Adamesque decoration is as noticeable as the architectural form; or the restrained, non-architectural designs for Kenwood and the new book room at Kedleston (both in **33** the late '60's).

CHIMNEY-PIECES

Almost invariably, the single item that springs most readily to mind when the Adam style is mentioned is the chimney-piece. Adam lavished a great deal of attention on this form, and the drawings for chimney-pieces, as well as executed examples, are valuable guides to his decorative style and its development. As with so much of Adam's work, the chimney-pieces present a picture of infinite variation upon relatively few types. Utilizing an imaginative mixture of three major components—side stile, frieze, and central tablet—Adam produced over 500 different designs for chimney-pieces. The early ones, like other interior architectural features, show clearly the force of tradition on the emerging Adam style. The mature examples similarly reflect the refining and classicizing of those influences along with the introduction of new styles.

The heavy, robust, and rather architectural chimney-pieces used by the Adam brothers in Scotland and by the Burlingtonians in England were strong influences on Robert during the first few years after his arrival in London. The **94** massive piece with caryatids employed in the Red Drawing Room at Hopetoun **98, 20** reappears in only slightly altered form at Hatchlands and at three other houses **3, 99–105** before 1765. Colonnettes and consoles and the mantel shelves resting on brackets, reminiscent of those at Hopetoun or Dumfries House, are also frequently encountered in Adam's early works in England. While the caryatids are used only rarely after the mid-'60's, the other inherited types of stiles are found often throughout Adam's career. The bold projection of these stiles is softened by Neo-classical detail—as when colonnettes are entwined with delicate foliage or **106** replaced by flat pilasters—but their recurrence effectively indicates the Early Georgian influence on Adam's chimney-pieces.

Yet his chimney-pieces also demonstrate the introduction of new designs and the drastic modification of old ones. Although decorative panels were occasionally used as stiles on early examples, they became among the most popular form of stile decoration during the 1770's and '80's. Instead of the early panels with simple heavy decoration, however, those of the mature period feature intricate linear designs, delicate and flat. And the single-panel stile gives way to wide stiles with central panels and side borders, the whole elegantly complex, as in the **111** Etruscan Room at Home House. The last type is very common during the last two **109, 110, 112** decades of Adam's career, not only in the great houses, but even in the speculative projects, such as Portland Place.

The variety of stiles noted here could be combined with numerous friezes and plaques, and therein lies the secret of Adam's infinite variation. Although certain types of supports, such as caryatids, tend to be used with specific kinds of lintels, on the whole there is no consistent correlation between frieze and stile **101, 105, 106** treatment. Most of the chimney-piece friezes are of a continuous pattern, whether **110–113** or not a central tablet obscures part of it, and they are closely related to the designs used by Adam in his room and door friezes. Much less common are the

24

friezes with decoration symmetrically balanced on each side of a central plaque. **102, 103, 114**
Here the motifs are similar to those on wall panels, as well as to those on friezes.

The third ingredient in Adam's chimney-pieces is the decorative tablet used **101, 110, 112**
on the centre of the lintel on a little more than half of his designs. Closely allied to
the wall and ceiling panels, these feature both narrative subjects and the usual
Adam motifs. In some instances, as for example the musical trophies in the music
room at Harewood or the putti and globe used in at least three different libraries
(Osterley, Kenwood, and Bolton House), tablets were related to the use of the room **92**
or to the client's insignia or tastes. But in general, there is little rationale of this
kind, a Neo-classical motif being the only requisite demanded.

CEILINGS

The ceiling was often the key to Adam's decoration of a room. Frequently, his first
drawings for a project were for ceilings, and their great diversity is the first specific
innovation claimed in the preface to the *Works in Architecture*.[31] The ceilings, too,
are guides to the carpets, for Adam generally related his floor coverings to them.
But, above all, it is in his ceilings that Adam demonstrated more effectively than
anywhere else the novelty and variety that he named among the principal
attributes of his style.[32] In no other sector of his work did Adam introduce such
a variety of new designs, and in no other part is his variation on basic schemes so
successful.

As with other aspects of his decorative work, there is similarly a development
from rather heavy, simpler ceilings to very flat and highly complex ones. The
somewhat more robust designs of the late 1750's and early 1760's are replaced by **115–120**
the mid-'60's by more delicate works in lower relief. From this point on, the **130**
ceilings become, on the whole, more linear and intricate, but also more elegant.
Many of the same patterns, albeit more refined, continue in use, together with
newer and more complex arrangements.

The development of Adam's ceiling designs is strikingly illustrated in the
previously noted contrast between the hall and gallery at Syon, where the simple, **14, 124**
high-relief format is superseded by the triumph of a two-dimensional decorative **15**
effect. Whereas these ceilings have utterly different designs, there are also
cases of Adam's transformation of an early scheme using a relatively simple
arrangement of boldly sculpted forms into a much more linear composition
filled with intricate and delicate detail. The dining room ceiling at Shardeloes **122**
(1761; repeated in the dining room at Osterley, *c*1766) is related in basic format
to the music room ceiling at 20 St. James's Square (1773). Both have central **39**
motifs with projections pointing toward the corners, an outer band, and ringed
medallions in the corners. But there the similarity ends. Where one is in pronounced
relief, the other is quite flat; and where one has a good deal of free space, the other
has a great quantity of fine, delicate decoration. The spirit and the execution are

utterly different. There are closer examples than these, and there are many far more distantly related, but these two designs indicate the trends and development of Adam ceilings.

Adam's wide variety of ceilings and their general progression from simple and heavy to complex and intricate can be seen within a few major types. Despite the enormous variation, all of the ceilings appear to fall into five basic categories: (1) simple concentric circular and oval rings, (2) compositions of concentric rings which emphasize the division of the rings and the treatment of their radial members, (3) ceilings in which the emphasis is upon the central motif and its relation to the edges, (4) triparite patterns, and (5) overall patterns. All of these were used throughout Adam's career, though the more complex designs—especially the X-shaped central motif of category three—were especially prevalent from the late-1760's on.

Any of the ceilings of the first three groups might also be used as the central panel of a three-part scheme, flanked by complementary end sections. One of Adam's favourite devices for treating the ceiling of a rectangular or apse-ended room was to design end units in such a way as to make the central panel a self-sufficient square, decorated in the manner of any square ceiling. Sometimes the three units are not related; at other times Adam integrated them into one design or ingeniously linked together three separately designed panels. Similarly, overall patterned ceilings might take the form of a continuous repeat of a small motif, as in coffered ceilings or those inspired by coffering, or of a more complex repeat of a compositional grouping, as for example in the gallery at Syon.

Adam used all of the various types of designs on flat ceilings, which were by far the most common variety, and in combination with coves; but only certain treatments, primarily overall patterns, were applied to vaulted rooms. These last, which Adam greatly admired, were used only rarely, the library at Kenwood being the most famous example.

CARPETS AND PAVEMENTS

For a number of his rooms, though actually only a fraction of his total output, Adam designed floor decoration as well as the adornment of walls and ceilings. A few of these floors were of marble or scagliola, but carpets were generally the decoration prescribed. In both cases, the idea of theme and variation effectively illustrated in Adam's ceilings is equally evident in the relationship between ceilings and floors. When designing a carpet, for example, Adam usually attempted to relate it to the ceiling. Hardly ever were the two identical; rather the carpets often echo the general composition but vary the detailed decoration. Typical of this treatment are the drawing room at Osterley and the great dining room at Cumberland House. There are, of course, other rooms such as the drawing room at Syon, where carpet and ceiling do not exhibit the same basic pattern, but even here the motifs and the spirit indicate at least a family relationship.

Like the carpets, Adam's pavements also tend to reflect the general design of the ceiling, though, again, they seldom, if ever, duplicate it. The hall and ante-room at Syon, the hall at Osterley, the gallery at Newby were all designed in this way. **27, 35** Although the general tendency was toward inter-relationship, there were exceptions here, too, as in the hall at Wormleybury.

DUPLICATION AND VARIATION

It is variation rather than duplication that characterizes Adam's decorative work. Despite the apparent sameness that the Adam style often conveys at first glance, very little actual repetition exists, though there is an enormous amount of combining of parts. Virtually exact duplication can be found in both ceiling and chimney-piece designs, but those with minor differences or with intermingling of elements are much more common.

Of the almost 650 different ceiling designs in the collection at the Soane Museum, I have found only five examples of absolute repetition, and all are **122, 123** within the first nine years of Adam's London career.[33] In all of these cases, there are slight differences of detail, of style of draftsmanship, or of colour, but the resemblance is astounding. This, however, is the exception. Far more typical is the mixture of parts, as when very similar central panels are flanked by quite different end sections or when the same format is used but within a circle in one and an oval in the other. The basic motif of the gallery at Harewood (1769) and the first drawing room at Chandos House (London, 1771), for example, is the **139, 138** same, though all of the specific details are different; but at Harewood it is only one segment of a continuous repeat along the ceiling, while at Chandos House it is the central panel flanked by two end pieces.

With chimney-pieces, too, the interest is more in the different combinations of similar elements than in the duplication of the whole. Cases of very close **111, 112** repetition are more frequent than with ceilings, but I have located only 29 examples of near duplication among the almost 550 different designs for chimney-pieces at the Soane Museum. As might be expected, many of these are for the large speculative projects, such as the Adelphi and Portland Place; and, indeed, almost twelve per cent of all chimney-piece designs for the Adelphi are duplicates of other Adelphi designs. In both the chimney-piece and ceiling repetitions, the two (or more) designs tend to be fairly close in date. In any case, such close duplication as this is a relatively limited practice with Adam, surprisingly rare for so prodigious an output as he had.

COLOUR

Colour, which Adam utilized to a far greater extent than did his predecessors, was one of his principal means of variation. Roundly criticizing the white ceilings often employed in the first half of the eighteenth century, the Adam brothers instead advocated backgrounds 'coloured with various tints to take off the crudeness of the white.'[34] In Robert's conception of decoration, colour was not an adjunct but an integral part, and many of his sketches were marked with a colour key to enable his draftsmen to execute his ideas exactly as he envisioned them.[35]

One of the delights of examining the Adam drawings is their colour, for there are many finely finished and beautifully coloured designs, especially after 1765. Very few of the early drawings are rendered in colour—most are in pencil or ruled ink, often accompanied by grey, pink and grey, or occasionally brown wash—but this is remedied after the middle of the decade. The most striking aspect of the coloured renderings is the richness and brightness of the colour. Although one can find the almost washed-out pastel tints frequently associated with the Adam style, far more typical are the strong blues and greens, the sumptuous reds, the lively apricots and lilacs.

From these drawings, from executed works in which the present colours have been documented by comparison with the drawings or by scraping down to the original coat, and from the Adam writings, certain conclusions can be reached about Adam's use of colour. It appears that Adam very early conceived of coloured grounds and white decoration, with judicious use of gilding; that his colours while sometimes pale were often full-bodied and strong; that the colours were not limited to the pastel tints generally thought of as 'Adam'; that the most important place for colour in an early Adam room frequently was the ceiling, but that by the mid-1760's his walls were equally colourful; and that he was not content with the mere 'picking out' of details with colour. There were rooms with relatively little colour, but the total effect at which Adam was aiming certainly relied upon colour as much as upon motif.

16
62
152
There can be no doubt of this when one examines a room such as the ante-room at Syon. The *verde antique* columns; the white and green chimney-piece; the gilded decorations set against the blue and green backgrounds of the capitals, frieze, and panels; and the blue, green, red, and gold pavement tell us that. While by no means typical of Adam's colour schemes, the Syon ante-room illustrates well the emphasis on colour and the use of strong pigment in his interior work.

FURNISHINGS

Unlike architects who restricted themselves to plan and exterior, or even included interior architecture, Adam designed, at one time or another, almost everything—façades, plans, outbuildings, interior walls and ceilings, furniture, carpets, silver, door furniture, stove grates, candlesticks, ink wells, and more. His concern with these items is shown by some of the engravings in the *Works* and by the great number of drawings at the Soane Museum related to the furnishings of his projects. He did not lavish this attention on all of his houses, but for many clients he designed tables and mirrors, a few pieces of silver, a fire grate or two, a sedan chair, door knobs and escutcheons, or a myriad of other objects that are normally beyond the purview of an architect.[36] For some clients, however, Adam literally designed almost the whole ensemble, the most famous example being Osterley.

In the realm of decorative furnishings, Adam's style and taste are as obvious as in any other aspect of his work. While Adam furniture has been considered in great detail in another volume of this series[37] and such large objects as bookcases and organs have already been mentioned in this volume, a glance at other examples of his furnishings will demonstrate both the character of these pieces and their function in an Adam interior. The curtain cornices designed for Derby House (23 Grosvenor Square, 1774), stove grates such as that for the Earl of Coventry (1765), the sconces in the saloon at Kedleston (1760's), and the candelabra provided for Sir Watkin Williams-Wynn (1773) all evoke the same Neo-classical spirit and exhibit the same motifs as larger and more integral Adam designs of the same dates. Perhaps the most extreme example of this co-ordination and of Adam's attention to minutiae in effecting a perfect ensemble is the door furniture that he designed. Reiterating on a minute scale the delicacy and elegance characteristic of the mature Adam manner, these pieces are often quite close to Adam grotesque decorations. All of the various elements had their roles to play in the 'almost total change' in interior decoration that Robert and James claimed for themselves.[38]

165, 160
164
161

162, 163

DECORATION IN THE GOTHIC TASTE

Although Adam was among the leading Neo-classicists in Europe, he occasionally produced designs in the Gothic manner, which should be included in a study of his decorative work. Adam's taste for Gothic was not founded on the study or theoretical allegiance that formed his Neo-classicism, but its roots go back even farther. His youthful landscape drawings and architectural sketches of the 1740's and early 1750's often featured the papery, gingerbread Gothic then in vogue, and on his trip to England in 1749–50, he noted medieval structures as well as Burlingtonian ones.[39] The romanticism implicit in his appreciation of Gothic and evident also in his love of landscape was an important force throughout his life.[40]

166, 167

Adam's medievalism in architecture was reflected in two ways—Scottish Baronial castles and Gothic interiors. The castellar designs, of which Culzean Castle (1777–90) is a fine example, illustrate Adam's romanticism rather than his archaeological bent. Despite its battlements and turrets, Culzean is a symmetrically designed house with classical arches and a thoroughly Neo-classical interior. And most of Adam's houses of this type were similarly unarchaeological. This

67, 113

same type of romantic Gothic, albeit sometimes more authentic than were his exteriors, characterized the Gothic interiors that occasionally emerged from the Adam office. In most cases, the choice of Gothic was the client's, but Adam's version of Gothic Revival decoration invariably reflected the delicacy and linear quality of his own style.

169, 170 In the mid-1760's Horace Walpole, the high priest of the Gothic Revival, commissioned Adam to design a ceiling and a chimney-piece for Strawberry Hill and even provided him with models to follow. The results, in spite of the authenticity of their inspiration, are akin to Adam's contemporary classical work. This is especially true of the chimney-piece, but even the ceiling has the complex radial arrangement and delicate detail of many Adam ceilings.

Far more extensive was Adam's work at Alnwick Castle, his most ambitious effort in the Gothic vein. Begun in the late 1760's and continued all through the '70's, the interiors of Alnwick and a number of its outbuildings were designed in the Gothic style at the behest of the Duchess of Northumberland, and Adam furnished her with decorations in the fanciful type of Gothic he had espoused in **168** the 1750's. Typical is the drawing of the library with its Tudor arches, crockets, and finicking decoration. All of Adam's work inside Alnwick, with the exception of a few chimney-pieces on the ground floor, was destroyed in a nineteenth-century reconstruction, but Adam interiors do survive in one of the buildings on the **171, 172** estate, Hulne Abbey (1778). Here and in the Adam drawings can be seen Adam's flirtation with Gothic, a brief and playful interlude in a thoroughly Neo-classical career.

Figure g. Design for the Frieze of the Tapestry Room at Croome Court, *c*1763. Sir John Soane's Museum, Vol. 53, No. 25a.

CHAPTER THREE

THE SOURCES OF ADAM'S DECORATIVE STYLE

The style of decoration that Robert Adam evolved in his first seven or eight years in London was derived from a wide variety of sources, and these remained his principal inspiration during his entire career. Just as his stylistic development after the middle of the 1760's was largely an elaboration and refinement of his early work, so, too, the basic influences of that period pervade his mature and late style, as well. Different aspects of the sources already evident by 1765 were introduced later, and there was a new influx of inspiration in the early 1770's, but the general areas of influence did not change. Of these, the most important was antiquity, primarily Roman. Mingling with and in certain cases independent of the ancient sources were those of Renaissance and Baroque Italy. The eighteenth century supplied the remaining influences—Italian, English Palladian, and French. The interrelationship of Adam's sources is complex, yet each, with the exception of the French, can readily be isolated. French influence on the Adam style was more a matter of spirit than of specific examples, and Adam was perhaps as influential on French Neo-classicism as the latter was on him.

The variety of the sources upon which he drew indicates Adam's widespread tastes. Selective in his choice of models, he was also individualistic in his use of them. Some of the prototypes were reproduced with little or no alteration in form, but most of them were modified and combined in such a way as to stamp them with a distinctly Adamesque imprint. Adam mixed his sources as he saw fit, uniting Burlingtonian and antique elements, Greek and Roman ones. Although certain details can be identified as derived from specific examples, the interpretation of the whole is always characteristic of Adam. In the best tradition of the Renaissance, he adapted and utilized in his own way the art of the past. His field of choice was very wide, and he made excellent use of it.

The means by which Adam came into contact with his sources were also diverse. From his father came Robert's introduction to Palladianism and the beginning of his taste for the English Rococo. Both interests were heightened through architectural books and through his journey to England in 1749–50. The Italian influences—antique, Renaissance, and contemporary—were the result of his Grand Tour and his study in Italy, supplemented by books and drawings. Robert's knowledge of French designs owes something to Clérisseau, but much also to prints and literary sources. His journeys, his library, and his collection, as well as comments in his letters and in the *Works*, are thus the best guides to the sources for his style.

Of his Grand Tour something has already been said, and the books that he owned can be seen in the volumes sold at the various Adam sales.[41] Supplementing the printed works was a vast assemblage of drawings, fragments, and casts, whose character and intended use are revealed in Adam's letters and the sale catalogues. In letters to his family from Rome, Adam told of collecting 'antique Cornishes, freezes, Figures, Basreilivs, Vases, Altars,'[42] both originals and casts, as well as 'employing painters Drawers &c. to do the Fountains, the Buildings, the Statues & the things that are of use for drawing after & for giving hints to the imagination of us modern Devils.'[43] He intended, in short, 'to send home a Collection of Drawings of Clerisseaus my own & our Myrmidons which never was seen or heard of either in England or Scotland before.'[44]

The majority of drawings, sculptures, and books are related to antiquity, which was by far the most important source of inspiration for Adam's decoration, as well as for his architecture in general. Because of the state of archaeological discoveries and the aesthetic theories of the late 1750's and because of the course of Robert's Grand Tour, the monuments of Rome and its environs assume the major role among ancient sources. Herculaneum and Pompeii; Baia, Pozzuoli, and Cumae; and Spalato each provided Adam with material roughly commensurate with the amount of time he spent there. Adam also supplemented his direct experiences of antique monuments with books, among the most influential of which was Robert Wood's *Ruins of Palmyra* (1753).

It was through books that Adam encountered the few Greek models that he used. Greece, although acknowledged by the Adams as the fountainhead of art,[45] was employed very little by them. Robert's only mention of a Greek source is the inscription 'Ionick of Le Roy' on a sketch of a gate house,[46] but he did use the Ionic order of the Erechtheum as illustrated in J.-D. Le Roy's *Les ruines des plus beaux monuments de la Grèce* (Paris, 1758) in a number of places, for example, the capitals and entablature of the ante-room at Syon. As is typical of Adam's use of his models, he borrowed the volutes and the mouldings but substituted a different design, a type found in Roman *thermae*, for the necking of the capitals at Syon. The decoration on the Erechtheum necking he used, instead, for the frieze of the entablature. This mixing, matching, and adaptation that characterize Adam's utilization of his sources is strikingly analogous to the way in which he varied his ceiling or chimney-piece designs.

In spite of his occasional use of Greek models, Adam most frequently turned for stylistic inspiration to the remains of ancient Rome. His plans and various features of his elevations reflect this influence, but it is even more strongly felt in the ceilings, panels, friezes, and myriad decorative details of his work. Adam readily, perhaps eagerly, acknowledged this influence when he labelled a drawing for the little drawing room at Audley End, 'Design of a Ceiling in the Stile of the paintings of the Ancients,' or when he charged Lord Coventry for a similarly designed ceiling for Coventry House. And in February 1762, he wrote to his brother James, still in Italy, requesting sketches of painted Roman ceilings.[47] The unexecuted design for Audley End just noted is an example of an Adam ceiling derived from a specific Roman source, the Baths (or Palace) of Augustus. Here the entire composition is very close; at other times, Adam used only the central motif or the general treatment, altering or adapting it to suit his purposes.

Although ancient painted ceilings interested Adam more, coffering also attracted his attention, to judge by the extensive appearance of it in his Italian drawings. In England, he used coffers in various interiors, as in the gallery at Croome, where he reproduced with only slight modification the coffering system of the Basilica of Constantine. While the pattern is the same, albeit elongated, the effect is totally different, for Adam converted the deep coffers of a vaulted surface into shallow coffers in a flat ceiling. Roman mosaics, too, were grist to his mill. The carpet that he designed for the gallery at Syon was probably inspired by a mosaic such as one of the second century A.D. found in Ostia, and there are ceilings similarly derived.

The specific details of Adam's decoration derived from Roman sources are very numerous. Many friezes, decorative plaques, narrative panels, and particular motifs had their origin in Rome; and their sources can often be identified. Others are so general as to be visible all over Rome, as for example the strigils on sarcophagi or the swirled columns that can be found lying in the Roman Forum even today. Characteristic of the more specific prototypes are a frieze from the Forum of Trajan found in the gallery at Croome and in the ceiling of the hall at Syon and the two trophies of Octavianus Augustus perched on the balustrade of the Capitol which were adapted for the ante-room at Syon. In the case of the trophies, Adam somewhat altered his models, 'restored' lost parts, flattened the composition, and produced thoroughly Neo-classical designs that offer instructive comparison with the antique originals.

Not nearly so numerous as the sources from the city of Rome are those from parts of the Empire, though they are of some significance. The only ancient monuments in Italy outside of Rome utilized by Adam to any degree were those of the area above and below Naples, and even these were little used. Both Robert and James visited Herculaneum, while James also saw Pompeii, but relatively little had been uncovered by the dates of the Adams' visits and sketching was generally prohibited. There are a few designs related to Adam decoration among the paintings subsequently unearthed, but no specific sources from Herculaneum or Pompeii have been found. The same is largely true of the monuments to the north and west of Naples, especially Baia, Cumae, and Pozzuoli. That they were influential on the Adams is attested to by the visits to these sites by both Robert and James and by their reference in the *Works* to 'the inimitable remains on the Baian shore.'[48] Very few of the Baian remains, however, have been illustrated, and in these there are related designs but little that is really specific.

Spalato, where Adam and his party had excavated, measured, and drawn, furnished Adam with sources for plans, elevations, and details, but they are fewer than might be expected. Actually, of course, he was there less than six weeks, as compared to two years in Rome itself. The one element at Diocletian's palace that left the strongest imprint on his decorative style was the capital on a pilaster in the corner of the peristyle. This fluted capital with leaves overlaid on its bottom half was employed by Adam in a number of places, including the saloon at Saltram and the dining room at Lansdowne House. There are other details from Spalato that may have served as Adam sources, but many of these were also present at Rome.

Known to Adam only through the pages of Robert Wood's book, the monuments of Palmyra were also an important inspiration, surprisingly so for a purely literary source. Adam especially turned to Palmyra for models for ceilings, and at least three or four specific examples can be identified. The most interesting of these is the drawing room ceiling at Osterley, which Adam adapted from a soffit in the Temple of the Sun. Whereas most of Adam's borrowing from Palmyra was characterized by relatively limited alteration, this model was radically changed, the square being converted into a rectangle and the circle into an oval, with the feathers dramatically stretched out to fit the new proportions. Adam's use of Palmyra was no secret, for the origin of the Osterley ceiling was guessed by Horace Walpole, though he specifically mentioned only the doorcases and frieze.[49]

One other ancient source that deserves mention is Early Christian art, principally the decoration of crypts. Adam, like most of his contemporaries, considered these third- and fourth-century designs to be antique and used them for their compositions and classical motifs, not their specifically Christian subject panels. Although not identical, the ceiling for the Duchess of Bolton's dressing room at Bolton House (London, 1770) is very close to a vault in the Crypt of Lucina in the Cemetery of St. Calixtus, *circa* A.D.220, and there are a few similar examples of an Adam-Early Christian relationship.

Adam's knowledge of ancient decoration and its influence upon his work were tempered by his acquaintance with the decorations of the Renaissance, another major source of the Adam style. This is especially true of Adam's grotesque panels and vertical pilaster strips, whose creation can only be explained in terms of both antique and *Cinquecento* examples, transformed into his own eighteenth-century style. Roman versions interested both Robert and James, who studied them and had them copied, but the brothers were also very cognizant of Renaissance examples, as evidenced by comments in their letters and by the large numbers of copies of Renaissance grotesques in the Adam Collection at the Soane Museum.

34

Although Robert saw the fifteenth- and sixteenth-century examples as illustrative of lost antique examples and used them to elucidate his concept of ancient grotesques,[50] he absorbed the Renaissance character to an important extent.

In the drawings for grotesque decoration by Adam and his draftsmen, the antique and Renaissance influences are combined in a presentation characteristic of eighteenth-century watercolour grotesques. This style of delineation, especially in such early Adam designs as those for Hatchlands or Castle Ashby, is quite close, **9, 12** for example, to certain tracings and copies after the plates of Pietro Santi Bartoli **76** at the Royal Institute of British Architects. In Adam's executed grotesques, as typified by the panels of the eating room at Osterley, the dual influences of **75** antiquity and the Renaissance have been suffused by a cold, flattening process.

From his study of antique decorations in such places as the Domus Aurea, the Baths of Livia, Hadrian's Villa, and the sepulchres near Rome and in the vicinity of Baia (most of which are no longer available to us), Adam derived both specific details and an interest in grotesques as an important form of interior decoration. Combining this with an examination of the grotesques of Raphael, Giovanni da Udine, and other *Cinquecento* masters whom he felt had access to more and better preserved examples of Roman stuccoes, he then evolved his own concept of how antique grotesques in their full glory must have looked. This conclusion was necessarily coloured by his own taste and by the spirit of eighteenth-century Neo-classicism. The result was grotesque decoration such as that at Osterley—involved and illogical, while at the same time flat, linear, and elegant. Adam's mature grotesques have the delicate, graceful movement of antique examples, such as the arabesques of the Ara Pacis; but their complexity and **77** illogical inclusion of griffins, urns, peltoid shields, and inset painted panels amid the arabesques tend to divorce them from the Roman grotesques. In their mixture of various elements, Adam's panels are more akin to the Vatican *loggie* **74** or other Renaissance examples than to the Ara Pacis reliefs, yet the *Cinquecento* vitality and exuberance are completely lacking. Compared to either predecessor, the Adam grotesques, despite their elegance and delicacy, are inorganic and very **75** much a product of the eighteenth century.

The related motif of vertical grotesque strips was probably evolved in a similar manner. Roman triumphal arches, such as the small Arcus Argentariorum, provided antique prototypes, while Adam had Renaissance examples in the Vatican *loggie* and elsewhere. Both influences can be seen in the gallery at Syon. **19**

The sixteenth century also furnished Adam with material not directly connected with antique sources, and the same is true of the seventeenth century. Adam's writings, both published and unpublished, include mention of a number of Renaissance, Mannerist, and Baroque artists, of whom two of the most consistently named are Pirro Ligorio and Alessandro Algardi. In praising Pirro Ligorio, Adam probably had in mind the Casino of Pius IV in the gardens of the Vatican and also his antiquarian studies. His praise of Algardi was undoubtedly based on the Villa Pamphili (now Doria-Pamphili), built 1644–52 under Algardi's general direction, although largely the work of Giovan Francesco Grimaldi.[51] The elaborate stucco decorations of the Villa Pamphili were a notable influence on Adam's earliest decorative work in England. At least two ceilings designed by Adam before 1760—a very early unidentified drawing and the dining room at Hatchlands—were probably inspired by ceilings in the Italian villa, and certain decorative details, including the panel decoration in the original drawing room at Hatchlands, were also adapted from this structure.

117–119

The other major source for the Adam style—in addition to antiquity and the artists of Renaissance and Baroque Italy—was the eighteenth century itself. This in reality is a three-pronged influence, stemming from Italy, England, and France. The Italian segment mainly centres on Piranesi, whose influence on Adam was complex and far reaching. They had known each other in Rome, and Piranesi had accompanied Adam on sketching expeditions and examined the young Scotsman's drawings. Coming during the formative period in the creation of the Adam style, Piranesi's acquaintance resulted in an important impact on Adam. The archaeological enthusiasm that pervades all of Piranesi's work struck a responsive chord in Robert Adam and impressed him with the enormous variety of Roman art. Adam's taste for the grand is surely similarly derived. And a large number of antique motifs used by Adam can be seen in the prints of Piranesi. But the Italian engraver's role as an inspiration to Adam did not end with Robert's departure from Rome in 1757, for the theories and designs that Piranesi published after the mid-1760's also had an important influence on Adam. This is evident in the theoretical concepts of genius and variety, as well as in the creation of Adam chimney-pieces and 'Etruscan' decoration of the 1770's. Elements of the elaborate chimney-pieces in Piranesi's *Diverse maniere* of 1769 were employed by Adam, though the fireplaces as a whole were far too involved for Adam's taste. This new (or renewed) inspiration is the force behind Adam's much more complex stiles of the '70's, as seen, for example, in the first drawing room at Wynn House.

107, 108

109–113

Adam's 'Etruscan' rooms were probably also inspired by the *Diverse maniere*, where Piranesi both defends the use of urns and bases as decorative sources for wall ornamentation and illustrates three examples of such decoration.[52] His defence may well have inspired Adam, with plates such as these serving as models. Adam developed his source a good deal, stylizing and regimenting it, but the trellis pattern springing from sphinxes and the scale and poses of the figures are similar in both the Etruscan Room at Osterley and the plates of Piranesi. Although Adam probably took his motifs and colours from illustrations of Greek vases or from actual specimens, the ultimate conception seems to have been derived from Piranesi.

46, 47

Aside from ancient art, Burlingtonian Palladianism in England was Adam's most significant source of inspiration. Despite his criticism of the architecture of his English predecessors and his disparagement of their two patron saints, Palladio and Inigo Jones,[53] Adam was heavily indebted to the work of Burlington, Kent, and their followers. He broke with this style in many ways and altered the features that he borrowed, radically changing the scale and character of many of them and overlaying them with a spirit derived from antiquity, but a large part of Adam's architecture is grounded upon the Palladianism of the Burlington circle. This is evident in his plans, his exterior compositions, and his exterior details, with his addiction to the Palladian motif within a relieving arch the most telling advertisement. It is also true of his interior treatment.

Adam ceilings, chimney-pieces, and decorative detail all owe some debt to English Palladianism and to the modified Rococo style that graced its interiors in the late 1740's and the 1750's. The ceiling of the hall at Shardeloes or the ante-room at Syon, for example, recalls the White Drawing Room at Houghton, and at least three ceilings at Holkham possibly exercised an influence upon Adam designs. There are differences between the Adam and the earlier examples, especially in scale, but the resemblance is strong. Similarly, a number of Adam's chimney-piece types—those with term, colonnette, console, and panelled stiles or bracket-supported mantel shelves—derive from Burlingtonian prototypes. Among other decorative features found in both Adam's works and those of his English predecessors are modillioned cornices, tabernacle frames, overmantels, and various friezes.

One of the most revealing examples of Robert Adam's interest in English decorative features of the earlier eighteenth century is his use of caryatid chimney-pieces. The role of the sculptor Rysbrack in the creation of the piece in the Red Drawing Room at Hopetoun and possibly in that at Hatchlands has been mentioned earlier, and the type was not at all uncommon in England. An early example, featuring terms as at Hopetoun, is the chimney-piece in the Stone Hall at Houghton (c1738), probably also carved by Rysbrack. Full caryatids, very close to those at Hatchlands, are to be found on a piece from Chesterfield House (c1748–50), now at the Metropolitan Museum of Art; and Isaac Ware, the architect of that house, illustrated and discussed this chimney-piece in his *Complete Body of Architecture* of 1756. Still another example is in the gallery at Corsham Court (1762–64). Adam's versions are more classical, often even employing copies of antique reliefs for the central tablet, but there is no doubt that the basic idea was derived from examples current in England about the middle of the eighteenth century.

Another instance of the Adam-Burlingtonian relationship is perhaps furnished by Adam's 'Estruscan' decoration, which was almost foreshadowed in certain of Kent's ceilings, such as that of the smoking room at Rousham (1738–41). It is unlikely that Adam's decoration comes from Kent, however, for perhaps the most striking aspect of the Adam 'Etruscan' rooms is their use of ochre, black, and white on a pale blue or green ground, whereas Kent's ceilings are brightly coloured.[54] The brilliant colouring also removes Kent's ceilings of this type from

120

99–105

94

98

97

Adam's grotesque decorations, where relatively simple colour effects are employed, especially in the earlier examples.

More related to Adam's grotesques are those in the Painted Room at Spencer **78** House, designed by 'Athenian' Stuart in 1759. The Spencer House grotesques are more complex and suave than Adam's of the same date, and even Adam later credited Stuart with having 'contributed greatly towards introducing the true style of antique decoration . . .'[55] Yet despite the general similarity to various Adam decorations, the specific influence of the Painted Room on Adam does not seem to have been decisive.

French decoration of the third quarter of the eighteenth century is the last source of the Adam style remaining to be considered. Unlike the other sources, however, the nature of its influence is highly complex. While the Adam style owes something to French inspiration, the Louis XVI style is also indebted to Adam. Although most of the difficulty revolves about the question of which country first employed various aspects of Neo-classicism, it must be realized that the influence in both directions was often more of spirit than of specific details. Neo-classical architecture and decoration as they developed on both sides of the English Channel are in reality rather different. They share a similar spirit toward antiquity and certain characteristic elements, but the visual configurations are not of the same kind. Neither French nor English Neo-classicism can be viewed as a derivative copy of the other.[56]

The overlapping tastes of the French and English in this period, the French interest in things English and the reverse, are also important to an understanding of the roles played by Adam and his French contemporaries in the development of Neo-classicism. Both sides of the coin are summed up in George Selwyn's remark on his return from Paris in 1762, as reported by Horace Walpole, that 'our passion for everything French is nothing to theirs for everything English.' [57] And there is abundant evidence to support the attraction in both directions.

All of the indications of this cross-interest seem to be in the 1760's and 1770's; in the 1750's, however, the tastes of the two countries were not on a par. The Rococo fashion appeared earlier and stronger in France, but so did dissatisfaction with it. By the mid-1750's its excesses were being ridiculed in France,[58] and a new vogue, the *Style Pompadour* or *Goût Grec*, was capturing Paris. It is reflected in the comments of both Grimm and Walpole,[59] as well as in the paintings of Greuze, Vien, Roslin, Drouais, and others. Most of this pictorial material is especially relevant to furniture rather than wall and ceiling decoration, and, in fact, some of the furniture illustrated in Greuze's portrait of Lalive de Jully has been identified.[60] This furniture and the others depicted in various paintings are much heavier than either fully developed Louis XVI furniture or that of Robert Adam, but they are nevertheless Neo-classical. Similar furniture was also illustrated in the plates of Jean-François Neufforge, published from 1757 on.

There is much less evidence for the nature of French interior decoration of the late 1750's and early 1760's, but from the designs of Neufforge and the description of Lalive de Jully's room designed by Louis Le Lorrain,[61] we can see that the French were at a roughly parallel point in the development of Neo-classicism as was Adam, or perhaps a year or so ahead. But they are not strictly comparable in style. Adam was almost certainly aware of these developments, and they would have encouraged him to press on with his new style. Perhaps there are a few motifs or ideas that influenced him, but at least in interior decoration there was relatively little explicit influence.[62]

Even in the early and mid-1760's when Adam's clients began buying Gobelins tapestries for use in Adam rooms, there is no noticeable French influence in his interiors. While he adapted the French designs for the tapestry rooms to suit his spaces, he neither suggested or designed the tapestries nor was he inspired by them.[63]

44

By the same token, many noted French interiors of the 1760's and 1770's, for example Mme. du Barry's pavilion at Louveciennes designed by Ledoux in 1770, are very different from contemporary Adam rooms. The Louveciennes room, preserved in a watercolour by Moreau le Jeune, was as thoroughly Neo-classical as Adam decoration of comparable date, but it was also utterly different.

173

Just as early French Neo-classical designs, such as those of Neufforge, may have encouraged Adam and even provided him with specific aids, so Adam may have served as an inspiration for more mature French examples. The introduction and development of Neo-classical grotesque panels is one area in which Adam definitely appears to have preceded the French, but the influence of his grotesques on the later French ones was, on the whole, probably in the form of inspiration rather than of specific design sources, and other counter-influences are possible as well. As early as 1759, in the designs for Castle Ashby and Hatchlands, Adam was utilizing grotesques; and by the middle of the 1760's, he had arrived at intricate and fully-developed grotesque panels (Osterley). None of the French examples known today dates before the mid-1770's. One, however, that has been cited as a possible exception is the decoration by Clérisseau of the salon of the Hôtel Grimod de la Reynière, on the Champs-Elysées. As a result both of uncertainty concerning its date and of Clérisseau's relations with Adam, these decorations have assumed an important role in the question of Adam and French Neo-classicism.

9, 12

75

79

The Hôtel Grimod, built in 1769, was decorated before 1782, when drawings of it were made by a Polish architect, J.-C. Kamsetzer. Dates ranging from 1769, immediately after Clérisseau's return to Paris, to 1775 or later, after his visit to England in the early 1770's, have been advanced. The earlier date suggested that the decorations were a consequence of Clérisseau's study and work in Italy; the later date implied that the decorations were a result of the Adam decoration seen by Clérisseau in London. Because of their general similarity to dated French grotesques of the later 1770's and early 1780's, the Hôtel Grimod grotesques seem more likely to date from the mid-1770's than earlier. Recent discovery of an article in the *Almanach des Artistes* of 1777 on the 'salon de M. de La Reynière, nouvellement décoré par M. Clérisseau' appears to confirm this stylistic impression.[64] In addition, the Hôtel Grimod panels are not unrelated to such mature Adam grotesques of the late 1760's as those in the dining room at Osterley. While the setting is French and various details are specifically Gallic, the individual grotesque panels are quite similar to Adam work. The illogical combination of inset plaques of various shapes with urns, cornucopiae, and arabesque foliage, as well as the elegant flatness, compare favourably with the Osterley panels or others by Adam. And the vertical arabesque strips are also to be found in Adam's work. As Adam's grotesques were not nearly so developed in 1757 when he left Clérisseau's tutelage, it is very possible that the Hôtel Grimod decorations were, at least to a certain extent, inspired by the work Clérisseau saw in London in the early 1770's. The complex nature of the Adam-Clérisseau interchange makes a simple explanation for the relationship of these two sets of grotesques difficult. Part of the answer lies in the antique and Renaissance sources behind both decorations. Yet it seems likely that a part of the solution is also to be found in the inspiration furnished Clérisseau by Adam's mature grotesques. The end result is not, of course, identical to Adam's work, but the similarity cannot be ignored.

The relationship between later French grotesques and those of Adam is by no means as close. At Bagatelle (1777), Fontainebleau (boudoir, 1783), and the *petits appartements* at Versailles (1779–83; 1788–89), there are some motifs similar to Adam; but none of the French rooms is really Adamesque. A comparison of the Bagatelle grotesques with those in the Vatican reveals a much closer resemblance, though an entirely different spirit. Very possibly the popularity of this form in England inspired French designers, but they looked to antiquity and the Renaissance, even more than to Adam, for specific sources.

The problem of the grotesque panels epitomizes the whole question of Adam-French relationship in regard to the birth and development of Neo-classical architecture, decoration, and furniture. The influences are involved and reciprocal, and the resulting styles are quite different, despite their common Neo-classicism. It is possible to see France as a source of the Adam style and the reverse, but only in the light of the complex relationship of Adam and French Neo-classicism.

Figure h. 'Tablet for an Eating Room Chimney with a Bas Relief of Bacchanalian Boys, 21ˢᵗ Janry 1775.' Sir John Soane's Museum, Vol. 6, No. 91.

CHAPTER FOUR

THE COLLABORATORS

The enormous output of the Adam office was the result of a highly-developed system. Robert, as the impresario, was assisted by his brother James, their younger brother William whose principal department was that of finances, a number of draftsmen, and scores of craftsmen. Even before James joined the firm on his return from the Continent late in 1763, Robert had established a well-organized and efficient office. Although Robert was undoubtedly very quick—James wrote in 1762 that, 'I think from what I can perceive he makes plans much faster than I can make Cornishes'[65]—he could not alone have produced the wealth of drawings that pre-date James's arrival nor could he have progressed so far on so many projects. The sketches that he made himself, together with the necessary visits to clients and supervision of accounts, indicate tremendous energy and enterprise. But the success of his early career in London, as well as of his subsequent efforts, was also due to his organizational ability.

While still in Italy Adam had realized the need for draftsmen and office assistants, and he assembled there a group to assist him in making views of ruins and drawings for his various publication projects. Of the men he employed in Rome, Robert chose two to bring back to England, Agostino Brunias and the man he called 'Liegois,' almost certainly Laurent-Benoît Dewez. Brunias, a Roman painter whom Adam and Clérisseau had converted into an architect, was acclaimed by his new employer for doing 'all my ornaments, & all my figures vastly well.'[66] The draftsman from Liege, whom Robert described as his 'plan man & Line drawer,' is never identified by name, but he would appear to be the Laurent-Benoît Dewez who was a pensioner of the Liegois Fondation Darchis in Rome from 1754 to 1757.[67] Although he is traditionally reputed to have worked under Vanvitelli at Caserta and to have travelled in Greece, Syria, Egypt, Sweden, Denmark, England, and other countries, all between 1757 and his arrival in Brussels in 1760, there is strong reason to believe that he was instead with Robert Adam on the Continent and in England. Dewez' Italian drawings are very close to Adam's, but even more convincing are his drawing of a chimney-piece at Whitton dated April 1758 and his use of Adam's favourite Palladian motif within relieving arch on the façade of the Abbey of Afflighem (begun 1764).[68]

In addition to Dewez and Brunias, Robert also requested James to recruit Scottish assistants of the type Dewez might supervise. Presumably with some of these Scottish draftsmen and with his two Continental assistants, Adam set up his office in London early in 1758. On 1 February, one member of the Adam family informed the others in Edinburgh of conversing in French with 'Mess.ᵗˢ Liegois & Romaine,'[69] but by the end of that year the Liegois had slipped away without telling Robert or even Brunias. He accused Adam of using him as a slave and vowed to return only if Robert assured him that nothing he had signed would be used against him. Although annoyed, Adam agreed, for, as he wrote James, his Liegois knew 'Adam's' way of drawing. Should he come back, Robert intended to use him to train others, in case this should happen again.[70] Whether or not he did return is unknown, but by 1760 he was in Brussels, where he became the leading Neo-classical architect of Belgium.[71] Brunias remained with the firm at least until the end of 1762, but his subsequent relations with Adam are not known. In 1763 and 1764 he exhibited landscapes at the Free Society and in 1770, at the Society of Artists. By that date he had gone to the West Indies, the results of his journey being exhibited at the Royal Academy in 1777 and 1779.[72]

In order to enrich and replenish the Adams' supply of Italian draftsmen, James recruited three more during his Grand Tour—a Florentine named Agostino Scara, Giuseppe Sacco from Verona, and a young man from Naples identified only as Benedetto.[73] In addition to these, James brought back George Richardson, whom he had taken with him to Italy. Richardson had been employed in the Adams' Scottish office, but joined, with James, the London establishment when they returned at the end of 1763. In the introduction to his *Book of Ceilings* of 1776, Richardson speaks of the many advantages he has had 'in the Study of Architecture, both at Home and Abroad, under these eminent Masters Messers. ADAM of the ADELPHI, for whom I was employed in Drawing and Designing upwards of eighteen Years,' and the Adam account at Drummond's Bank contains numerous payments to him from 1764, when the account began, to 1769.[74]

From this group of draftsmen, primarily Italian and Scotttish, came the finished drawings of the early years that Adam presented to his clients and the office duplicates which, together with some of the returned or rejected copies, fill many of the volumes of Adam drawings at the Soane Museum. The use of both native and imported delineators continued all through Adam's career. Italian inscriptions appear on certain later drawings,[75] and there is abundant documentation for payment to specific Italians.

The first of these to appear in the Adam accounts is Giuseppe Manocchi, to whom four payments were made in 1766, totalling £134.[76] While the exact relationship of Manocchi to the Adam firm is obscure, there are a sizeable number of Manocchi drawings, almost exclusively finished renderings of arabesques or of ceiling decorations, among the Adam drawings at the Soane Museum. Many of these are signed and dated 1765 or 1766, and there are also many sketches by

Manocchi at the Royal Institute of British Architects and at the Metropolitan Museum of Art which are dated in London between 25 April 1765 and 29 July 1766, one day after the last payment recorded in the Adam bank account.[77] A number of the sketches are inscribed 'di Mia invenzione,' suggesting that most of his work in London was merely copying or the working out of someone else's designs. Certain of the sketches were utilized in the execution of the finished drawings at the Soane Museum, but none of Manocchi's renderings appear to have served as sources for specific Adam decorations.

Much less elusive than Manocchi was Antonio Zucchi, who not only served Adam as his principal decorative painter but also seems to have done both drafting and designing. Zucchi (1726–92) had accompanied James Adam on his tour of Italy and had executed for him many drawings, some of which were sent to Robert. Although James left him in Italy, he was in London at least by 1767, when he painted ruin scenes for Osterley. Recorded Adam payments to Zucchi begin only on 27 May 1768, after which they are very numerous. Most of these payments were for the decorative pictures painted by Zucchi for a number of Adam houses, but some remittances were probably also for designing and drafting. An example of this latter type of work is seen in a bill from the Moorfields carpet-maker Thomas Moore to Sir Watkin Williams-Wynn, which includes, 'Paid M.ʳ Anthony Zucchi by M.ʳ Adam's order for painting a small pattern of the Carpet . . . £10. 0. 0.'[78]

Similarly, Zucchi possibly designed or made elaborate drawings for detailed decoration, as for chimney-pieces at 20 St. James's Square or the bas-relief panels desired for the hall at Nostell.[79] But Zucchi's activities as a designer were definitely secondary to Adam's. His work in this field appears to have been limited to the design of inset paintings and possibly of bas-reliefs. Most of the decorative paintings are indicated on the Adam drawings in a stock, schematized fashion, and whereas the majority of Adam drawings were followed very closely, the inset paintings are almost invariably quite different from those on the drawings. The major exceptions are when Zucchi himself had sketched in the prospective pictorial decoration.[80]

107

134, 138, 141

A third Italian whose name figures in the Adam bank account was Joseph Bonomi (1739–1808), to whom payments were made in 1770 and 1771. Born and educated in Rome, he came to England about 1767, reputedly at the invitation of the Adams.[81] After a few years in their office, he worked for Thomas Leverton and later established himself as an architect in his own right.

Adam also continued to employ British delineators, and even after his death architects advertised themselves as former draftsmen in his office. Two such men published advertisements in Philadelphia in 1794 and 1797 proclaiming their experience under Adam as an indication of their worth. One, in fact, to illustrate his ability and thorough training, included an extensive list of Adam's last works.[82]

Although the assistants changed with time, the procedure in the office seems to have remained fairly constant. It is possible to form an idea of the system from the large number of drawings in the Adam collection at the Soane Museum. There are sketches, finished renderings, office duplicates, and detailed studies for all types of commissions from the earliest days in London to the death of James in 1794. Taken together, they furnish repeated examples of the working method of the office and of the roles of the architects Robert and James, of the draftsmen, and also of the craftsmen who executed the work. A complete dossier does not exist for every project—in fact, for none of the major executed works is every step represented by drawings in the collection—but there are enough examples of each type of drawing to illustrate the system followed.

This can probably be seen most effectively in ceilings and carpets, where about 100 of the almost 680 different designs represented in renderings at the Soane Museum can be related to existing preparatory sketches. These range through Adam's career, beginning with Hatchlands in 1759, although they are less full for the late 1780's and early 1790's. Most of the sketches are in pencil or charcoal, sometimes with colour notations. They may take the form of tiny, though careful models or of large drawings, either hastily sketched out or fairly carefully delineated. They may even be no more than lightly-drawn designs on the floor plan of a house. But regardless of the form or degree of finish—often only a quarter of the pattern is sketched in—the ideas of the architect were followed quite closely in the finished drawings. Very little room was left for creativity on the part of the draftsmen.

Perhaps the best example of a single design with a complete set of drawings is that of a carpet for Coventry House, London, about 1767. The earliest sheet in
154 the group is a charcoal sketch, roughly drawn by Adam himself, with notations for all the colours, except for part of the border. The next step is probably a more
156 careful pencil sketch by one of the draftsmen for two different carpet designs. The right half, for Coventry House, indicates how Adam's charcoal sketch would appear in an overall pattern. The other part is not an alternate scheme, but, rather, large- and small-scale sketches for the gallery carpet at Syon, upon which Adam was also engaged at about this time. The Coventry House carpet as envisioned in the two sketches was then illustrated in a coloured rendering, which would be sent
155 to the client. An office copy, only partially filled in and coloured, would at the same time be filed away. In both design and colour, it follows very closely the charcoal sketch by Adam, although also offering an alternate colour scheme. The process
157, 158 is carried one step further in two large-scale details by the same draftsman, probably produced for the guidance of the weaver. They are very similar, with the exception of the background colour in the border. Both versions of the background colour are shown on the office copy of the rendering, and a pencilled note on one of the detail drawings relates this apparent indecision on the part of the draftsman to
157 the original Adam sketch: 'Mr Adam had not time to fix the Colours of the Border But thinks that need not Stop the Estimate from being made . . .' As
154 certain areas of the border were the only parts of the charcoal sketch for which

44

no colour was indicated, the draftsmen's great dependence on Adam's sketches is very apparent.

This process, albeit with many of the steps missing, can be seen in a number of other carpet and ceiling designs, as well as in other types. The draftsmen elaborated the sketchy original idea, but they seldom made changes of any substance. The only exception to this practice has been alluded to previously—the design of inset paintings and occasionally of bas-relief panels. The sketches for ceilings which include subject panels frequently leave those blank, and even on finished renderings they are usually indicated merely by three or four stock figures. The actual design of the pictures was probably left to the painter, though the subject or colour might be suggested by Adam.

These decorative painters were among the principal members of the group of craftsmen that Adam assembled for the execution of his commissions. Just as the office draftsmen were necessary to the production of designs for so many works, so the painters, plasterers, stone and wood carvers, and furnishers of all kinds were essential to the creation of the interiors that are the crux of the Adam style. Adam's success was due as much to his ability to find and employ expert artists and artisans to carry out his designs as to his own skill as an architect and designer. Thus they, too, are important collaborators.

Of all these assisting craftsmen, the most prominent were the painters of decoration whose role we have just considered. Robert employed a good many decorative artists, but the most famous of these and the most used was Antonio Zucchi. From his arrival about 1766 until his departure in 1781 after his marriage to Angelica Kauffmann, Zucchi was constantly engaged upon work for Adam. His painting is documented in at least thirteen Adam houses, and there are late eighteenth- or early nineteenth-century references to his work in six more.[83]

29, 32, 33 39, 48, 75

Despite the fact that almost all decorative painting in Adam houses is frequently ascribed to the woman that Zucchi married, only two works can definitely be assigned to Angelica Kauffmann (1741–1807)—the signed medallions in the back drawing room at Chandos House and two overdoors in the first drawing room at Derby House, Grosvenor Square.[84] Although she undoubtedly did other work for Adam, it appears to have been far smaller in quantity and frequency than is often assumed.

Among the other well-known foreign painters whom Adam used in the decoration of his interiors were Giovanni Battista Cipriani, Michael Angelo Pergolesi, Biagio Rebecca, and Francesco Zuccarelli. Cipriani (1727–85), who came to England in 1755 with William Chambers and the sculptor Joseph Wilton, had met Adam in Florence. There Adam described him as 'the Best natur'd lad in the World who draws in the most delightful Manner imaginable in the Stiles of all the Great Masters'.[85] In England, Adam probably used Cipriani to paint the many small panels in the ceiling of the drawing room at Syon, while Cipriani's bill to Lord Shelburne of 6 February 1771 identifies five inset ceiling paintings and

125

135   eight wall paintings in the drawing room at Lansdowne House as his work.[86] Later diaries and journals mention Cipriani's work on other Adam projects—Buckingham House, the drawing room at Bowood, and 19 Arlington Street.[87] Although Pergolesi is often considered one of Adam's principal decorators, the only documented work by him under Adam is the painting of the pilasters in the

19   gallery and minor work at Syon,[88] and his name does not appear in the Adam bank account. Rebecca (1735–1808), who came to England in 1761, definitely worked at two Adam houses, Audley End and a London house in New Burlington Street, for both of which documents survive; and visitors of a slightly later date

24   credit him with three others—Harewood, Kedleston, and Kenwood—as well.[89] Zuccarelli was really a landscape painter, rather than a decorative artist, but his paintings were planned for at least three Adam interiors, Syon, Lansdowne House, and Saltram.[90]

     Although Cipriani was working for Adam by 1763 or earlier, most of the other decorative painters were not employed before the middle of the decade. Preceding all of these, however, was William Delacour, who painted a set of ruin panels for the saloon at Yester in 1761. And three years earlier Delacour had submitted an estimate for painting a room for Lord Milton's house in Edinburgh with arabesques for the Brothers Adam.[91]

     A list of Adam's decorative painters would also include William Hamilton, Andrea Casali, and possibly Pietro Maria Borgnis. Hamilton (1751–1801), the son of a Scottish assistant of the Adams, figures extensively in the Adam bank account, where many payments to him are noted from 1765 on. There is no documentation for his specific work for Adam, but three different descriptions in the early

24
18   nineteenth century credit him with decorative paintings at Kedleston.[92] Casali (c1720/24-after 1783) painted the grisailles in the dining room at Syon in 1769; and, according to Mrs. Lybbe-Powys, the decorator of the Etruscan Room at

46   Osterley was 'Berners,' perhaps P. M. Borgnis (1743–1810), son of the painter at West Wycombe.[93]

     Vying in significance with inset paintings in the Adam decorative scheme were bas-relief decorations, primarily in plaster. Robert's letters from Rome are filled with references to the importance of bas-reliefs, and their inclusion is characteristic of most of his post-Italian designs. Although plasterwork was designed for his earliest completed interior, General Bland's drawing room at

11, 15   Isleworth of 1758–59, it was not in the antique manner, a lapse that Robert attributed to his inability to find English stuccoers who could execute such work.

12   For Hatchlands, Adam designed grotesque panels, but these were not executed, due to either lack of money or lack of competent workmen, though other elaborate if less classical plasterwork was completed.[94]

     In the early 1760's Adam found it necessary, or desirable, to have made in Rome Neo-classical reliefs for important commissions. These included plaques for

18   monuments, as well as the relief of the three graces for the dining room at Syon,

Rbt. Mylne pd. — money to Wm. Hamilton of Diary, 23 May 1783

which was being made by Luc-François Breton (1731–1800) in 1762.[95] But before this last work was completed, Adam had found a firm of English plasterworkers both able to carry out his designs and amenable to his tastes, the firm of Joseph Rose.

The existence in the firm of two men named Joseph Rose, an uncle and a nephew, complicates the problem of the individual principally responsible for various Adam commissions, but together and in succession they produced the stucco decoration of almost all of the major Adam houses. Joseph Rose I (c1723–80), was apprenticed to the Yorkshire stuccoer Thomas Perrit in 1738 and at some point after leaving Perrit moved to London. He was joined, and on his death succeeded, by his nephew Joseph Rose II (1746–99), who was probably Adam's principal stuccoer.[96]

The first record of the Roses' work for Adam is a bill covering activity at Shardeloes from 10 October 1761 to 19 February 1763.[97] After that, the work of the Roses is documented at all of the great succession of Adam houses—Croome Court, Bowood, Syon, Kedleston, Mersham-le-Hatch, Harewood, Audley End, Kenwood, Nostell Priory, Newby, Luton, Saltram, and Alnwick, as well as in all of the important London houses.[98] Adam payments to the Roses are also extensive, from the opening of the account at Drummond's Bank in 1764.

13, 120

60, 70, 75
80–82, 130, 131

As with Adam's other craftsmen, the plasterworkers carried out the Adam designs with virtually no alteration. This can be seen by comparing any of the drawings at the Soane Museum with the executed works for which they were intended. The only difference—but it is a highly significant one—is that between the character of three-dimensional plasterwork and the lines of the Adam draftsmen.

28, 29

Whereas almost all of his plasterwork was executed by one firm, Adam ranged very widely in his choice of stone carvers for chimney-pieces and medallions. The first of these was Michael Rysbrack (1694–1770), whom we have already seen as the carver of the caryatid chimney-piece at Hopetoun in 1756 and probably the similar one at Hatchlands three years later. He also collaborated with Adam on two English monuments, those of Sir Nathaniel Curzon at Kedleston, c1763, and of Admiral Edward Boscawen at St. Michael Penkevil, Cornwall, dated 1763.

94
98

Michael Henry Spang (d.1762), a Dane who came to London about 1756, was another early stone carver used by Adam. There are two drafts to Spang, both dated 1760, among the Adam correspondence with his first bankers, and Spang is credited with carving the sculptural detail on the Admiralty Screen, the monument to James Thomson in Westminster Abbey, and chimney-pieces at Kedleston, all c1759–60.[99]

23

Among the stone carvers whom Adam employed from the 1760's on were the brothers Benjamin and Thomas Carter, William Collins, William Tyler, John Moore, John Devall, Joseph Wilton, Joseph Nollekens, John Hinchliff, and Peter (or Patrick) Henderson. Benjamin Carter (d.1766) and his younger brother Thomas

100–101 (d.1795) submitted detailed bills for chimney-pieces carved for Shardeloes, Croome, Bowood, Lansdowne House, and Mersham-le-Hatch;[100] and much of their work can be identified in existing pieces and on the Adam drawings. Benjamin, along with a number of other craftsmen used by Adam, subscribed to the *Ruins of Spalatro,* while payments to Thomas are recorded in the Adam bank account in 1768 and 1769. William Collins (1721–93), who also received payments in those years as well as in 1767, made the medallions on the north façades of Harewood and

91 Kedleston, 1760 and 1761, and the chimney-piece tablet for the library at Nostell in 1767.[101] Both William Tyler (d.1801) and John Moore (d.1809) carved chimney-pieces at Audley End.[102]

As with Joseph Rose, there were two John Devalls (or Deval) who worked for Adam, John Devall I (1701–74) and his son (1728–94). Payments are recorded to them in the Adam bank account from 1766 to 1769 and again in the mid-1770's. Documented chimney-pieces by the Devalls include work at Coventry

102 House and Nostell Priory, *c*1767, and at Sir John Griffin Griffin's in New Burlington Street a decade later.[103]

Two famous sculptors not generally associated with Adam but actually used by him were Joseph Wilton and Joseph Nollekens. Wilton (1722–1803), whom Adam had met in Florence, carved the caryatid chimney-piece in the gallery at

20 Croome (for which he charged £300 in 1766) and is mentioned in connexion with bas-reliefs in the gallery at Syon in the Duke of Northumberland's memorandum book, *c*1767. He also designed a rather unclassical chimney-piece for the hall at Osterley, but it was not executed.[104] Nollekens (1737–1823) appears to have worked at Harewood, for his name appears on an Adam drawing of a chimney-piece for the first drawing room which was executed.[105] Less famous are John Hinchliff

106, 107 (d.1796), who supplied chimney-pieces for 20 St. James's Square, *c*1773, and Peter (or Patrick) Henderson of Edinburgh, who was responsible for marble

113 chimney-pieces at Culzean.[106]

Adam's wood carvers, as distinct from cabinet-makers, were somewhat fewer than the quite numerous stone sculptors whom he employed. During the early years in London, Adam's major carver of wooden decorations, mouldings, bookcases, chimney-pieces, and frames was Sefferin Alken, whose name is also given as Saffron and as Alkin and Alkan. There are two drafts to him from Adam in 1759 and 1760, and his name appears in the accounts for Shardeloes and Croome between 1761 and 1765. Among his more notable works were the library bookcases

90 for Croome. At Croome, too, he also carved in stone—both chimney-pieces in the house and decoration on garden buildings—and he appears to have done some work at Coventry House as well.[107]

From the mid-1760's on, Adam used such wood carvers as John Gilbert, John Minshall, John and/or William Adair, and William Cairncross. Payments to Gilbert appear in the Adam bank account as early as 1764, and his work is documented at Lansdowne House and Osterley. Minshall (or Minshull) was employed at Kenwood in the late 1760's, while Cairncross worked at Culzean twenty years later. For the name Adair there are at least two references—as the carver of a picture frame for Lord Shelburne in 1772 and for substantial amounts of fine wood carving, including the ante-room chimney-piece, for Sir John Griffin Griffin's house in New Burlington Street in 1778–79, the latter specifically by W. R. Adair.[108]

Some of the wood carvers also made furniture for Adam's clients, but in this they were largely secondary to more famous cabinet-makers. The relationship of Adam to the fashionable makers of furniture who supplied pieces for his clients has been considered in some detail by Eileen Harris, who distinguished between Adam-designed furniture and that made by such well-known cabinet-makers as Chippendale or Ince and Mayhew.[109] In the execution of Adam's own furniture designs, he often used the wood-carvers who were already engaged by him on other tasks, but he might also supply designs to professional furniture-makers, such as William France (at Croome and Kenwood).[110] Adam's relations with carvers, cabinet-makers, and even painters is often highly complex; and it is important, as Dr. Harris has emphasized, to realize that the appearance of Neo-classical furniture by Chippendale or other famous cabinet-makers in an Adam house by no means indicates Adam's authorship of the furniture designs.

Just as the wood carvers overlap into the category of cabinet-makers, at the other end of the spectrum they begin to merge with the carpenters and contractors. Of these, perhaps the best known is John Hobcroft, who was the master carpenter at Croome, Coventry House, Sir John Griffin Griffin's New Burlington Street house, and probably Mamhead.[111] Adam kept a check on this work, examining and approving bills, as he did for scores of other workmen—plumbers, glaziers, slaters, bricklayers, and suppliers of such commodities as pulleys, hinges, and wire.[112] Of course in all these cases, the actual measuring and checking was usually done by a supervisor or clerk of the works, but Adam was certainly aware of them.

Far more interesting than these craftsmen, however, were the makers of decorative objects to Adam's designs. Not only did Adam design carpets, door furniture, stove grates, stair rails, and myriad other pieces, but he also selected craftsmen and approved their work. Bills for work at 20 St. James's Square amply demonstrate this. In 1773 and 1774 William Kinman & Co. charged Sir Watkin Williams-Wynn for balconies, fanlight, stair railing, hall lantern, and candle branches in the music room; while Hopkins & Co. supplied fenders, tongs, and stove grates, including one for the front drawing room with '4 round fluted term feet with rams heads on Do., the whole to Mr Adams Designs & Curiously embossed.'[113] Thomas Blockley, whose name appears on Adam drawings for door furniture and in the Adam bank account in 1769, also billed Sir Watkin Williams-Wynn for locks, as well as for sash pulls and other assorted items.[114] And among the charges of the Moorfield's carpet maker Thomas Moore to Sir Watkin was the

159

payment to Zucchi on Adam's order for painting a small pattern of a carpet noted earlier. Adam similarly mentioned Moore in his bills, as when he charged Sir Laurence Dundas £6. 0. 0 'To painting in Oyl all the parts of the Carpet at Large for Mr. Moor' for the saloon at 19 Arlington Street.[115] Other Adam houses for which Moore made or sold carpets were Croome, Coventry House, Syon, and Mersham.[116] As was the case in other areas, Adam did not rely solely on Moore for carpets. The drawing room carpet at Saltram, designed by Adam in 1769, was woven at Axminster, and John Parker paid £126 for it on 2 October 1770.[117]

There were, of course, many more craftsmen employed by Adam than those enumerated here. Among the more famous were Richter and Bartoli who supplied scagliola-inlaid tables 'According to Mess.rs Adam's Disaing' for the saloon at Nostell, as well as for Croome and possibly for Ashburnham House.[118] But there were scores of others who are less renowned or whose names have not come down to us. All of them, the fashionable and the more obscure, made up Adam's 'regiment of artificers,' as Mrs. Montagu called them in 1779.[119]

Adam's decorative work as we know it owes a great debt to the painters, plasterworkers, carvers, and host of other craftsmen that Adam employed. Without the assistance of skilled artists capable of carrying out his designs in three dimensions, Adam would have been unable to achieve the 'kind of revolution in the whole system of this useful and elegant art,' which he and James claimed. But, with the possible exception of some of the decorative painters, these men were not creative artists; they were simply expert and sensitive craftsmen. Robert may have accepted some suggestions from his craftsmen, but they were essentially collaborators in execution, not in creation. The same was largely the case with Adam's office assistants. They collaborated in the production of the drawings, but they did not invent the designs. All contributed to the production of the Adam projects, but Robert himself remained the dominant force.

Trained by his father, educated and broadened by Clérisseau, aided by James and by the assistance of scores of delineators and craftsmen, Robert evolved the Adam style of decoration and supervised its execution. Without any of these, it would not have been the same, but it principally owes its creation and development to one man—Robert Adam.

50

Figure i. Detail of Design for a Temple at Audley End, Essex, 1772.
Courtesy of the Hon. Robin Neville, Audley End.

FOOTNOTES

1 (London, 1792), I, 40.

2 Letter to Lord Kames, 31 March 1763 (Register House, Edinburgh, Abercairny Papers, No. 564).

3 THE GENTLEMAN'S MAGAZINE, LXII (March 1792), 282–83. See also Robert Adam, 'Account Book of a Trip to Scotland,' 15 May 1791–11 January 1792 (Register House, Edinburgh, Clerk of Penicuik Papers, No. 4968).

4 Robert and James Adam, *The Works in Architecture* (London, 1773–78), I, i, 3.

5 *Ibid.*

6 For a discussion of this phenomenon, see John Summerson, *The Classical Country House in 18th-Century England*, JOURNAL OF THE ROYAL SOCIETY OF ARTS, CVII (July 1959), 567–68, esp.

7 *Works*, I, i, 3.

8 For these early sketches, see James Adam's sketchbook at Penicuik House (Coll. of Sir John Clerk, Bart.) and Robert Adam's drawings in Sir John Soane's Museum, London, Adam Drawings, Vol. 9, Nos. 1–71.

9 'Draft Notes of a Life of Robert Adam' (Register House, Edinburgh, Clerk of Penicuik Papers, No. 4981).

10 Adam wrote frequently about 'the true the Simple & Grand Architecture' (Letter to Helen Adam, Rome, 23 Oct. 1756; Register House, Edinburgh, Clerk of Penicuik Papers, No. 4823), and one of the great disappointments of his life was that he was never really able to build a great public edifice commensurate with his love for the grand.

11 *Works*, I, i, 5–6.

12 For information on Adam's youth and early career in Scotland, see John Clerk, 'Draft Notes of a Life of Robert Adam' (Register House, Edinburgh, Clerk of Penicuik Papers, No. 4981), and John Fleming, *Robert Adam and His Circle* (London, 1962), Chapter 3.

13 Noted in a letter of Rev. Richard Pococke, 10 Sept. 1760, in his *Tours in Scotland: 1747, 1750, 1760*, ed. D. W. Kemp (*Publications of the Scottish History Society*, Vol. I, Edinburgh, 1887), p. 298.

14 See below, page 37. For Rysbrack's description of this piece and his two drawings related to it, as well as for Adam's letters and his specific statements concerning the chimney-piece sketch, see the notes to Fig. 94.

15 Letter to James Adam (Register House, Edinburgh, Clerk of Penicuik Papers, No. 4764). For information on Adam's Grand Tour, I have mainly utilized the letters in the Clerk Papers. For a more detailed description of the trip, see Fleming, *Robert Adam and His Circle*, Chapters 4–6.

16 Letter to James Adam, 19 Oct. 1755 (Register House, Edinburgh, Clerk of Penicuik Papers, No. 4789).

17 *Ibid.* For Adam and Winckelmann, see letters from Winckelmann to H. D. Berendis and to Anton Raphael Mengs, 29 Jan. 1757 and 28 July 1762, in J. J. Winckelmann, *Briefe*, ed. Walther Rehm (Berlin, 1952–57), I, 267, and II, 255.

18 Letter from Robert to James Adam, 24 July 1756 (Register House, Edinburgh, Clerk of Penicuik Papers, No. 4811). For the trip to Spalato, see other letters from Robert to James Adam, 6 Aug. and 1 Nov. 1757 (Clerk Papers, Nos. 4841 and 4843) and the preface to R. Adam, *Ruins of the Palace of the Emperor Diocletian at Spalatro in Dalmatia* (London, 1764). For a more detailed discussion, see John Fleming, *The Journey to Spalatro*, ARCHITECTURAL REVIEW, CXXIII (Feb. 1958), 103–107.

19 Letter to James Adam, 24 July 1756 (Register House, Edinburgh, Clerk of Penicuik Papers, No. 48/11).

20 Letter to James Adam, probably Nov. or Dec. 1758 (Register House, Edinburgh, Clerk of Penicuik Papers, No. 4853/1).

21 Dates given here and in the following paragraphs are those for interior decorative designs and work; they do not include exteriors, outbuildings, or furnishings.

22 Letter to Sir Horace Mann, 22 April 1775 (*The Letters of Horace Walpole*, ed. Mrs. Paget Toynbee, Oxford, 1903–1905, IX, 186). A decade earlier Adam had been designing for Walpole at Strawberry Hill (see Figs. 169–170), and as late as 21 June 1773, Walpole described Osterley up to that time as 'the palace of palaces!' (Letter to Countess of Upper Ossory, *Letters*, VIII, 291).

23 James Adam, *Practical Essays on Agriculture* (London, 1789), I, iii.

24 An example of Adam's decreasing use of certain interior architectural features is furnished by full overmantels, of which 14 can be dated between 1758 and 1763, but relatively few thereafter. *How many: "relatively few"?*

25 Register House, Edinburgh, Abercairny Papers, No. 564.

26 Some decorative paintings can be dated before 1765, but the vast majority were executed later. For discussion of Adam's decorative painters, see below, pp. 45–46. For Joseph Rose's plasterwork for Adam, see pp. 46–47.

27 The only dated ruin panels executed for an Adam commission before the mid-1760's are those in the saloon at Yester, signed by William Delacour and dated 1761.

28 The other rooms decorated in the 'Etruscan' style were those at Derby House, Grosvenor Sq.; Apsley House; Home House (all mentioned in the *Works in Architecture*, II, i); the drawing room at Byram (Fig. 55); the great dining room at Cumberland House (Fig. 56); 'Mr Adamson's Parlor' (Soane Mus., Adam Drawings, Vol. 14, Nos. 136–37), probably in the Adelphi; and a small room under the stairs of the garden façade of Osterley (*Ibid.*, Vol. 14, No. 54). Part of the 'Etruscan' decoration has been restored in Home House (now the Courtauld Institute of Art), and the small garden room at Osterley also survives.

29 Eileen Harris, *The Furniture of Robert Adam* (TIRANTI CHAPTERS IN ART, Vol. XXXVIII; London, 1963).

30 For the organ cases that are not illustrated see *Works*, II, ii, 8 (20 St. James's Sq.) and Soane Mus., Adam Drawings, Vol. 25, No.

14 (Great Saxham). For the cabinets, see Soane Mus., Adam Drawings, Vol. 17, Nos. 213 (Coventry) and 216 (Lansdowne).

31 I, i, 5. Shardeloes furnishes a good example of a commission that began with ceilings. The earliest reference to Adam is the contractor's statement that he had 'delivered the Plans of your best Rooms to Mr Adams, . . . And as soon as He has made Designs, for the Ceilings &c (which you approve) I will immediately send as many Plaisterers as can be employed' (Letter from Stiff Leadbetter to William Drake, 13 Feb. 1761; Buckingham County Record Office, Aylesbury, Shardeloes MSS).

32 *Works*, I, i, 6.

33 Library at Shardeloes and dining room at Syon (both 1761); dining room at Shardeloes (1761) and 2 duplicates—dining room at Osterley (*c*1766) and unexecuted design for Green Drawing Room at Harewood (1765); gallery at Syon (1763) and great drawing room at Audley End (1764); and unidentified room at Compton Verney (1763) and Charles Rogers' dining room in Laurence Pountney Lane (London, 1765).

34 *Works*, I, iii, 4.

35 For an example of this, see below, pp. 44–45.

36 For more on this, see Harris, *The Furniture of Robert Adam*, p. 25.

37 *Ibid.*

38 *Works*, I, i, 3.

39 See, *e.g.*, Soane Mus., 'Miscellaneous Sketches and Drawings by Robert Adam and Others,' No. 36.

40 All through his life he made sketches of medieval structures or variations based on them, as *e.g.*, a drawing made near Coblenz, 1 Dec. 1757, or a watercolour of the façade of Wells Cathedral dated 1792, the year of his death (Soane Mus., Adam Drawings, Vol. 54, Part iv, No. 2; and Vol. 2, No. 68).

41 For Adam's Grand Tour, see Chapter I, above; and for more specific details, see Fleming, *Robert Adam and His Circle*, Chapters 4–6. The Adam sales relevant to a discussion of Adam's sources are as follows: (1) 26–27 Feb. and 1–2 Mar. 1773; (2) 9–13 June 1785; (3) 20–21 May (library and drawings) and 22 May (collection) 1818; (4) 9 July 1821. All sales were handled by Christie's, where copies of the sales catalogues are still available. Most of the books and a number of the other objects are listed by Arthur T. Bolton, *The Architecture of Robert*

and James Adam (London, 1922), II, 324–37.

[42] Letter to his mother, 24 Jan. 1756 (Register House, Edinburgh, Clerk of Penicuik Papers, No. 4797).

[43] Letter to Peggy Adam, 5 Mar. 1755 (Register House, Edinburgh, Clerk of Penicuik Papers, No. 4766).

[44] *Ibid.*

[45] Demonstrated by the arrangement of the map of the Mediterranean on the frontispiece of the Adam *Works in Architecture*. First noted in F. Saxl and R. Wittkower, *British Art and the Mediterranean* (London, 1948), p. 71.

[46] Soane Mus., Adam Drawings, Vol. 9, No. 195.

[47] Copy of a letter of 8 Feb. 1762 (Register House, Edinburgh, Clerk of Penicuik Papers, No. 4926). The Audley End drawing, signed and dated 1763, is in a scrap book at Audley End, p. 110; the charge to Lord Coventry in June 1765 is in a bill covering Mar. 1764 to June 1765 (Croome Estate Office, Worcs.).

[48] I, i, 4.

[49] Letter to Countess of Upper Ossory, 21 June 1773, in Walpole, *Letters*, ed. Toynbee, VIII, 292. Probably also derived from Palmyra are ceilings at Bowood, Compton Verney, and Audley End (*cf.* Wood, Pls. XXXVII B, VIII, and XLII C).

[50] *Works*, I, i, 5.

[51] Rudolf Wittkower, *Art and Architecture in Italy, 1600 to 1750* (Harmondsworth, 1958), p. 360, note 36 (viii).

[52] P. 9 and Pls. 2, 3, and 55. For a more detailed account of the Adam-Piranesi relationship, see Damie Stillman, *Robert Adam and Piranesi*, in ESSAYS IN THE HISTORY OF ARCHITECTURE PRESENTED TO RUDOLF WITTKOWER, Ed. D. Fraser, H. Hibbard, and M. J. Lewine (London, 1967).

[53] See *Works*, I, i, 4–5, and letter to Helen Adam, 23 Oct. 1756 (Register House, Edinburgh, Clerk of Penicuik Papers, No. 4823).

[54] Saxl and Wittkower, p. 73.

[55] *Works*, I, i, 5. Adam's private comments at the time were much less complimentary. See letters to James Adam, 5 Sept. and 11 Dec. 1758 (Register House, Edinburgh, Clerk of Penicuik Papers, Nos. 4852 and 4854).

[56] For a recent discussion of the English-French problem, especially as it relates to furniture, see Harris, pp. 9–13. The strongly pro-Adam side is best seen in various writings by Fiske Kimball, *e.g.*, *Les influences anglaises dans la formation du style Louis XVI*, GAZETTE DES BEAUX-ARTS, 6th Ser., V (1931), 29–44 and 231–55; and *The Moor Park Tapestry Suite of Furniture by Robert Adam*, PHILADELPHIA MUSEUM OF ART BULLETIN, Vol. XXXVI, No. 189 (Mar. 1941).

[57] Letter from Walpole to Sir Horace Mann, 30 Nov. 1762, in Walpole *Letters*, ed. Toynbee, V, 280.

[58] An article by C.-N. Cochin in the MERCURE DE FRANCE in Dec. 1754 does just that.

[59] F. M. Grimm's famous 'tout est à Paris à la grecque' of 1763 is in *Correspondance littéraire*, . . . , ed. M. Tourneux (Paris, 1877–82), V, 282. Walpole's remarks are seen, *e.g.*, in letters to Sir Horace Mann and to Miss Anne Pitt, 9 Apr. 1764 and 1 Mar. 1766, in Walpole, *Letters*, ed. Toynbee, VI, 47 and 426.

[60] Svend Eriksen, *Lalive de Jully's Furniture 'à la grecque,'* BURLINGTON MAGAZINE, CIII (Aug. 1961), 340–47. For the paintings illustrating furniture at this date, see Jean Seznec and Jean Adhémar, eds. *Diderot Salons* (Oxford, 1957–60), Vol. I, Figs. 31, 52, 72, and 83.

[61] C.-N. Cochin, *Mémoires inédits*, ed. Charles Henry (Paris, 1880), p. 143.

[62] Adam's awareness of French Neo-classical designs of the late 1750's is indicated in his probable use of French courtyard screens as inspiration for the Admiralty Screen of 1759. *Cf.*, *e.g.*, Neufforge *Recueil élémentaire d'architecture . . .* (Paris, 1757–80), Vol. I, Pl. 43. Adam's concepts of planning were also partially derived from France, as he himself admitted 15 or 20 years later (*Works*, I, i, 10 and II, i, 1) and as is quite evident by looking through the plates of Neufforge.

[63] In Jan. 1764 Adam charged Lord Coventry for 'a Design for finishing the Sides of the Tapestry Room (Not finished)' and for 'Altering the French Designs of the Tapestry room in Colours' in a bill to Lord Coventry covering Aug. 1760 to Feb. 1764 (Croome Estate Office, Worcs.). For Adam and the French tapestries, see Eileen Harris, *Robert Adam and the Gobelins*, APOLLO, LXXVI (Apr. 1962), 100–106. The four Adam clients who purchased the sets were the Earl of Coventry (Croome), Sir Laurence Dundas (Moor Park), William Weddell (Newby), and Robert Child (Osterley). The situation in respect to furniture, as Dr. Harris has shown, appears to be somewhat different than that discussed here for interior decoration.

64 E. Croft-Murray. *The Hôtel Grimod de la Reynière: The Salon Decorations.* APOLLO, LXXVIII (Nov. 1963), 379–381. For references to dates suggested by others, see notes to Fig. 79.

65 Letter to Peggy Adam, 22 Oct. 1762 (Register House, Edinburgh, Clerk of Penicuik Papers, No. 4945).

66 Letter to James Adam, 11 Sept. 1756 (Register House, Edinburgh, Clerk of Penicuik Papers, No. 4817). In 1754 Brunias had won the third prize in the second class of painting at the Accademia di San Luca (Fleming, *Robert Adam and His Circle*, p. 360).

67 Letter to James Adam cited in preceding note. For Dewez in Italy, see Simone Ansiaux, '*Les dessins d'Italie' de Laurent-Benoît Dewez*, BULLETIN DE L'INSTITUT HISTORIQUE BELGE DE ROME, Fasc. XXVII (1952), pp. 7–15.

68 Dewez reputed travels are inscribed on his tombstone, the epitaph of which is printed in Léon Dewez, *Laurent-Benoît Dewez Premier Architecte de la cour de Bruxelles sous Charles de Lorraine*, ANNALES DE LA SOCIÉTÉ ROYALE D'ARCHÉOLOGIE DE BRUXELLES, XXXV (1930), 93. This tradition was accepted by H. Gerson and E. H. Ter Kuile, *Art and Architecture in Belgium*, 1600 to 1800 (Harmondsworth, 1960), p. 33; but Ansiaux, BULL. DE L'INST. HIST. BELGE DE ROME, XXVII, 9, is not very satisfied with it. For drawings by Dewez related to Adam, see Archives Générales du Royaume, Brussels, Dept. of Maps and Plans, Fond Dewez, *e.g.*, Nos. 10, 13, 18, and 64a. The possibility of Dewez identification with 'Liegois' was first suggested to me by John Fleming, who subsequently published this information. See his *Robert Adam and His Circle*, pp. 216, 255, and 359–60. For Dewez design for the Abbey of Afflighem, see Léon Dewez, ANNALES, SOC. ROY. d'ARCHÉOLOGIE DE BRUXELLES, Vol. XXXV, Fig. 12 and p. 75.

69 Register House, Edinburgh, Clerk of Penicuik Papers, No. 4847. The author is not identified.

70 Letter of 11 Dec. 1758 (Register House, Edinburgh, Clerk of Penicuik Papers, No. 4854).

71 Gerson and Ter Kuile, p. 33.

72 Letter from Betty to James Adam, 21 Dec. 1762 (Register House, Edinburgh, Clerk of Penicuik Papers, No. 4950). Algernon Graves, *The Society of Artists* (London, 1907), p. 42; and Graves, *The Royal Academy of Arts* (London, 1905–06), I, 321.

73 Letters from James to his mother, to Betty, and to William Adam, 26 Dec. 1760, 26 Dec. 1761, and 8 Jan. 1763 (Register House, Edinburgh, Clerk of Penicuik Papers, Nos. 4880, 4919, and 4955). For the full names, see Fleming, *Robert Adam and His Circle*, pp. 371 and 373.

74 Richardson's introduction is dated 22 Mar. 1774. For Adam's payments, see the Cash Ledgers at Drummond's Branch, Royal Bank of Scotland, London.

75 *E.g.*, a partially coloured duplicate for the back drawing room at Sir George Colebrooke's in Arlington St. with the notation, 'A di 4= Maggio 1771 Cominciato questo Lavoro' (Soane Mus., Adam Drawings, Vol. 12, No. 86).

76 Drummond's Bank, Cash Ledgers, 1766, pp. 320–21.

77 These 2 drawings are, respectively, Metropolitan Mus., New York, Album No. 47.112, p. 10a; and R.I.B.A., Hardwick Album III, No. 62a. Manocchi died in Rome, 29 June 1782, at the age of about 52 (Register of Deaths for S. Nicola in Arcione, Vol. XVI, 1780–91, at Archivio del Vicariato, Vatican City).

78 Item dated 29 Dec. 1774 (National Library of Wales, Aberystwyth, Wynnstay MSS, Box 115/17). For Adam's payments to Zucchi, see Drummond's Bank, Cash Ledgers.

79 Bill from Zucchi to Sir Watkin Williams-Wynn, receipted 15 June 1776 (Natl. Library of Wales, Aberystwyth, Wynnstay MSS, Box. 115/17); letter from Zucchi to Sir Rowland Winn, 16 Aug. 1776 (Nostell Priory Archives, C3/1/5/3A/5).

80 For more on Zucchi and the other decorative painters, see below, pp. 45, 46. In my investigation of Zucchi's role in the Adam productions, I have benefited greatly from discussion of the problem with Mr. Edward Croft-Murray.

81 H. M. Colvin, *Biographical Dictionary of English Architects* (London, 1954), p. 83.

82 Joseph Bowes in the GENERAL ADVERTISER, Philadelphia, 16 Oct. 1794. Also, Christopher Minifee in the FEDERAL GAZETTE, Philadelphia, 16 Nov. 1797. Noted by Alfred Coxe Prime in unpublished MSS, Henry Francis duPont Winterthur Museum, Winterthur, Del., U.S.A.

83 His work is documented through bills, letters, and signed paintings at Osterley, Mersham-le-Hatch, Kenwood, Harewood,

Luton, Saltram, Nostell Priory, Newby, and the following London houses: 29 Sackville St. (for John Parker), Lansdowne House, 20 St. James's Sq. (Wynn House), 23 (later 26) Grosvenor Sq. (Derby House), and 20 Portman Sq. (Home House). The 6 houses referred to in somewhat later writings are Compton Verney and Kedleston and the following London houses: Coventry House, Buckingham House, and Nos. 3 and 4 Royal Terrace (Adelphi). For references to the undocumented work, I am indebted to Mr. Edward Croft-Murray's kindness in allowing me to see the typescript of Vol. II of *Decorative Painting in England, 1537–1837*.

[84] Soane Mus., Adam Drawings, Vol. 54, Part vii, No. 267, is inscribed 'Frame for Mrs Angelicas Two pictures over the Doors in the first Drawing room at Lord Stanleys, Gros. S^q' For the Chandos House paintings and others attributed to her, see Lady V. Manners and G. C. Williamson, *Angelica Kauffmann, R.A.: Her Life and Her Works* (London, 1924), pp. 131–34.

[85] Letter to James Adam, 19 Feb. 1755 (Register House, Edinburgh, Clerk of Pencuik Papers, No. 4764).

[86] For Syon, see the rough draft of a letter from the Earl of Northumberland to Robert Adam, 4 Nov. [1763], in Alnwick Castle Library, Vol. XCIV, p. 45. Cipriani's bill to Lord Shelburne is reprinted in Fiske Kimball, *Lansdowne House Redivivus*, PHILADELPHIA MUSEUM BULLETIN, Vol. XXXIX (Nov. 1943).

[87] Croft-Murray, typescript.

[88] Payments for the gallery and closets off it were noted from 15 July 1766 to 25 July 1768 in 'An Account of net Receipts and Disbursements by Thos Butler' (Alnwick Castle Archives, U. I, 44).

[89] Agreements, bills, and receipts for his work at Audley End and in New Burlington St., both for Sir John Griffin Griffin, are preserved in the Essex Record Office, Chelmsford, Braybrooke Papers, D/DBy A27, A30, and A32. References to comments by later visitors to Harewood, Kedleston, and Kenwood are listed in Croft-Murray, typescript.

[90] Memorandum book of work at Syon to be carried out, 1767, lists Zuccarelli's landscapes for the gallery (Alnwick Castle Archives, U. I. 59); Diary of Lady Shelburne, p. 241, quoted by Bolton, II, 312; Croft-Murray, typescript (for Saltram).

[91] John Fleming, *Enigma of a Rococo Artist*, COUNTRY LIFE, CXXXI (24 May 1962), 1225–26.

[92] J. P. Neale, *Views of the Seats of Noblemen . . .* (London, 1818–23), Vol. I, No. 28; R. Warner, *A Tour Through the Northern Counties* (Bath, 1802), I, 122; G. Lipscomb, *A Description of Matlock-Bath* (Birmingham, 1802), p. 114. Brought to my attention by Croft-Murray, typescript.

[93] For Casali at Syon, see *Syon House Book*, pp. 41, 213–14. For Borgnis (or Berners) at Osterley, see *Passages from the Diary of Mrs. Philip Lybbe-Powys*, ed. E. J. Climenson (London, 1899), p. 231. For both of these references I am indebted to Croft-Murray, typescript.

[94] For both of these early projects, see above, pp. 15, 16.

[95] Letter from James to Helen Adam, 7 Mar. 1762 (Register House, Edinburgh, Clerk of Penicuik Papers, No. 4929).

[96] See Geoffrey W. Beard, *New Light on Adam's Craftsmen*, COUNTRY LIFE, CXXXI (10 May 1962), 1098–1100; and Beard, *A Family's 50-Year Supremacy*, COUNTRY LIFE, CXXVIII (8 Dec. 1960), 1428–29. I am greatly indebted to Mr. Beard for sharing with me the results of his research before publication.

[97] Buckingham County Record Office, Aylesbury, Shardeloes MSS.

[98] For all of these I have found bills by the Roses or references in contemporary documents. Further evidence is furnished by entries in a sketchbook by Joseph Rose II, now at Harewood, which includes details of work on many of these houses.

[99] Rupert Gunnis, *Dictionary of British Sculptors, 1660–1851* (London, 1953), p. 361. As with the other works, the Kedleston chimney-pieces are generally given to Spang, but the exact documentation is uncertain. Gunnis refers to a bill of £990. 0. 0 for chimney-pieces in the four principal rooms, but this document, as abstracted at the end of a book kept by Samuel Adams (Kedleston Archives, Vol. '3R), does not give the carver's name.

[100] Bills at Buckingham County Record Office, Aylesbury (Shardeloes MSS); Croome Estate Office; Kent County Record Office, Maidstone (Mersham Accts.). Bills for Bowood and Lansdowne House excerpted in Bolton, I, 213–14; II, 344.

[101] Gunnis, p. 111; letter from Robert Adam to Sir Rowland Winn, 18 Aug. 1767 (Nostell Archives, C3/1/5/2).

[102] Letter and bill from Robert Adam to Sir John Griffin Griffin, 13 Oct. 1763 and Dec. 1762–Jan. 1764; bill from Moore to Griffin in 'Book of Payments for Audley End' (Essex Record Office, Chelmsford, Braybrooke Papers, D/DBy C30, A365, and A259, respectively).

[103] Bills at Croome Estate Office; Nostell (C3/1/5/4/7); and Essex Record Office, Chelmsford (Braybrooke Papers, D/DBy A37).

[104] Croome Estate Office; Alnwick Castle Archives, U. I. 59; and Soane Mus., Adam Drawings, Vol. 22, No. 210 (undated).

[105] Soane Mus., Adam Drawings, Vol. 22, No. 198 (dated 1771).

[106] Bills: National Library of Wales, Aberystwyth (Wynnstay MSS, Box 115/17); and Register House, Edinburgh (Ailsa Muniments, Misc. Box X).

[107] Drafts on Innes & Clerk and Innes & Hope (Guildhall Library, London, No. 3070, pp. 37 and 38a); receipts for Shardeloes (Buckingham County Record Office, Aylesbury); bills from Adam and Alken to Lord Coventry (Croome Estate Office).

[108] For Gilbert, see Drummond's Bank, Cash Ledgers; Bolton, II, 334; and Osterley bills at the Victoria and Albert Museum, Dept. of Woodwork. For Minshall, see his bill in Bolton, II, 348. For Cairncross, see bill in Register House, Edinburgh, Ailsa Muniments, Misc. Box X. For Adair, see Ralph Edwards and Margaret Jourdain, *Georgian Cabinet-Makers* (London, 1946), p. 73; and bills in Essex Record Office, Chelmsford (Braybrooke Papers, D/DBy A37).

[109] *The Furniture of Robert Adam*, pp. 25–30.

[110] Adam's bill for Aug. 1760–Feb. 1764 (Croome Estate Office) includes 'Design of a Bed given to Mʳ France' (Dec. 1763); and France charged Lord Mansfield for furniture 'perform'd from Mr. Adam's design' (printed in Edwards and Jourdain, p. 79).

[111] Hobcroft's bills for Croome and Coventry House are at Croome Estate Office, that for New Burlington St. is at Essex Record Office, Chelmsford (Braybrooke Papers, D/DBy A37). For Mamhead, Hobcroft submitted estimates in 1766 and c1775 and signed estimates of other builders, 1772–c1775 (Coll. of Sir Ralph Newman, Bart., Blackpool, Devon).

[112] For an example of plumber's work, see bill from William Chapman to Lord Le Despencer for house in Hanover Sq., 24 Mar.–27 Nov. 1767 (Royal Institute of British Architects, MSS Box 14). For the other workmen and suppliers, see the bills of James Lloyd, John Pratt, Edward Gray, Edward Gascoigne, and William Sparrow for 20 St. James's Sq. (National Library of Wales, Aberystwyth, Wynnstay MSS, Box 115/17).

[113] National Library of Wales, Aberystwyth, Wynnstay MSS, Box 115/17. The stove grate appears to be on Soane Mus., Adam Drawings, Vol. 17, No. 126. Adam's account at Drummond's Bank, includes payments to William Kinman from 1766 to 1769.

[114] Soane Mus., Adam Drawings, Vol. 25, No. 57 (for Sir Watkin Williams-Wynn); Drummond's Bank; and National Library of Wales, Aberystwyth (Wynnstay MSS, Box 115/17: 14th July–12 Nov. 1773). Blockley's bill for work at Shardeloes, 13 Dec. 1764–18 Mar. 1765, has also been preserved (Buckingham County Record Office, Aylesbury, Shardeloes MSS).

[115] 'Scroll of an Accᵗ', probably submitted 18 July 1765. Printed by Bolton, II, 345. For Zucchi and Moore at Wynn House, see above, p. 43.

[116] The drawing room carpet at Syon, still in place, is signed on the border 'by·Thomas·Moor·1769.' The others can be documented through Moore's bills, 1765–69, at Croome Estate Office, and an entry in Sir Edward Knatchbull's Account Book, 1762–1784 (Kent County Record Office, Maidstone), under date of 14 Oct. 1779.

[117] Acct. Book of John Parker, Lord Boringdon, 1770–1778 (Saltram Park, Devon), p. 11; Soane Mus., Adam Drawings, Vol. 17, No. 178 and Vol. 8, No. 99.

[118] Bill to Sir Rowland Winn, 28 Feb. 1777 (Nostell Archives C3/1/5/4/5); Bill to Lord Coventry, 6 Dec. 1768 (Croome Estate Office); note on Soane Mus., Adam Drawings, Vol. 23, No. 22 (library chimney-piece, Ashburnham House, 1773).

[119] Letter to the Duchess of Portland, 20 July 1779. Quoted by R. Houchon, *Mrs. Montagu, 1720–1800: An Essay* (London, 1906), p. 213.

BIBLIOGRAPHY

The most valuable source for the study of Robert Adam's decorative work is the collection of Adam drawings at Sir John Soane's Museum, London, for among the almost 9,000 drawings by Adam and his staff are sketches and renderings for a large percentage of the decorative projects. Other drawings can be found in the archives of a number of the houses upon which Adam worked, as well as small quantities in various collections, including those of Capt. Charles Adam, Sir John Clerk, the Royal Institute of British Architects, the Victoria and Albert Museum, and the Metropolitan Museum of Art.

Documents are also preserved at a number of the Adam houses, the most significant collections being those as Croome, Nostell Priory, Alnwick Castle (including Syon MSS), Kedleston, Harewood, Hopetoun, and Saltram. Important documents are also located in the following public depositories: the Register House (Clerk of Penicuik, Ailsa, and Abercairny MSS) and National Library of Scotland, Edinburgh; National Library of Wales, Aberystwyth (Wynnstay MSS); Essex Record Office, Chelmsford (Braybrooke MSS); Buckingham County Record Office, Aylesbury (Shardeloes MSS); Kent County Record Office, Maidstone (Mersham-le-Hatch MSS); Guildhall Library, London; Drummond's Branch, Royal Bank of Scotland, London; Royal Institute of British Architects; and Victoria and Albert Museum (Dept. of Woodwork).

There are, in addition, a great many books and articles that deal with Robert Adam, his decoration, and his individual houses. Most of these cannot be included here, though some will be found in the footnotes and notes to the illustrations, as will references to Adam and his work in published journals, diaries, and collections of letters. Especially valuable for the study of Adam's decorative work are the articles on individual houses in COUNTRY LIFE *and, to a lesser extent, in* THE CONNOISSEUR, *and the following works:*

ADAM, R[obert]. *Ruins of the Palace of the Emperor Diolcetian at Spalatro in Dalmatia.* London, 1764.

ADAM, Robert and James. *The Works in Architecture.* 2 vols. London, 1773–78; 3rd. (posthumous) vol., 1822 (Reprints: Thezard, 1902; Tiranti, 1939 and 1959).

BEARD, Geoffrey W. *A Family's 50-Year Supremacy,* COUNTRY LIFE, CXXVIII (8 Dec. 1960), 1428–29.

—————. *New Light on Adam's Craftsmen,* COUNTRY LIFE, CXXXI (10 May 1962), 1098–1100.

—————. *Robert Adam's Craftsmen,* CONNOISSEUR YEAR BOOK, 1958, pp. 26–32.

BOLTON, Arthur T. *The Architecture of Robert and James Adam.* 2 vols. London, 1922.

CROFT-MURRAY, Edward. *Decorative Painting in England, 1537–1837.* 2 vols. London, 1962—.

EDWARDS, Ralph, and JOURDAIN, Margaret. *Georgian Cabinet-Makers.* Rev. ed. London, 1946.

FLEMING, John. *Robert Adam the Grand-Tourist*, THE CORNHILL, CLXVIII, No. 1004 (Summer 1955), 118–37.

————. *Robert Adam and His Circle in Edinburgh & Rome*. London, 1962.

HARRIS, Eileen. *The Furniture of Robert Adam*. London, 1963.

————. *Robert Adam and the Gobelins*, APOLLO, LXXVI (April, 1962), 100–106.

HUSSEY, Christopher. *English Country Houses: Mid-Georgian*, 1760–1800. London, 1956.

KIMBALL, Fiske. *Les influences anglaises dans la formation du style Louis XVI*, GAZETTE DES BEAUX-ARTS, 6th Ser., V (1931), 29–44, 231–55.

————. *Lansdowne House Redivivus*, PHILADELPHIA MUSEUM BULLETIN, Vol. XXXIX (Nov. 1943).

————. *The Moor Park Tapestry Suite of Furniture by Robert Adam*, PHILADELPHIA MUSEUM BULLETIN, Vol. XXXVI, No. 189 (Mar. 1941).

LEES-MILNE, James. *The Age of Adam*. London, 1947.

PARKER, James. *Croome Court: The Architecture and Furniture*, METROPOLITAN MUSEUM OF ART BULLETIN, XVIII, No. 3 (Nov. 1959), 79–93.

SAXL, F., and WITTKOWER, R. *British Art and the Mediterranean*. Oxford, 1948.

STILLMAN, Damie. *Robert Adam and Piranesi*, in ESSAYS IN THE HISTORY OF ARCHITECTURE PRESENTED TO RUDOLF WITTKOWER, Ed. Douglas Fraser, Howard Hibberd, and Milton J. Lewine.

SUMMERSON, John. *Architecutre in Britain*, 1530 *to* 1830. Rev. ed. Harmondsworth, 1955 (a later revised ed., 1963, further amplifies the material).

SWARBRICK, John. *Robert Adam & His Brothers*. London, 1915.

NOTES TO THE ILLUSTRATIONS

The photographs for this volume have been selected with two purposes in mind—to illustrate the text and to provide a visual survey of Adam's decorative work. As a result, the notes are by no means uniform. In some cases, emphasis is placed on the role in the development of Adam's decorative style of the work illustrated; in others, a description and analysis of the work itself have been given primary attention. The aim has been to make of the notes useful adjuncts to both the photographs and the general text. For this reason, most of the documentation has been reserved for the notes, with as much documentary evidence as possible in the form of bills, letters, and drawings being included here.

Aside from the first and last plates, the illustrations have been arranged into nine main groupings:

The Work of William Adam and of the Adam Brothers Prior to Robert's Grand Tour; and the Drawings of the Grand Tour (Figures 2–8)

Wall Elevations and General Interior Views (Figures 9–60)

Details of Wall Elevations—panels, entablatures, doorways, etc. (Figures 61–86)

Wall Furniture—organs and bookcases (Figures 87–93)

Chimney-pieces (Figures 94–114)

Ceilings (Figures 115–150)

Carpets and Pavements (Figures 151–158)

Decorative Furnishings—railings, grates, candelabra, door furniture, sconces, curtain cornices (Figures 159–165)

Designs in the Gothic Taste (Figures 166–172)

Within these groupings and the sub-groups of which certain of the major categories are composed, the illustrations are largely in a chronological order. I have, however, disturbed this chronological sequence whenever I felt that the arrangement of photographs for comparative purposes warranted it. For the same reason, illustrations of possible Adam sources or of comparable work by Adam's contemporaries have been placed together with the Adam material to which they relate. In all cases, I have tried to give cross-references to illustrations that might be usefully compared.

All illustrations are the work of Robert Adam and/or his staff unless otherwise labelled.

1. 'CHIMNEY BOARD FOR THE ETRUSCAN DRESSING ROOM AT OSTERL[E]Y,' MIDDLESEX, 1777. Sir John Soane's Museum, Vol. 17, No. 137.

Dated 2 June 1777. This design for a panel to be used in summer to cover the fireplace opening illustrates both the quality of the renderings that issued from the Adam office and Robert Adam's attention to detail. Such relatively minor elements in the total ensemble were accorded the same care as much more significant and grandiose ones. How closely Adam guided his draftsmen can be seen by comparing this drawing with the pencil and ink sketch for it (Soane Mus., Vol. 24, No. 221). The central vertical section of the sketch is virtually identical to the rendering illustrated here, even to the horizontal subject plaque at the top. Adam's drawing contains alternate suggestions for the side panels, with the left-hand proposal being the one adopted for both sides in the finished version. Aside from this change, the only differences are those of colour and modelling. The shading employed on the individual motifs in this drawing is not indicated on the ink sketch, but the suggestion of a spatial relationship between the vertical lines is already apparent through the placement of the lower central vase slightly farther back than the two stands next to it. This hint of three-dimensional placement and the shading of the forms is in contrast to the general flatness of the panel as a whole, a contrast emphasized by the garland swags which join the three major vertical streams. But the ambiguity is overshadowed by Adam's typically elegant flattening process, which is as obvious in his sketch as in the draftsman's rendering.

The finished version, in 'Etruscan' colours on a pale blue ground, was designed *en suite* with the walls (*cf.* Fig. 46) and includes similar motifs, but Adam varied the composition. Rather than reproducing a portion of the wall decoration, he chose the course of theme and variation. The same linear elegance, the same elongation and rhythm, the same colours, and a related group of classical motifs have been used in both the walls and the chimney-board design; yet this panel, while an integral part of the total composition, has an existance of its own. In its role as a related yet distinguishable part of a general ensemble, as well as by its stylistic character, this design epitomizes Adam's decorative work, especially in the decade of the 1770's.

The chimney-board, if executed, no longer survives at Osterley.

2. WILLIAM ADAM. Arniston, Midlothian. Hall, begun *c*1726.

The hall at Arniston with its monumental architectural quality and heavy florid plasterwork is characteristic of William Adam's interior decoration. The conception of a large two-storey hall with galleries serving as corridors was derived from Vanbrugh's halls at Castle Howard and Blenheim, and the treatment of the detail is equally Baroque. The colossal traditional orders; the giant keystones; and the three-dimensional quality of the scrolls, fruit, foliage, and other decorations are part of the robust manner from which Robert Adam was to turn completely. Yet, the father's attention to the design of the interior and certain of his treatments (swags, for example) were to inspire the Adam brothers in their early Scottish work (*cf.* Fig. 3) and Robert in his early work in England (*cf.* Figs. 10 and 11). The stuccowork was executed by James Enzer, who was probably Dutch (see C. Hussey in COUNTRY LIFE, LVIII, 257).

3. ADAM BROTHERS. Dumfries House, Ayrshire. Drawing room, *c*1754–59.

In contrast to their father's hall at Arniston (Fig. 2), this room by John, Robert, and James Adam illustrates the lighter Rococo decoration characteristic of the 1750's. The architectural treatment of the doors and overmantel, the thick naturalistic carving on the door entablature and overmantel stiles, and the swags show a certain bow in the direction of William Adam's decorative work; yet the whole conception is flatter, more restrained, and less robust than the senior Adam's interior decoration. A number of the features at Dumfries House—the modillioned cornice, loosely-flowing foliage frieze, and chimney-piece with console stiles, as well as the architectural quality of the doors and overmantel—are also typical of Robert's earliest work in England after his Grand Tour (*cf.* Figs. 10, 11, and 12). Only the classical motifs are missing. The ceiling, too, serves as a transition to Adam's later style, for it combines rich curvilinear foliage with both coffer shapes and the general composition of a central motif surrounded by subsidiary elements that was to be exploited by Adam throughout his career. The foliage in medium relief also lies between the heavy florid plasterwork of William Adam and the flat, linear quality of Robert Adam's mature work. The stuccowork here is reputed to be by Clayton, who had worked for William Adam in the 1740's. For reference to Clayton as a stuccoer and for documentation for Dumfries House itself, see J. Fleming, *Robert Adam and His Circle*, pp. 94–97, 338.

4. ADAM BROTHERS. Hopetoun House, West Lothian. Yellow Drawing Room, ceiling detail, begun *c*1752.

The extravagant Rococo cartouches in the four corners of the cove of the Yellow Drawing Room ceiling announce clearly the new taste of Robert Adam and his brothers in the early 1750's. These motifs, with their S- and C-curves, floral sprigs, heads, and asymmetrical elements, are again evidence of the change from William Adam's more Baroque decoration and of Robert's coming abreast of current English taste. The Hopetoun cartouches also demonstrate the Adams' lively sensitivity, for the design is handled with consummate skill. Rather than straggling assortments of loose curves, these corner ornaments are unified and coherent compositions. The series of small curves at the bottom are answered by the two larger bold curves on top, and the foliage curling away at the ends is countered by the heads facing

60

back toward the centre. At the corner, in the midst of the exuberant decoration is a void, but the shape of the void has been as felicitously planned as the complex curves of the scrolls and sprigs. By means of these striking examples of Rococo decoration, the Adams effectively bridged the corners of the coves and at the same time rhythmically carried the eye of the beholder from the cornice to the central flat of the ceiling. The modillioned cornice and the flowing frieze beneath it, related to the slightly later work at Dumfries House (Fig. 3), are characteristic of the Adams' early Scottish work, but also of Robert's first works in England. The lightness and gaiety in evidence here were also to continue to serve him in England, though the Rococo manner was to be supplanted by the host of classical motifs he encountered in Rome.

5. ADAM BROTHERS. Hopetoun House, West Lothian. Red Drawing Room, ceiling, c1754–60.

The Rococo style of the cartouches in the Yellow Drawing Room (Fig. 4) is reiterated in the shells, scrolls, and foliage of the Red Drawing Room ceiling. The central motif of the ceiling also has the same combination of curvilinear freedom and artistic control. The lively asymmetrical curves projecting from the central motif are parts of a unified whole, which is further accentuated by the outer ring of foliage that echoes the heavy circular border while differing from it substantially. The cove here is less successful, but again the corners have been rhythmically bridged. In addition to the dominant Rococo spirit, there are also present intimations of *Chinoiserie*, as in the flat of the ceiling. This interest in things Chinese was also manifested at just about the same time in sketches by James Adam preserved at Penicuik House. These two tastes are employed in a basic framework of sub-divided panels and pronounced mouldings that are also typical of the decorative treatments of the 1750's. Significant here, also, as in the cartouches of the Yellow Drawing Room, are the variations in thickness in the decorative plasterwork. For the caryatid chimney-piece that dominates this room, see Fig. 94.

6. ADAM BROTHERS. Arniston, Midlothian. Drawing room, ceiling, begun c1754.

7. ADAM BROTHERS. Arniston, Midlothian. Drawing room, ceiling detail, begun c1754.

Shortly after the succession in 1753 of Robert Dundas, the Adam brothers began work on a western wing to be added to the house erected by their father in 1726. In September 1754 Robert wrote of his need to stop there before setting off for Italy, and Arniston was still in progress four years later when it was specifically mentioned as a work under construction (Letters from Robert Adam to his sisters, Inverary, 21 Sept. 1754, and to James Adam, London, undated but probably late Nov. or early Dec. 1758; Register House, Edinburgh, Clerk of Penicuik Papers, Nos. 4745 and 4853/1). It is from this addition that the drawing room comes. Its rinceau frieze, modillioned cornice, guilloche-decorated mouldings, wide cove, and Rococo decoration are all typical of the Adam work of the 1750's. The exquisite Rococo scrolls of foliage and birds in the flat of the ceiling (especially visible in Fig. 7) demonstrate the accomplishment of Robert's decorative work— even before his more typical Neo-classical style appeared a few years later. The general arrangement of the main part of the ceiling and the sense of rhythm in the decoration also foreshadow Adam's work in England. As in the Red Drawing Room at Hopetoun, the cove is less effectively handled than the flat of the ceiling, but again the corners are the most successful sections of the cove. For Adam's early designs in England that demonstrate the continuation of the general composition exhibited here, with the motifs and asymmetrical curves replaced, *cf*. Figs. 115 and 116.

8. RECONSTRUCTION BASED ON ROMAN BATHS, c1755–57. Sir John Soane's Museum, 'Miscellaneous Sketches and Drawings by Robert Adam and Others,' No. 145.

Adam's study in Rome under Clérisseau together with the influence of Piranesi and others inspired him to produce such grandiose conceptions as this reconstruction of antique *thermae*. This drawing demonstrates not only Adam's feeling for the grand and his sense of space but also a host of classical motifs that were to become the mainspring of his decorative vocabulary. Screens of columns, long subject panels, skull-and-swag friezes, niches, coffers, arabesques, medallions with classical figures all appear here and in much of Adam's decorative work in England. There are no prototypes of this kind of study in Adam's Scottish drawings. The details are basically Roman, the scale is Piranesian, and the finish and the perspective treatment indicate the influence of Clérisseau.

9. 'SKETCH OF A SECTION FOR THE EARL OF NORTHAMPTONS HALL AT CASTLE ASHBY,' NORTHANTS., 1759. Sir John Soane's Museum, Vol. 54, Part i, No. 56.
10. 'WINDOW SIDE OF A GREAT HALL FOR THE RIGHT HON^BL THE EARL OF NORTHAMPTON AT CASTLE ASHBY,' NORTHANTS., 1759. Sir John Soane's Museum, Vol. 29, No. 21.

None of the three finished elevations for the hall (Soane Mus., Vol. 29, Nos. 20–22) are dated, but the sketch bears the date 4 June 1759. In both the sketch and the finished drawing are seen the diverse elements out of which Adam created his style. These include the *aedicular* doorways, modillioned cornice, and Palladian motif within relieving arch that Adam inherited from Burlingtonian Palladianism; as well as the panels, plaques, motifs, and screens of columns that he encountered during his study in Rome. The relatively thick quality of the grotesques also indicates the earliness of the designs, but just as these were smoothed out, so, too the other ingredients in the Adam style seen here were brought closer together into a tighter and more coherent syle in succeeding works. Neither these designs, nor Adam's proposed new layout of the gardens and park (1760; drawing at Castle Ashby) were executed.

11. 'SECTION OF THE DRAWING ROOM FOR GENERAL BLANDS HOUSE AT THISTLEWORTH,' MIDDLESEX, 1758. Sir John Soane's Museum, Vol. 32, No. 63.

Among Adam's first clients in London was Gen. Humphrey Bland, who approached him in late January 1758, concerning the addition of a large drawing room to his house in Isleworth. Work evidently began fairly shortly thereafter, for by November of that year, the stuccoing was complete (Letters from one of the younger Adams to Helen Adam and from Robert to James, 1 Feb. and Nov. or Dec. 1758; Register House, Edinburgh, Clerk of Penicuik Papers, Nos. 4847 and 4853/1). Reminiscent of his earlier Scottish work are the elaborately framed doors, the cornice, the overmantel, and the coved ceiling. But more classical features are to be found among the decorative details, as in the

trophy, anthemia, and putti with urn. For Adam's dissatisfaction with the lack of antique spirit in the stuccowork, see p. 16 above. For the ceiling of this room, dated 1759 on the drawing, see Fig. 115.

12. HATCHLANDS, SURREY. Design for the Great dining room, 1759. Sir John Soane's Museum, Vol. 35, No. 83.

Signed and dated 'Robt Adam Architect 1759.' Late in 1758 or early in 1759, Adam took over the decoration of the house begun for Admiral Edward Boscawen early in 1757. The house was completed only shortly before Boscawen's death on 10 Jan. 1761. The finest of the rooms created by Adam was the dining (now drawing) room, although it would have been infinitely grander had Adam's full scheme been carried out. Neither the ruin paintings nor the arabesques were executed, but sketches for the grotesques exist beneath the wall hangings (H. S. Goodhart-Rendel, *Guide to Hatchlands*, p. 16). As designed, the room represents the first synthesis of Adam's Scottish style with his new Italian tastes. Mingling with the door cornice on brackets and the modillioned cornice are the classically-inspired panels. The ruin scene can be related to many sketches drawn by Adam in Italy (*e.g.*, Soane Mus., Vol. 55, Nos. 98, 99, and 107) and even to the reconstructed *thermae* drawing in Fig. 8. The arabesques, among Adam's earliest, are loose, fairly thick, and relatively simple; yet they point the way to his more mature examples. The liveliness of the arabesque scrolls and even some of the forms can be related to the Adam brothers' decorations in Scotland, with a new symmetry present at Hatchlands. The rapid development of this type of decoration can be seen by comparing these panels with those actually exectued at Shardeloes in the early 1760's (Fig. 13) and at Osterley in the latter part of the decade (Fig. 75). Similarly, the frieze is tighter than the Scottish ones, and classical motifs abound; but its relation to those at Arniston or Dumfries is recognizable.

13. SHARDELOES, BUCKINGHAMSHIRE. Dining room, *c*1761–64.

The grotesque panels in the dining room at Shardeloes appear to have been the first decorations of this type to be executed by Adam. Although there are designs that precede those at Shardeloes (Castle Ashby, Hatchlands), no executed examples can be dated earlier than these. Yet, the exact date for the Shardeloes dining room grotesques is not known. Adam's first connexion with this house for William Drake was his commission to design 'Ceilings &c,' reported by the contractor-builder Stiff Leadbetter in a letter to Drake, 13 Feb. 1761 (Buckingham County Record Office, Aylesbury, Shardeloes MSS). The drawing for the ceiling of this room (Soane Mus., Vol. 11, No. 69) is dated 1761, as are the designs for the chimney-piece (Soane Mus., Vol. 22, Nos. 28–30). While Adam's wall elevations (Soane Mus., Vol. 31, No. 105) are not dated, Joseph Rose's plasterwork in the house was completed by 19 Feb. 1763 (Shardeloes MSS).

Both the delicacy and the complexity of the grotesques executed here are in sharp contrast to the thicker, simpler grotesques designed for Castle Ashby and Hatchlands (Figs. 9 and 12). Adam's drawings for the Shardeloes dining room do not include grotesques in the wall panels, but grotesque panels are shown (though they were not executed there) in the design for the hall (Soane Mus., Vol. 31, No. 102). Like those for Castle Ashby and Hatchlands, the grotesques planned for the Shardeloes hall show the illogical combination of candelabra, urns, and cornucopiae amid the arabesque foliage; and, like the earlier designs, they are broadly and simply drawn. The panels in the dining room, however, shown here, seem far more advanced and developed. Such extraneous elements as urns, sphinxes, and a rectangular subject plaque are still to be found, but the total effect is now one of elegance and delicacy, unified design and flatness. The curvilinear rhythms of Adam's Rococo decorations in Scotland have been retained yet transformed in the service of Neo-classicism. The complexity and the finesse, as well as the restraint, are among the most striking features here, combined, of course, with the antique inspiration and the sensitivity evinced in his early Scottish decorations. In his mixture of divergent sources, as well as in his tendency toward a complex yet flat depiction and a subtle intertwining of forms, Adam here demonstrates his first mastery of the elements of his mature style and foreshadows the course of his future development. For this development, cf. Fig. 75; for a comparison with antique grotesques, see Fig. 77.

Despite the obvious Neo-classical character of this room, the legacy of Adam's pre-Grand Tour manner—e.g., the modillioned cornice and the bracketed doorway cornices—should not be overlooked.

14. SYON HOUSE, MIDDLESEX. Entrance hall, begun c1761.

For the first room that the visitor to Syon would encounter, Adam designed an imposing hall in his grand Roman manner. The two-storey height was determined by the Elizabethan and Jacobean house that he was remodelling, but the treatment is purely Neo-classical. Adam's design for the hall (Soane Mus., Vol. 39, No. 3), dated 1761, was executed very nearly as designed, with the exception of the wall toward the ante-room, as shown here. In the Adam drawing this end of the room is depicted as a flat wall, with the same treatment as the two long walls and a doorway echoing those on the two long walls. Probably before 1761 was over, however, he had decided instead on the highly effective screened apse which was actually executed. For it is this view that appears in the *Works* (Vol. I, part i, Pl. 6B) with the date 1761. The plate in the *Works* is virtually identical to the executed wall, including the medallion, portrait heads, and urns in the plaques and even the reproduction of the *Dying Gaul* in the centre of the screen. The curved stairs behind the screen, the Doric order, the coffers, and the decorative details are all characteristic elements of Adam's Neo-classicism. Likewise Roman in inspiration are the columns with swirled fluting and the frieze around the ceiling whose antique prototype can be seen in Fig. 71. All of these elements are combined with a truly Roman *gravitas* to produce a highly auspicious and effective introduction to one of Adam's finest houses.

If the details and character are the result of Adam's Grand Tour, the general heaviness is due to his earlier training and predilections. It is the only evidence of his pre-Italian manner in the room. Adam's preference for a somewhat more masculine entrance hall is demonstrated in many of his later houses—Osterley (Fig. 27), Mersham-le-Hatch, Harewood, Newby (Fig. 35), and many others—but in none of these is the relief as high or the heaviness so pronounced. The contrast is especially striking if one compares this room with the long gallery at Syon (Fig. 15) of only a few years later. For the ceiling of this room, see Fig. 124.

15. SYON HOUSE, MIDDLESEX.
Long gallery, c1763–68.

Although Adam had begun to think about the ceiling for this room by August 1761 (Soane Mus., Vol. 11, No. 22), the executed design, as well as an alternate, date from August 1763 (*Ibid.*, Vol. 11, No. 23). In the latter year, also, the Earl of Northumberland wrote Adam that he wanted the gallery 'proceeded upon with all possible expedition' and also commented upon certain questions raised by his architect, such as 'the twisted Flutings under the Book Cases' and the material to be used for the pedestals and dado (Rough draft of letter, dated 4 Nov.; Alnwick Castle Library, XCIV, 44–45). On 16 July 1765 an agreement was signed with Thomas Davis 'to Gild the Gallery at Syon in the best and most Compleat manner,' and payment was made to Pergolesi between 15 July 1766 and 16 May 1768 for painting the pilasters in the gallery (Alnwick Castle Archives, U.I. 46 and U.I. 44). By 1767, when Lord Northumberland recorded in a memorandum book work remaining to be carried out at Syon, the listing for the gallery included only decorative items—furniture, carpet, locks, Zuccarelli's landscapes over the chimney-pieces, other inset paintings, Wilton's bas-reliefs, and more minor items (Alnwick Castle Archives, U.I. 59). In addition to the documents and drawings noted here, there are various designs for the walls (Soane Mus., Vol. 39, Nos. 1–2; Vol. 1, Nos. 162–63), but none are dated.

The room, as executed, illustrates the elegant flatness of Adam's developed style. By a series of overlapping motifs, both in the ceiling and along the walls, Adam transformed the immensely long Jacobean gallery into a unified and coherent space. This is especially true of the ceiling, where the complex overlapping of octagons and the judicious variation of individual motifs produce a balanced synthesis of repeated pattern and general overall design. Along the walls, too, Adam has combined the groups of arabesque pilasters with triumphal arches and *aediculae* in order to achieve a subtle rhythm rather than a dull repetition. The low-relief decoration inspired by his Italian sojourn contributes to his success and to the overall effect at which Adam was aiming.

For a detail of this room, see Fig. 19.

16. SYON HOUSE, MIDDLESEX.
Ante-room, c1761–65.

Adam's sense of the whole composition, of the relationship of one room to the next, was demonstrated quite early in his career in England, and Syon is one of the best examples. This is obvious in the plan (Fig. d) with its continuous variation of room shapes, but it is equally noted in the decoration of the different rooms. To move from the largely monochromatic entrance hall (Fig. 14) into the brilliantly coloured ante-room is to realize Adam's conception of the whole. The sumptuous dark green columns; the blue- and green-backed capitals, panels, and frieze with gilded decoration; the white and green chimney-piece; and the scagliola pavement of green, yellow, red, and blue mark this chamber as a very different conception from the preceding hall. And yet, the antique sources unite the two, producing Adam's typical immense variation upon a few basic themes. The role of antiquity in the ante-room is emphasized by the columns procured in Rome, the trophies (*cf.* Fig. 17), the statues, and the capitals and entablature (see Figs. 62–64). The combination is Adam's contribution—and achievement.

As early as the beginning of 1761, James Adam was already looking in Rome for the columns of the ante-room. Found only after a great deal of effort, they were shipped from Italy on 27 March 1765 (Letter from James to Jenny Adam, 4 March 1761, Register House, Edinburgh, Clerk of Penicuik Papers, No. 4890; letter from Jas. Adam to Earl of Northumberland, 22 April 1765, Alnwick Castle Library, XCIV, 46).

Adam's models for the two large trophy panels flanking the doorway from the hall were the Roman trophies on the Campidoglio in Rome. Called the Trophies of Marius by Montfauçon and the Trophies of Octavianus Augustus by Piranesi, these imposing vestiges of Roman grandeur were much admired by Adam, who saw them in Rome and owned large brown wash renderings of them (Soane Mus., Vol. 26, Nos. 89–92), as well as reproductions in books. While Adam made some changes in his models, including the supplying of missing elements, the resemblance is very striking.

17. TROPHY OF OCTAVIANUS AUGUSTUS (Trophy of Marius). Roman Imperial sculpture, as engraved by G.-B. Piranesi,

Trofèi di Ottaviano Augusto (Rome, 1753), Pl. 6. See Fig. 16.

18. SYON HOUSE, MIDDLESEX.
Dining room, *c*1761–69.

After the brilliantly coloured ante-room with its spatial sleight-of-hand, one passes into the longitudinal dining room with screened apses at each end. The colour is somewhat subdued, but this room differs as much from the hall as from the ante-room. Adam's love of small-scale decorative detail is here combined with many antique or antique-inspired elements. The ancient statuary or copies of them supplement the Neo-classical grisaille panels, bas-relief, screens of columns, and grotesques. Yet despite all of this evidence of Adam's Grand Tour, there are numerous references to his earlier work. The modillioned cornice, the rinceau frieze, the elaborate over-mantel and its panel with crossette corners, and the chimney-piece all derive from the Adam brothers' Scottish work, albeit masked by Neo-classical detail. Here, we are still conscious of this mixture, whereas in the gallery the integration has begun to take place.

The earliest dated drawings for this room are two designs for the ceiling, an earlier idea (1761) and the executed version, dated Dec. 1761 (Soane Mus., Vol. 11, Nos. 16 and 18). Chimney-piece designs (Soane Mus., Vol. 22, Nos. 42 and 43) close to those executed, though with some differences, date from the following year. In 1762, also, Luc-François Breton was at work in Rome on the relief of the Graces in the overmantel (Letter from James to Helen Adam, 7 Mar. 1762, Register House, Edinburgh, Clerk of Penicuik Papers, No. 4929). Most of the work appears to have been completed by 1767, and in 1769 Andrea Casali was paid £200 for the grisaille panels simulating classical reliefs (Lord Northumberland's Memorandum Book, Alnwick Castle Archives, U.I. 59; E. Croft-Murray, typescript for Vol. II of *Decorative Painting in England*, 1537–1837, who cites *Syon House Book*, p. 41, pp. 213–14). There are undated drawings for the walls in the Adam collection at the Soane Museum (Vol. 1, Nos. 160–62).

19. SYON HOUSE, MIDDLESEX.
Long gallery, detail of southwest corner, *c*1763–68.

For documentation, see Fig. 15.

The elegance and delicacy, as well as the strongly Neo-classical character of Adam's developed style is already apparent in the gallery at Syon. The overall surface quality of the flat, delicate decoration is as striking here as are the arabesque pilasters that articulate the wall. The presence of both antique and *Cinquecento* influence on the pilasters is reinforced by the strigils on the dado derived from Roman sarcophagi and by the Michelangelesque motif of small orders flanking large ones. The walls abound with evidence of Adam's delight in the stuccoes and painted decorations of both Imperial and High Renaissance Rome. All of these elements, plus the tabernacle door frame utilized in the Adams' Scottish work, are subjected to Adam's sense of two-dimensional surface decoration, foreshadowing the linear elegance of his work of the 1770's.

The extent of the client's participation in Adam's work is well illustrated by a letter from the Earl of Northumberland in which he comments to Adam about the decoration here: 'I very much approve of having the twisted Flutings under the Book Cases and pedestals to the Pillasters to be of Wood, & the Rest of the Dado I think may be of Stocho' (Rough draft dated 4 Nov. [1763], Alnwick Castle Library, XCIV, 44–45).

20. CROOME COURT, WORCESTERSHIRE. Gallery, 1761–*c*1766.

Originally conceived as a library, the gallery at Croome Court evolved instead into a classical sculpture hall related to the dining room at Syon (Fig. 18). A ceiling for this room was the first interior work undertaken by Adam for the Earl of Coventry, for in September 1760 Adam charged his client £12. 12. 0 for this design. By March 1761, however, another design had been substituted, and it was this one that was executed (Soane Mus., Vol. 11, Nos. 34 and 36; Adam's first bill to Lord Coventry, Croome Estate Office). Adam's conception of the gallery as a library dates from November 1761, but it was not until June 1763 that he charged Lord Coventry £16. 16. 0 for 'A New Section of the Gallery finished in the Antique Taste with Statues Bas Reliefs &c' (Soane Mus., Vol. 50, Nos. 10 and 9, respectively; bill at Croome Estate Office). In 1764 Joseph Rose executed the plasterwork of the gallery, and in 1766 Joseph Wilton submitted a bill for £300 for the 'large

[handwritten marginal note: Good contrast – esp. overmantle, lack of moulding on niches, + cornice. – cf. also fig 31]

Statuary Chimney piece composed of Statues, representing Nymphs of Flora, holding a Wreath, &ca.' (both bills at Croome Estate Office). Adam's last charge for the gallery was in January 1766 for the grisaille paintings above these chimney-pieces. *By whom ??*

Classical in much of its inspiration, the gallery at Croome Court nevertheless has allusions to the Scottish works of the Adam brothers in the general heaviness, the modillioned cornice, and the caryatid chimney-piece. Noted at Hopetoun, this type of chimney-piece appears in a number of Adam's early houses in England (see Figs. 94 and 98). More antique are the grisaille panels, both narrative and decorative; the bas-relief panels of griffins, urn, and rinceau; the anthemion frieze perhaps derived from the Forum of Trajan (see Figs. 70 and 71); and the coffered ceiling modelled after the vaults of the Basilica of Constantine. Adam utilized the Constantinian coffering pattern with very little change, but by transferring the coffers from a tunnel vault to a flat surface and by suppressing the three-dimensional quality of his model, he created a substantially different effect. This change is highly typical of Adam's eighteenth-century classicism, for his tendency is always to make of his inspiration something more elegant, more refined, and more linear.

21. KEDLESTON HALL, DERBYSHIRE.
Hall, west elevation, c1761–70.

The hall at Kedleston is the most imposing and most architectonic room that Adam ever created, but he was not responsible for the original conception of such a grandiose hall. The first architect of this new house for Sir Nathaniel Curzon (created Lord Scarsdale on 9 April 1761) was Matthew Brettingham, whose plans were examined by Adam in December 1758 (Letter from Robert to James Adam, 11 Dec. 1758; Register House, Edinburgh, Clerk of Penicuik Papers, No. 4854). Early in 1759 demolition of the old house was already under way, and by 1760 there are payments for work on the new one (Accounts in Muniment Room at Kedleston: Vol. III, pp. 126–59). At some point, probably earlier than 1761, the date that he himself gives, James Paine also made plans for Kedleston. He reported that although foundations were laid, he had to give up the commission due to pressure of other works (Paine, *Plans, Elevations, and Sections of Noblemen and*

Gentlemen's Houses, II [1783], 14). His place was taken by Adam, who had received commissions for temples, bridges, and an organ at Kedleston as early as December 1758. By the middle of 1760 Adam claimed to be in full command of the work at Kedleston, and some of his interior designs date from that year (Letters from Robert to James Adam, 11 Dec. 1758 and 24 July 1760; Clerk of Penicuik Papers, Nos. 4854 and 4866). His only dated drawing for the hall is inscribed 1761, and Adam seems to have been responsible for this room—and the whole project—from this point on. The basic scheme of a great Egyptian hall had been set by Paine, but the actual decoration is Adam's, as can be seen by his cross-section, unfortunately not dated but with a ceiling corresponding to that on the 1761 drawing (Soane Mus., Vol. 40, No. 3; and Vol. 11, No. 45, respectively). This ceiling was not executed—George Richardson was responsible for that feature—but the rest of the hall design is quite close to the room as it now exists.

Given the format of a grand pillared hall, Adam turned to antiquity for specific inspiration. The Temple of Mars as illustrated by Palladio (Book IV, Part xv, Pl. 5) was his source for the niches with square subject panels above them; and included there, too, is the colonnade. Yet the combination of these features with the decorative panels and the frieze is Adam's contribution. The chimney-pieces and their overmantel decoration, while in the Adam style, appear to be later in date than the rest of the wall elevations.

Although the hall at Kedleston demonstrates Adam's feeling for the grand and his use of antique prototypes, it is not typical of his work. Both its architectonic treatment and its rather close dependence on Roman models make of it a room apart from the linear elegance of the Adam style. While perhaps inspired by the magnificence of Rome and the ideas of Piranesi, it is even more likely that Adam here yielded to the exigencies of a previous plan and the desire of his patron.

22. KEDLESTON HALL, DERBYSHIRE.
Drawing room, begun 1760.

Both the ceiling and chimney-piece in this room were designed in 1760, and the elaborate doorways with tabernacle frames appear on the east-west cross-section drawing for the house (Soane Mus., Vol. 40, No. 4).

These doorways and the Palladian window, all executed in beautifully veined alabaster, contribute substantially to the characteristic early Adam decorative style. Their three-dimensionality and architectural emphasis are consonant with the treatment in Robert's first designs in England (*e.g.*, Thistleworth or Castle Ashby), and the same is true of the chimney-piece and ceiling. Though not shown in this view, the caryatid chimney-piece (executed as designed on the drawing at the Soane Museum, Vol. 22, No. 15, with the right hand alternate used) is closely related to those at Hatchlands and Croome Court (Figs. 98 and 20). The ceiling is also comparable to Adam designs of the late 1750's and 1760's, but at the same time it illustrates Adam's skill in varying and combining elements and themes. The central panel of the ceiling features an overlapped loop motif very close to that of a square ceiling designed a year earlier for Hatchlands (Soane Mus., Vol. 11, Nos. 4–5), though the putti have been moved from one of the loop chains to the other and that loop has been somewhat altered. This same pattern, again slightly changed and minus the putti, was re-used a year later in the ante-room at Syon, where the side panels of the Kedleston ceiling flat, somewhat modified, also appear (see Soane Mus., Vol. 11, No. 17, dated Dec. 1761). But neither of these rooms had a coved ceiling. A parallel for this can be found in General Bland's drawing room of 1759. The general arrangement of the decoration, the free but heavy arabesques, the inset subject panels, and the type of corner elements—though not, of course, specific details—of both coves are similar. In the ingenious combination of a few basic themes, as much as in the nature of its decoration, the drawing room ceiling at Kedleston is typical of the Adam style. The ceiling was executed as designed on the grey-wash drawing at the Soane Museum (Vol. 11, No. 43); a partially filled-in and coloured version is preserved in the Muniment Room at Kedleston. The plasterwork was by Joseph Rose, who charged £345. 6. 5¼d. for his work in this room (Kedleston Archives, Vol. 3R, pp. 64–68).

23. KEDLESTON HALL, DERBYSHIRE.
Dining room, begun 1760.

Although Adam's first designs for this room are the same date as those for the drawing room, the two rooms are by no means similar or even comparable in style. The chimney-piece (with terms instead of full caryatids) parallels that of the drawing room, and the doorways with pediments or bracket-supported cornices are akin to the much more architectural door enframements there, but that is the extent of the real similarity. While the general arrangement of this ceiling is not unlike that in the drawing room—central square with flanking side panels, series of narrative panels amid arabesques in the outer border—the treatment is very different. The emphasis is on flat, complex, and delicate decoration, as opposed to the simpler, thicker forms in the other room. Where Adam used bas-relief panels in the drawing room, he substituted painted scenes here. The delicate, intricate arabesques and related classical motifs contrast strongly with the heavier forms of the drawing room. There is a difference in the depth of relief and in the scale of details. Even the borders between panels testify to the former, while the whole treatment of decoration eloquently demonstrates the difference in scale. Whereas the principal feature of the walls in the drawing room is the impressive Palladian window, here that role is assumed by the niche with its refined Neo-classical decoration. The concern for space and the elegant small-scale plasterwork within the niche are indicative of Adam's new tastes and the development of his style.

Drawings exist for the walls, the chimney-piece, and the ceiling. All were executed more or less as designed, though with some changes. The chimney-piece and ceiling drawings (Soane Mus., Vol. 22, No. 16; and Vol. 11, No. 53) are dated 1760 and 1761, respectively; the four wall elevations (Vol. 40, Nos. 20–23) are not dated. The most noteworthy alteration between the drawings and the execution was in the niche, where Adam changed the decoration to radiate down from the crown, rather than up from the centre of the bottom. The stuccoer was Joseph Rose, whose bill for this room totalled £270. 3. 3½d. (Kedleston Archives, Vol. 3R, pp. 64–68). The chimney-piece was one of the four included in a bill for £990, and Michael Henry Spang (d. 1762) was probably the carver (an abstract at end of Vol. 3R gives the cost, but no sculptor's name; but Rupert Gunnis, *Dictionary of British Sculptors*, p. 361, says that Spang was paid the money for this work). While no documents exist for the decorative painters, certain eighteenth- and nineteenth-century visitors credit Zucchi with the four ceiling roundels, William Hamilton with the four oblong ceiling panels, and Henry Morland with the central ceiling panel (E. Croft-Murray, typescript for Vol. II of *Decorative Painting in England, 1537–1837*).

24. KEDLESTON HALL, DERBYSHIRE.
Saloon, begun *c*1761.

The saloon at Kedleston is one of the rooms created by Adam that most clearly proclaims the strong Roman influence on his style. The grandeur of the Pantheon-type room, the coffered dome, and the diamond-coffered niches are easily related to Adam's Italian studies, as are the ruin scenes by William Hamilton and the grisailles by Biagio Rebecca (painters reported by George Lipscomb, *A Description of Matlock-Bath* . . . , Birmingham, 1802, pp. 114–15). Although executed at a slightly later date, the paintings were indicated on Adam's cross-section drawing, which must date at the beginning of 1761, if not earlier, as it is inscribed for Sir Nathaniel Curzon, Bart., who was created Lord Scarsdale on 9 April 1761 (Soane Mus., Vol. 40, No. 3). The general conception of the saloon was carried out in accordance with this drawing, though many of the specific details were altered. These include the doorway pilasters, the niche treatment, the frieze, and the decorations between niches. Swirled Corinthian columns gave way to Ionic pilasters with green scagliola shafts; diamond coffering replaced delicate decoration within vertical strips in the niches; the frieze became tighter and more complex; and the elegant candelabra-and-plaque sconces took the place of square niches with classical statuary. (For a detail of the sconces, see Fig. 164). On the whole, these changes reflect the increasing flatness, elegance, and complexity of Adam's style, though within a context that still evokes feelings of grandeur and space.

25. SYON HOUSE, MIDDLESEX.
Design for the circular closet off the long gallery, 1764. Sir John Soane's Museum, Vol. 39, No. 15.

Although labelled at a later date as a design for Alnwick, this drawing is an unexecuted design for the circular closet off the long gallery at Syon. It corresponds very closely to the unexecuted ceiling design dated Sept. 1764 (Soane Mus., Vol. 11, No. 24) and to the walls of the existing closet, minus some of the detailed decoration. The small-scale quality of the decoration, the delicate arabesque lyres, and the general flat, overall character are quite typical of Adam's work in the mid-1760's. Despite the profusion of surface decoration—ranging from Greek key and double-guilloche to anthemia, dolphins, lyres, and valeria—there is already the tendency toward a linear, two-dimensional effect that is to characterize Adam's mature designs.

26. OSTERLEY PARK, MIDDLESEX.
Cross-section of the first scheme, 1761. Drawing at Osterley.

In 1761 Adam designed a major addition to the Osterley house of Francis Child. His proposal consisted of exterior elevations, plans, and one cross-section, illustrated here. Some finished drawings are preserved at Osterley, while other sheets are in the Soane Museum (Vol. 43, Nos. 92–98). These designs were superseded in the mid-1760's, when Adam began to remodel substantially the house for Robert Child, Francis' brother. The only interior shown in any detail in the 1761 scheme is the hall, and it is typical of Adam's first few years in London. The elaborate overmantel with broken pediment, the inset picture with crossette corners, the chimney-piece with console sides, the modillioned cornice, the bracket-supported door cornices, and the grotesque panels are all elements in the early Adam manner. The simple and thick grotesques, the oval plaques over the doors, and the ruin scene over the mantel reflect the influence of the Grand Tour, but their treatment indicates the tentative nature of Adam's early use of them. Adam's rapid development between the early- and mid-1760's is readily evident when one contrasts this design with that executed in the latter part of the decade (Fig. 27).

27. OSTERLEY PARK, MIDDLESEX.
Hall, designed 1767–68.

The hall at Osterley demonstrates the synthesis that Adam had achieved by the mid-1760's. The basically flat treatment, the subjugation of the parts to the whole, the refinement have all been attained. The coffered alcoves introduce variety into the rectangular room, while the ceiling and pavement illustrate the unity arrived at by variation on a theme. As was often Adam's plan, the floor and ceiling mirror each other, yet without the slightest duplication of motif. The compositions are the same, the details completely different. The handsome trophy panels (flatter than those at Syon), the lyrical rhythm of the various rinceau or arabesque panels, and the restraint are all evidence of Adam's success at creating one unified effect. He has combined elements from his Scottish work in the 1750's (door cornice on brackets, double-guilloche borders) with inspiration from Rome (the trophy and arabesque panels, alcoves, coffering, peltoids) and Spalato (pilaster capitals; see Figs. 65 and 66). But instead of an undigested mixture, he has presented here a beautifully integrated whole. Even the general impression—refined yet not too delicate—and the colour—pale blue, medium blue, and white—have been carefully keyed to the role of the room as the entrance hall. It is a very effective preview of the rooms that lie ahead.

A number of drawings for the hall have survived. Preserved at Osterley are a plan with four wall elevations and a design for the ceiling (both dated 1767), while the Soane Museum has a slightly different ceiling design of 1767 and a chimney-piece drawing of 1768 (Vol. 11, No. 203; and Vol. 22, No. 211, respectively). The Osterley version of the ceiling design is slightly earlier than that at the Soane, for it contains martial trophies in place of the boy-in-rinceau panels shown on the version at the Soane and in the executed ceiling. Similarly, the only significant difference between the drawings for the walls and the present elevations are in the four large panels on the entrance wall—arabesques instead of trophies. The chimney-pieces were also altered, with the existing pieces reflecting the 1768 drawing at the Soane rather than the 1767 wall elevations.

28. 'DESIGN FOR FINISHING THE EATING PARLOUR AT OSTERLY,' MIDDLESEX, c1766–68. Drawing at Osterley.
29. OSTERLEY PARK, MIDDLESEX. Dining room, c1766–68.

Adam's mature use of two types of wall panels that had intrigued him since his arrival in London—grotesques and ruin scenes—is finely illustrated in the dining room at Osterley. Inset paintings depicting classical ruins had figured in his designs for interior decoration from his first works in England. Although a few may have been executed in the early 1760's (those at

Yester signed and dated 1761 by William Delacour are the only documented examples), Adam was waiting for a painter who could answer to his tastes and his needs. That man was Antonio Zucchi, whose first datable works for Adam are the two large ruin fantasies in the dining room at Osterley, signed and dated 1767. Zucchi also did the overdoors and the small inset paintings amid the grotesque decoration. The grotesques, too, are probably Adam's first mature ones, though earlier, less developed grotesque panels were designed (Castle Ashby, Hatchlands) and executed (Shardeloes). For a detail of the Osterley panels and a more complete analysis of them, see Fig. 75. Other features in this room are closer to Adam's earlier work—the door hoods, the bolection-moulded frieze, and the ceiling. The rather thick and relatively simple ceiling design is actually a duplicate of that in the dining room at Shardeloes, designed in 1761 (cf. Figs. 122 and 123), and its simplicity and three-dimensionality are in sharp contrast to the delicate intricacy of the grotesque panels or the foliage above the overmantel.

Adam drawings exist only for the walls (undated) and the curtain cornices (Soane Mus., Vol. 17, No. 105; dated 1768). As can be seen by a comparison of the two illustrations here, the walls were executed largely as designed, with three minor but significant exceptions. The simple Doric frieze of the chimney-piece was made more elaborate and more decorative, the grotesque panels became more delicate and involved, and the inset paintings are quite different. This latter is customary with Adam drawings, for usually the drawings give only a general idea of subject painting, not an exact model as is the case with the rest of the decoration. With the grotesques, we have only the further refinement of an already well-developed and intricate design, not the difference between an early and a mature example.

30. LANSDOWNE (SHELBURNE) HOUSE, BERKELEY SQ., LONDON. Design for the ante-room (south-wall), 1766. Sir John Soane's Museum, Vol. 39, No. 58 (detail).

In August 1766, Adam charged the Earl of Shelburne £12. 12. 0 for 'a Design of a section of 4 sides for the ante room,' of which this is a detail of one side (Bill excerpted by Bolton, *Arch. of R. and J. Adam*, II, 340). It represents the elegant, assured style achieved by Adam by the middle of the 1760's. The complex, yet refined arabesque panels and pilaster strips; the classical inset paintings; the frieze of alternating bell-flowers and anthemia within delicate lyre scrolls; the soft lilac colour are all indicative of this achievement. And the rectangular room with one apsed end is also typical of Adam's concern for varied and interesting room shapes.

Except for slight modifications and, of course, the inset paintings, the ante-room was executed as designed. In a memorandum probably dating from February 1777, Lord Shelburne described the completed room as containing four Neo-classical subject paintings 'just finish'd by Cipriani—to suit the panels, which are ornamented according to a design of Adam's in arabesque stucco, with some small compartments painted by Zucchi' (A. H. Smith, ed., *A Catalogue of Ancient Marbles at Lansdowne House*, London, 1889, p. 80). The room was destroyed when the house was mutilated in the early 1930's, but the large inset paintings and the chimney-piece were re-installed in a reproduction of the ante-room in the area to the west of the original room.

31. LANSDOWNE (SHELBURNE) HOUSE, BERKELEY SQ., LONDON. Dining room, 1766–68. As re-installed in the Metropolitan Museum of Art, New York (Rogers Fund, 1932).

Related to the ante-room, though somewhat colder due to the use of statuary rather than inset paintings, is the dining room from Lansdowne House. Also included under August 1766 in Adam's bill to the Earl of Shelburne (four wall elevations, £12. 12. 0; ceiling design, £10. 10. 0), the dining room was probably more or less complete by August 1768, when Shelburne moved into the house (Excerpt of Adam's bill in Bolton, *Arch. of R. and J. Adam*, II, 340; letter from Lord Shelburne to his wife, 'Shelburne House,' 11 Aug. 1768, Wm. L. Clements Library, Univ. of Michigan, Shelburne Papers).

Designed to hold part of Lord Shelburne's growing collection of ancient statuary, the dining room also displays Adam's fascination with antiquity. The capitals derived from Spalato, the elegant grotesque panels, the urns and putti amid rinceau, and the medallion above the chimney-piece indicate the architect's taste as clearly as the statues would have

announced the client's interests. The complex, yet delicate and highly organized, ceiling is also characteristic of Adam's mature manner, as is the use of the screen of columns to vary the spatial effect.

Drawings exist for both the ceiling and the walls, and both were executed more or less as designed. This is especially true of the ceiling (Soane Mus., Drawer 32, Set 4, No. 3). The walls were slightly altered—in the overmantel and medallion above it, in the chimney-piece (simplified, with frieze changed to conform to room frieze), and in the large grotesque panels (Soane Mus., Vol. 39, No. 56). In the executed grotesque panels, such non-naturalistic forms as a peltoid shield and a classical medallion were added to the rhythmic arabesques of foliage. The luxuriant plasterwork of the room was by Joseph Rose, who charged £298. 15. 9½d. (Bill printed in Bolton, II, 342–44).

When installed in the Metropolitan Museum, the two long walls were reversed, with the fireplace wall now to the right of the screened end, rather than the left, as designed and built.

32. HAREWOOD HOUSE, YORKSHIRE. Music room, c1765–71.

Grotesque panels in bas-relief, classical fantasy paintings, and a complementary ceiling-carpet arrangement are the most striking features in the Harewood music room. Like other Adam rooms conceived in the second half of the 1760's, it shows both Adam's mastery of Neo-classical design and the unified composition at which he aimed. The grotesque panels, like those of the dining rooms of Osterley and Lansdowne House, are delicate, intricate, rhythmic, and flat. Again, as at Lansdowne House, peltoids and medallions were added to the arabesques on the design (Soane Mus., Vol. 14, No. 118). Except for minor modifications of this type (including different inset paintings, as usual) and a different chimney-piece, the room was carried out as Adam planned it. The drawing of the wall elevations is not dated, but the other drawings range from 1765 for the ceiling to 1770 for chimney-pieces; and one of Zucchi's paintings is dated 1771. The ceiling follows Adam's drawing (Soane Mus., Vol. 11, Nos. 132–33), except for elimination of decoration inside the scalloped ring and in the corners. None of the chimney-piece designs, however, corresponds to the executed version, though parts of them are related to the one shown in the illustration (see Soane Mus., Vol. 22, Nos. 177–80). Adam's unification of floor and ceiling through closely related yet variant designs is beautifully demonstrated here. Each of the bands and circles has a counterpart, but not a duplicate.

Of the colours in the room today, probably only the carpet actually reflects Adam's ideas as expressed in his drawings. The wall elevations call for multi-coloured grotesques on white walls, whereas the room now has light green walls with panel details in white. Adam's ceiling design also calls for white background, relieved by blue-background medallions, orange Vitruvian scroll, gold trim, and multi-colour arabesques. At the present, the background is peach with light green Vitruvian scroll and trim, and, of course, inset paintings in the medallions.

The inserted paintings are probably by Zucchi, as are the large wall paintings. The stuccowork was executed between 1766 and 1770 by Joseph Rose, who charged £165. 8. 0, including £35. 5. 0 for 'extra work not in the first Estimate, Viz. Ornamen^{td} Panels over two doors, & two ditto next Picture frame' (Harewood Archives).

See Fig. 61 for a detail of the plasterwork.

33. KENWOOD, HAMPSTEAD, LONDON. Library, 1767–69.

The library at Kenwood is perhaps Adam's finest room. Grandeur of proportions and a tunnel-vaulted ceiling are combined with an extremely effective spatial treatment using screened apsed ends; and the decoration, both in general and in detail, is sensitively and beautifully handled. The result is a truly impressive room, one evocative of Adam's aims and ideals. The inspiration of Roman antiquity is eloquently acknowledged in the tunnel vault, the screen of columns, and the apses. It is also apparent in the multi-panelled ceiling, the stucco panels, the inset paintings, the anthemion frieze, and the details of the chimney-piece. But it is all combined with consummate skill into a highly original conception. Adam's willingness to modify classical precedents is seen, and even advertised (*Works*, Vol. I, Part ii, p. 9), in the alteration of a Roman frieze to accommodate the insignia of his client, the Earl of Mansfield: lions replaced griffins, and heads of deer supplanted ox-heads. The arabesque panels (see also Fig. 80) are eighteenth-century creations after an antique theme.

Although James Adam had made drawings for this room in 1764 (Soane Mus., Vol. 43, Nos. 3–4; Vol. 11, Nos. 110–11), the executed ones are those created by Robert three years later (Soane Mus., Vol. 14, Nos. 113–15; Vol. 11, Nos. 112–13; Vol. 22, No. 234). The room follows the 1767 set of drawings very closely. These drawings are brilliantly coloured, with pinks, greyish blue-green, and gold predominant, and with white columns. While related, the present colour is somewhat different, especially in the columns, which are now maroon. Other subsequent changes include the introduction of bookcases in the alcoves of the chimney wall in place of mirrors with sofas beneath them.

The plasterwork was, as usual, by Joseph Rose (Adam, *Works*, Vol. I, Part ii, p. 10), and Antonio Zucchi submitted a detailed bill for the many inset paintings in 1769 (reproduced in J. Swarbrick, *Robt. Adam & His Brothers*, 1915, Fig. 128).

34. KEDLESTON HALL, DERBYSHIRE. Design for the painted breakfast room, 1768. Sir John Soane's Museum, Vol. 14, No. 125.

In 1768 Adam designed for Kedleston a circular breakfast room (25 feet in diameter) with niches. Although no longer extant, it was described in 1802 as a room 'finished with fresco paintings, and antique ornaments, after the Baths of *Dioclesian*' (Geo. Lipscomb, *A Description of Matlock-Bath . . .*, p. 113). A very good idea of the room and its proposed decoration can be had from Adam's two drawings at Kedleston (ceiling, chimney wall) and the six at the Soane Museum (Vol. 11, No. 48; Vol. 14, Nos. 124 and 125; Vol. 27, Nos. 31 and 32; Vol. 40, No. 18). The attenuated pilasters with their elegant painted grotesques are characteristic of Adam's increasing refinement and flatness in the late 1760's, and the rest of the decoration—maidens, stands, anthemia, rinceau—is marked by a similar linear rhythm and elongation. The liveliness of the decoration is echoed in the colours employed—blue, gold, brownish pink, and apple green. The breakfast room is also a foil for the saloon (Fig. 24), for the similar shape of the two rooms only serves to emphasize the difference in decoration—flat and painted here, grander and more three-dimensional in the other.

35. NEWBY HALL, YORKSHIRE. Entrance hall, c1769–72.

Adam's penchant for a somewhat more masculine or martial entrance hall is well

71

illustrated in the hall at Newby. Like those of Harewood, Mersham, and Mellerstain, *e.g.*, this room employs the enriched Doric order with ornaments in metopes (and fluted columns when the full order is used), which Adam felt 'very proper in Halls,' rather than the heavier, plainer variety (Letter to Lord Kames, 31 Mar. 1763, Register House, Edinburgh, Abercairny Papers, No. 564). And he gave to the room an abundance of military decoration, again noted in a number of his halls, *e.g*, Osterley and Harewood. The large trophy panels on the walls are supplemented by smaller groups of trophies on the walls and in the ceiling and by peltoid shields in the door entablatures, chimney-piece, and ceiling. Yet the martial air is tempered by the delicacy of the decoration and the especially refined character of the ceiling. As was frequently his custom, Adam used the same basic pattern for the main outline of both floor and ceiling design, but where the ceiling is finely detailed, the pavement is very simple and plain.

No drawing survives for the wall elevations, but there are designs for all of the other features. The earliest of these is the ceiling design of 1769, which was executed two years later almost exactly as conceived (Soane Mus., Vol. 11, No. 238. The date 1771 is incorporated in the executed ceiling by Joseph Rose, as I learned from an unpublished MS on 'English Decorative Plasterwork' by Geoffrey Beard). Unlike the ceiling, the pavement design (Soane Mus., Vol. 41, No. 78; dated 1772) was not executed as envisioned, but rather was altered to correspond more closely to the general ceiling composition. There are two designs for the chimney-piece— one unexecuted and one carried out (Soane Mus., Vol. 22, Nos. 260 and 261, respectively)—both dated 1772.

36. OSTERLEY PARK, MIDDLESEX. Drawing room, begun late 1760's–completed by 1773.

'A drawing-room worthy of Eve before the Fall,' was Horace Walpole's judgment of this room on his first sight of it, in June 1773 (Letter to Countess of Upper Ossory; Walpole, *Letters*, ed. Toynbee, 1903–05, VIII, 291–92). At that time the room had probably been finished only a short while, for it is the last of the state rooms that he mentions, the next chamber being included in his visit of 1778 (*Ibid.*, X, 282). And the date of 1773 is the only one we have for this room, for none of the drawings, either at Osterley or the Soane Museum, is dated.

The most remarkable features of the room are the ceiling and carpet and their relationship. The ceiling, derived from one at Palmyra, is an effective illustration of Adam's very successful use of ancient sources (*cf.* Fig. 37). His model was substantially altered, as he transformed the square into a rectangle, changed the circle to an oval, and elongated the petals or feathers. The ingredients are the same, the effect totally different. The relation of the carpet to the ceiling similarly reflects Adam's ingenuity, for while the general patterns are the same, the details vary substantially. The writhing central flower of the ceiling became a stylized one, and the extended petals inspired geometric counterparts on the floor. In place of the wide Greek-key band above, Adam substituted a frieze of anthemia below. The octagonal coffers of the ceiling are answered by circles in the carpet. It is theme and variation carried to impressive heights.

Adam also planned the colours carefully, for both the ceiling drawing and the design for the carpet include colours or colour notations (Soane Mus., Vol. 11, No. 204; Vol. 17, No. 186, respectively). The carpet was woven with the colours indicated by notes on the drawing— yellow, brown, and blue—as well as other colours (red, green) not indicated. The ceiling design uses a great deal of gold in place of the yellow of the carpet, but there are also pink, apple green, pale blue-green, and white. The painter of the ceiling, David Adamson, enumerated the various colours on his bill for work at Osterley, 1772–74: 'Sup of ornamented Ceiling 4 oil flatts white/the Grounds round the ornaments which are in Small parts is picked in with Superfine Green, Pink, dark purple & sky blue Colours . . . £33. 15. 6' (preserved at Victoria and Albert Museum, London, Department of Woodwork). Adding to the richly coloured effect were the crimson and gold frieze and the gilded door enframements.

The ceiling and carpet designs at the Soane Museum and the chimney-piece drawing at Osterley were executed as designed. The wall elevations, however, were greatly changed from the drawing preserved at Osterley.

37. PALMYRA, TEMPLE OF THE SUN. Soffit, early first century A.D. As engraved by Robert Wood, *Ruins of Palmyra* (London, 1753), Pl. XIX B.

See Fig. 36 for Adam's use of this design.

38. WYNN HOUSE, 20 ST. JAMES'S SQ., LONDON. Stairhall, c1772–74.

The London house that Adam built for Sir Watkin Williams-Wynn is one of only three of his major town houses to survive in good condition. The stairhall shown here demonstrates the care and attention that Adam gave to the project, as well as the elegant linear style that was his hall-mark in the 1770's. The delicate decoration in the panels and niche is both small in scale and finely detailed, but it is relieved by the substantial amount of plain wall space. And the plainest level, at the top, serves as a foil for the elaborate, though not minutely decorated, ceiling. Basically, each floor within the staircase is treated individually, and yet the whole space is united through the nature of the decoration. The large niche with flanking rectangular doorways on the first floor is echoed on the floor above by the arcade whose side arches have only rectangular openings. While three different friezes are used, all are variations on Adam's device of alternating motifs. Neither overpowering nor over-ornamented, the stairhall represents the synthesis of forces that was Adam's aim.

39. WYNN HOUSE, 20 ST. JAMES'S SQ., LONDON. Music room, 1772–c1776.

The music room for Sir Watkin Williams-Wynn's town house is unified not only by the composition of the room and the character of the decoration, but also by a theme. Bearing in mind the purpose of this room, Adam keyed much of the decoration to the subject of music. All of the grotesque panels, as well as the ceiling, emphasize the lyre, and the inset paintings continue the musical theme. Originally, Adam had planned fewer grotesque panels and more paintings, all with musical subjects— St. Cecilia, heads of great musicians, and the muses honouring the torch of Orpheus (pencilled note on Soane Mus., Vol. 40, No. 71). This last was to have been over the door at the end of the room, but, as detailed by Zucchi in his bill, it became 'Shepherds & Nimphs doing honor to the ashes of Correlli or Handell' (National Library of Wales, Aberystwyth, Wynnstay MSS, Box 115/17). The decoration itself illustrates the finesse of Adam's work of the 1770's. The grotesque panels are excellent examples of the intricate linear design that

marks Adam's maturity, and the same is true of the vertical strips of grotesques and bell-flowers. The ceiling combines minute detail and areas of plain space within a unified composition. And apsed ends relieve the severity of the straight sides of the room.

Drawings survive for all of the major features of the room. The chimney-piece and ceiling (Soane Mus., Vol. 23, No. 6; and Vol. 12, No. 47; dated 27 Aug. 1772 and 23 May 1773, respectively) were executed as designed, but the wall elevations were somewhat altered, though the general effect was retained (Soane Mus., Vol. 40, No. 71; dated 14 Aug. 1773). Both wall and ceiling designs are coloured, and these have served as a guide for the present redecoration. Light green walls are complemented by a pink frieze and lilac panels with white stucco decoration. These same colours (though without the pink) are shown on the ceiling drawing, but the tinted engraving in the *Works* (Vol. II, Part ii, Pl. 7) shows a different colour-scheme—light green for most of the ceiling, with the outer band and the edges of circles and ovals sky blue.

The house is now owned by the Distillers Company, who have preserved and restored most of the original decoration. For a detail of the grotesque panels, see Fig. 82.

40. LLOYD'S COFFEE HOUSE, LONDON. Design for the interior, 1772. Sir John Soane's Museum, Vol. 30, No. 59.

Adam's delight in spatial arrangements and elegant decoration was not restricted to domestic architecture, as can be seen in this unexecuted project for Lloyd's Coffee House. In both plan and decoration, it is comparable to the houses which he created during the same period of his career. His favourite device of a screened apse was employed here very effectively, together with the delicate linear decoration that characterizes all of his work in the decade of the 1770's. The lithe arches of the back wall with their attenuated supports, the arabesque and bell-flower strips, the complex alternating frieze, the capitals inspired by Spalato, the Neo-classical subject panels, and the small-scale decorative panels of the apse and vault are all in keeping with Adam's most exciting decorative projects of the same years (*e.g.*, Derby House or Northumberland House). And the rich colouring is equally characteristic.

41. DERBY HOUSE, 23 (LATER 26) GROSVENOR SQ., LONDON. Great drawing room, c1773. *Works in Architecture*, Vol. II, Part i, Pl. 5.

The town house that Adam redecorated for Lord Stanley (succeeded in 1776 as 12th Earl of Derby) was one of his finest works. As such, it beautifully demonstrated Adam's mastery of problems of planning (see Fig. e), as well as his elegance of decoration. The groin-vaulted ceiling with its barrel-vaulted lateral panels is typical of the elaborate treatments favoured by Adam in the 1770's. Yet despite the multitude of small panels, the whole ceiling is perfectly unified. The same is true of the carpet which echoes the ceiling, without, of course, duplicating it. The small delicate decoration of the mirrors and wall panels is relieved by the expanse of plain surface on which it appears, just as the elaborate torchères are set off by the pilasters behind them. The relatively traditional frieze is an antidote to the small-scale detailing of the tympana and ceiling. By these means, Adam achieved the almost brittle linear elegance, the triumph of two-dimensional elaboration that was his hall-mark in the central decade of his career.

Although demolished in 1862, this room is preserved for us in a number of drawings at the Soane Museum, as well as in the engraved pages of the Adam *Works in Architecture* (Vol. II, Part i, Pl. 6 includes a detail of the chimney-piece and overmantel). The Soane Mus. drawings are Vol. 50, No. 80; Vol. 23, Nos. 48–49; Vol. 12, No. 144; and Vol. 17, No. 184 (walls, chimney-piece, ceiling, and carpet, respectively).

42. NORTHUMBERLAND HOUSE, CHARING CROSS, LONDON. Design of wall elevation for the Glass Drawing Room, c1773. Sir John Soane's Museum, Vol. 39, No. 7.

The redecoration of the drawing room for the Duke of Northumberland's London house is typical in style of Adam's other work of the 1770's, but its use of material was an experiment that Adam did not repeat. Featuring green-painted glass for the pilasters, frieze, and dado, the room also has glass walls painted red to simulate porphyry. Superimposed on all of this is gold decoration with the delicate, linear character at which Adam aimed. Grotesque pilasters, a frieze with alternating motifs, and exquisitely detailed door panels contribute to this effect of elegant two-dimensional surface decoration, while the mirror over the sofa and the panels between the pilasters are beautiful displays of the intricate, yet refined decoration that Adam had achieved by this date. Designs for the window and chimney walls are also preserved at the Soane Museum (Vol. 39, Nos. 5 and 6). The drawing illustrated here is probably the one listed under 9 June 1773 in Adam's bill for drawings to the Duke of Northumberland (Alnwick Castle Archives, U.I. 46).

This wall was executed more or less as designed, but with some changes, as can be seen from a watercolour drawing of the room as it existed before the demolition of the house in 1874 and from the parts of the room as reassembled at the Victoria and Albert Museum (see Fig. 43).

43. NORTHUMBERLAND HOUSE, LONDON. Detail of the Glass Drawing Room, c1773–75. As exhibited at the Victoria and Albert Museum, London.

The Glass Drawing Room was probably executed in 1774–75, as indicated in a few tradesmen's bills that have survived (Alnwick Castle Archives, U. III. 6). It followed fairly closely the designs by Adam (Soane Mus., Vol. 39, Nos. 5–7; Fig. 42), but there were some alterations. These were largely minor changes, such as in the frieze of the door entablature, the overdoor compositions, and the pilasters. The circular bell-flower wreath around the overdoor painting became a square, with decorations added between the corners of the frame and the wreath. And the more varied grotesque decorations of the pilasters were replaced by a continuous vertical repeat. Other changes included the doors and door frames. On the whole, however, the novel conception envisioned by Adam in the drawings was carried out. From the surviving pieces, it is difficult to imagine the overwhelming effect that this room must have created, but the Adam drawings and a later watercolour showing the room before its destruction in 1874 certainly testify to the brilliance of the room.

44. OSTERLEY PARK, MIDDLESEX.
Tapestry Room, c1772–76.

The sumptuous crimson Gobelins tapestries on the walls and the furniture are the most striking feature of this room, which Walpole acclaimed as 'the most superb and beautiful that can be conceived' (Letter to William Mason, 16 July 1778, *Letters*, ed. Toynbee, X, 282). This was the fourth house in which Adam and/ or his clients utilized this type of decoration, the others being Croome Court, Moor Park, and Newby. The idea of a tapestry room seems not to have been Adam's, but rather the Gobelins factory's (see E. Harris, *Robert Adam and the Gobelins*, APOLLO, LXXVI, 100–106); yet he integrated the tapestries here into a highly effective composition. The French tapestries, with subject medallions designed by Boucher, were executed in 1775 and delivered to Osterley the following year. (The panel over the chimney-piece is signed 'Nielson ex. 1775'; and an entry under 5 July 1776 in an 'Acc^t of Labbourers time Employed in ye farm Work at Osterly' lists a charge 'for ye Waggon to Lond^n for ye tapestry,' Victoria and Albert Museum, London, Dept. of Woodwork).

The only Adam drawings that exist for this room are the ceiling and carpet designs, dated 1772 and 1775 respectively (Soane Mus., Vol. 11, No. 206; and Vol. 17, No. 187), which complement each other in general conception. Similarly, Adam has used the same motif for the room frieze and that of the chimney-piece but has treated it differently. In the frieze, the urns and heads are raised, whereas in the chimney-piece they are inset in coloured stones in the white piece. This small-scale decorative treatment was Walpole's only complaint about the room, though apparently he thought the inset stones were actually bronze (*Letters*, ed. Toynbee, X, 282).

45. HOME HOUSE, 20 PORTMAN SQ., LONDON. Design for Etruscan Bedroom, c1775. Sir John Soane's Museum, Vol. 14, No. 134.

The bedroom for the Dowager Countess of Home was one of the rooms designed by Adam in his 'Etruscan' manner, a style that was among his most significant innovations. The delicate and intricate decoration composed of sphinxes, medallions, urns, garland swags, and overlapping circles is typical of Adam's mature manner of the 1770's. It is the colour that marks

this as a very special type of treatment. The reds, browns, and blacks were derived from Grecian urns, and it is this colouring that gives the room its 'Etruscan' character, as the vases were called in the eighteenth century. Drawings also exist for the wall with the bed and for the chimney-piece (Soane Mus., Vol. 14, No. 132; and Vol. 23, No. 69). See Fig. 111 for the chimney-piece, which continues the 'Etruscan' colour scheme. The room is now used as a private office in the Courtauld Institute of Art. It has been partially restored, though a good deal of the decoration is lost.

46. OSTERLEY PARK, MIDDLESEX.
Etruscan Dressing Room, 1775–77.

Of the eight or more rooms designed by Adam in the 'Etruscan' style, the dressing room at Osterley is the only one preserved substantially in its original condition. The total ensemble —walls, ceiling, doors, furniture, carpet, chimney-board, and curtain cornices—was designed together to reflect this taste that Adam had introduced in the early 1770's. Certain of the features survive only in the Adam drawings, but even as extant, the room is an excellent example of both the 'Etruscan' manner and a completely unified design. The keynote is set by the walls with their delicate arabesque arches, urns, sphinxes, medallions, horizontal panels, and maidens in carelessly abandoned poses. The lightness and fragility, coupled with the terracotta and black colouring on pale blue ground, complete the setting.

By the repetition of the motifs and colours, both together and separately, throughout the room, Adam achieved a remarkable composition. The panels of the doors are closely related to the walls, while the door friezes are similar in colour and general spirit, though not in specific details. The chimney-piece frieze is virtually the same as that over the doors, but is not coloured. While the window pelmets (Soane Mus., Vol. 17, No. 107) repeat these friezes, the room frieze differs from them, yet is certainly related in its repetitive motifs. The chimney-board (Fig. 1) is very close to the wall pattern but by no means duplicates it. The basic format of the ceiling and of the carpet as designed (Soane Mus., Vol. 17, No. 189; it no longer survives) is the same, though the details vary. This is seen, for example, in the borders: the border on the carpet follows the design of the door frieze, whereas the ceiling border differs completely. The urns of the back splat and the colours of the chairs again relate to the general theme. It is, above all, the colour that unites the room. The ceiling and carpet both employ various other hues, but the 'Etruscan' colours are important there, too.

Although the ceiling designs date as early as 1772 (Soane Mus., Vol. 11, Nos. 210–12), the wall elevations that set the character of the room bear the date 1775, and all other drawings fall between 1775 and 1777. The wall elevations (Soane Mus., Vol. 14, Nos. 128, 130, 131; Vol. 27, Nos. 72–73; and Vol. 50, No. 71, some of which are duplicates of each other) were executed as designed in October 1775. There are two versions of the ceiling, different though closely related (Soane Mus., Vol. 11, Nos. 210–11 and No. 212), with the latter executed as Adam conceived it.

There is no documentary evidence concerning the painter of the 'Etruscan' decoration, but Mrs. Lybbe-Powys, who visited the room on 22 May 1788, reported that the housekeeper told her the decorative painter was 'Berners.' E. Croft-Murray feels that this may be Pietro Maria Borgnis (1743–1810), son of the painter at West Wycombe (*Passages from the Diary of Mrs. Philip Lybbe-Powys*, ed. E. J. Climenson, London, 1899, p. 231; Croft-Murray, *Decorative Painting in England*, typescript for Vol. II).

Of even greater interest, however, is Adam's source for his design. While he may have derived the specific motifs and the colouring from classical vases (as he states in the *Works*, Vol. II, Part i, preface), the actual inspiration seems to have been Piranesi's *Diverse maniere d'adornare i cammini* (1769). There, the Italian supports this type of decoration (p. 9) and gives three examples. A comparison of the Etruscan Dressing Room at Osterley with a detail from Piranesi (see Fig. 47) reveals a similarity of general conception and scale, as well as of such details as arabesques rising out of sphinxes and the attitudes of the maidens. The differences are also striking, for Adam's more fragile and less naturalistic forms are typical of the tendency toward elegance, refinement, and attenuation that are always to be found in Adam's mature work.

47. GIOVANNI BATTISTA PIRANESI. Design for a chimney-piece and wall. From *Diverse maniere d'adornare i cammini* . . . (1769), Pl. 2 (detail).

See Fig. 46.

48. HOME HOUSE, 20 PORTMAN SQ., LONDON. Stairhall, first floor level, 1775–77.

49. HOME HOUSE, 20 PORTMAN SQ., LONDON, Stairhall, detail of dome, 1775–77.

50. HOME HOUSE, 20 PORTMAN SQ., LONDON. Design for stairhall, *c*1775. Sir John Soane's Museum, Vol. 14, No. 116.

Executed as designed with a few minor changes, the stairhall of the Dowager Countess of Home's town house is highly characteristic of Adam's style, especially in the mid-1770's. The circular shape demonstrates Adam's feeling for space and its manipulation, and the decoration shows Adam's sense of linear and elegant classical design. Although presented in shades of grey on the drawing, the stairhall combines light blue and cream with two different varieties of marbleizing. The upper ground floor walls (bottom half of Fig. 48) and the columns, pilasters, entablature, and dado of the second floor are painted in imitation of yellowish veined marble. The dado of the first floor is veined in a grey-blue manner. Slightly brownish-pink marbleizing is also used. In the dome the decoration is white on light blue panels, with cream serving as the background here, as well as throughout the stairhall.

The rhythmic pattern of the stuccowork decoration of the dome illustrates the linear quality of Adam's mature work and the various classical motifs with which he loved to play. The linear elegance is continued in the decoration of the skylight, where the spirit is the same though the details quite different.

The addition of this decorative ironwork was one change from the original design, as was the magnificent stair-railing at the lowest level. The decoration also was somewhat altered, the large lamps on the first floor level being replaced by grisaille figures and some of the bas-reliefs being eliminated. The figures, panels, and lunettes were painted by Antonio Zucchi.

Home House is now occupied by the Courtauld Institute of Art, which has restored such sections as the stairhall with both sensitivity and authenticity.

51. 'LADY HOMES BACK PARLOR,' 20 PORTMAN SQ., LONDON, *c*1775. Sir John Soane's Museum, Vol. 14, No. 119.

A rectangle with one apsed end; delicate decoration featuring arabesques, grotesques, swags, and related forms; and peach and apricot colouring make the ground floor rear parlour of Home House both a very fine and a typical example of Adam's work at the height of his career. Also characteristic of this style of the 1770's are the attenuation, the dramatic exploitation of arabesque pilasters, and the beautifully-rendered (and executed) small-scale Neo-classical details. And the unity and overall control are very striking. This room, which was executed with relatively few changes, is now the lecture hall of the Courtauld Institute of Art. Carefully restored a few years ago, it is now decorated in shades of pink, the colour discovered when subsequent layers of paint were scraped off. For details of the decoration, see Figs. 68, 85, and 86.

52. HOME HOUSE, 20 PORTMAN SQ., LONDON. Music room, c1775–77.

Designed by late January 1775, the Countess of Home's music room was executed largely in conformity with the Adam drawings (Soane Mus., Vol. 50, Nos. 33–36; and Vol. 12, No. 164; dated 27 Jan. 1775). The delicate overall decoration, the niches, the mirrors, and the extremely attenuated pilasters convey a lightness and brittle elegance that epitomize Adam's style in these years. Many of the motifs had appeared earlier—urns, paterae, palmettes, garland swags, boys in rinceau, medallions—but they are here combined in a very linear and two-dimensional treatment, despite the alcoves created in the walls. The contrast between this room and one of less than ten years earlier is quite striking. In the library at Kenwood (Fig. 33; 1767–69), we still see a certain amount of relief, a strength that is not present here, where flatness and exquisite detail are the major characteristics. Although the designs are mainly in grey wash, the room is now painted in green with gilded decoration. The ceiling drawing is rendered in shades of green and is thus closer to the present colouring. The chimney-piece design (Soane Mus., Vol. 23, No. 66) was altered in execution, as were the elongated lunettes on the short walls. The laurel wreaths on the mirrors are a later addition. This room is presently the reading room of the Courtauld Institute of Art. For the organ designed for this room, see Fig. 87.

53. WORMLEYBURY, HERTFORD-SHIRE. Dining room, 1777–79.

Elegant and intricate detail set against a relatively plain background is the keynote sounded by Adam in the rooms that he decorated for Sir Abraham Hume's country house. In the dining room, this is seen in the delicately entwined arabesques at the sides of the alcoves and in the two friezes of heads and anthemia, both placed within tiny arches. The arabesque and urn of the large panel on the side and the stands and medallion in the alcove tympanum are similarly indicative of Adam's taste and handling. Evocative, too, of Adam's manner is the variation on a theme, demonstrated in the simultaneous similarity and difference of the decoration in the square panel on the right and the narrow arabesque panel flanking the mirror.

Adam's design for the wall elevation (Soane Mus., Vol. 50, No. 23; dated 23 Sept. 1777) was followed fairly closely, the major change in this detail being the addition of two arabesque panels at the sides of the arches and the mirror between them. The pale green walls with white decoration still exist, but in the drawing the room frieze and the bas-relief medallion have greyish-blue backgrounds rather than the light green of the present paint. For the ceiling of this room, see Fig. 145.

54. NO. 17 HILL ST., LONDON. Design for the great drawing room, 1779. Sir John Soane's Museum, Vol. 50, No. 25 (detail).

In January 1779 Adam designed a magnificent drawing room for Sir Abraham Hume's town house. A rectangle with curved ends, it was decorated at the height of Adam's elegant, linear manner. Although it still survives, it no longer exhibits the grandeur or the éclat shown here—or executed. Adam lavished a great deal of attention on this room, and many large-scale drawings survive to attest to this. There are, for example, both sketches and finished renderings for the grotesque panels of the doors and shutters. And an enormous rendering exists for the grotesque pilasters (Soane Mus., Vol. 49, No. 6). It conforms closely to the pilasters shown on this elevation, but with their design worked out in minute detail. The upper frieze, which is repeated over the doors, and the lower frieze of stands and garland swags heighten the effect of elegance and refinement. The same is true of the mirrors, the subject paintings, and the lively, imaginative capitals. The chimney-piece was not executed, but most of the design was carried out as conceived.

55. BYRAM HALL, YORKSHIRE. Design for the drawing room, c1780. Sir John Soane's Museum, Vol. 50, No. 70 (detail).

Adam's decorations for Sir John Ramsden no longer survive, but the drawings at the Soane Museum relate them closely to extant Adam work of the same date. The drawing room, decorated in the 'Etruscan' style, had the elegant elongated pilasters with grotesque decoration (shown filled on another section of this drawing), the grotesque panels of the doors, and the classical scenes of such schemes as the great drawing room of Sir Abraham Hume (Fig. 54). The coupled pilasters can be seen in the music room at Home House (Fig. 52). And the lively yet elegant grotesques between the pilasters and in the frieze are typical of Adam. The chimney-piece and overmantel-mirror with their decoration related to the frieze and pilasters are also shown on a larger-scale drawing (Soane Mus., Vol. 23, No. 151).

56. CUMBERLAND HOUSE, PALL MALL, LONDON. Design for the great dining room, 1780. Sir John Soane's Museum, Vol. 14, No. 138.

Dated August 1780. Among the largest and most imposing rooms designed by Adam in the 'Etruscan' fashion was the great dining room for the Duke of Cumberland's house in Pall Mall. There are many drawings for this room, including wall elevations, details of the frieze, many studies for the chimney-piece, and designs for the ceiling, carpet, and curtain cornice (Soane Mus., Vol. 14, Nos. 138–40; Vol. 49, No. 17; Vol. 23, Nos. 148, 185, 252, 253, and Vol. 24, No. 145; Vol. 14, No. 79; Vol. 17, Nos. 207 and 118). Taken together, they demonstrate Adam's ability to integrate all the aspects of a room into a unified whole while at the same time maintaining for each of the parts an interest of its own. For the chimney-piece, see Fig. 112; for the ceiling, see Fig. 149; for the frieze, see Fig. 73.

The total ensemble also illustrates Adam's expert and sensitive system of variation on a few themes. In its colouring, as well as in its composition and motifs, the Cumberland House dining room is related to the Etruscan Rooms at Osterley (Fig. 46) and Home House (Fig. 45); yet it is also quite different. The orange and black decoration, for example, is set against a pale green background rather than against pale blue, as at Osterley. The trellis pattern is akin to that at Osterley, but the actual formations are not at all the same. Osterley's horizontal bands with arabesques and sphinxes have

disappeared, along with the medallions and panel above them. They are replaced by large subject panels. The sphinxes of the walls at Osterley have been moved to the frieze, which is in turn very different from the earlier examples. The dado at Cumberland House with its parade of circles is obviously related to the dado at Home House, but the overlapping has been eliminated. Strikingly different, also, are the proportions of the rooms and the treatment of space. The longer, narrower room at Cumberland House is articulated by columnar screens at each end. All of these variations produce an effect that shows family resemblance, but nothing closer.

Cumberland House has been demolished, and its design survives only in these drawings.

57. CUMBERLAND HOUSE, PALL MALL, LONDON. Design for the third drawing room, c1780. Sir John Soane's Museum, Vol. 49, No. 18.

The rooms which Adam designed for the Pall Mall house of the Duke of Cumberland at the beginning of the 1780's show that Robert was at the height of his powers at this time. Elaborate and elegant decorations in his manner of the 1770's are the order of the day. Here, for example, Adam exploits the complex yet linear grotesque panels that he had enjoyed for the last fifteen years. Like those of the dining room at Osterley (Fig. 75), as well as scores of others, these panels are an intricate mixture of urns, sphinxes, circular and rectangular subject medallions, and delicate arabesques. During the 1770's Adam tended to emphasize the flatness and refinement that are very evident here. Both the chimney-piece and mirror also relate to Adam's work of the 1770's, the chimney-piece being particularly close to that in the first drawing room at Wynn House (Fig. 107). The pilasters with their intricate small-scale decoration and the rinceau frieze embodying such royal insignia as the lion and the unicorn are also characteristic of Adam's work. The tendency to reduce the orders to frames for decorative display is seen in the pilasters here, especially in a large scale detail (Soane Mus., Vol. 24, No. 271) that delineates the series of vertical strips with their delicate guilloche and floral infilling. And the idea of a frieze exemplifying British symbolism had attracted both Robert and James Adam as early as 1761, Robert in a design for a chimney-piece for the king and queen (Soane Mus., Vol. 22, No. 58; *Works*, Vol. I, Part v, Pl. 4A) and James in his conception of a British order. James's designs for the British order date 1762, but when engraved in the *Works* (Vol. I, Part v, Pl. 2), this design was described as being for the gateway of Carlton House. (James's design is seen in drawings at Avery Library, Columbia University; and the Metropolitan Mus. of Art, both in New York; and Soane Mus., Vol. 7, No. 69). It was appropriate—and typical of Adam—that the drawing room of a member of the royal family should be adorned with this type of frieze.

Cumberland House has been demolished.

58. DESIGN FOR AN OPERA HOUSE, HAYMARKET, LONDON, *c*1789. Sir John Soane's Museum, Vol. 47, No. 7.

Transverse section through the assembly rooms designed to be attached to the rear of the opera house. In 1789 Vanbrugh's opera house in the Haymarket burned down, and this drawing is part of the comprehensive set of designs that Adam appears to have submitted for the new theatre. They were not, however, accepted, as the building that arose in 1790 was designed by Michael Novosielski (1750–95). In addition to the opera house proper, Adam designed a group of assembly rooms, and the section illustrated here represents that part of the project. Shown in Adam's drawing are (from left to right) the entrance from the Haymarket with stairhall and lobby, the oval ball-room, and one of the assembly halls. Both the room shapes and the decoration are typical of Adam's work and show how closely related to his domestic designs were his projects for public buildings. The circular and oval rooms, the alcoves and columned screens are all familiar aspects of his work. So, too, are the coffers of the dome and alcoves, the circular and rectangular subject panels, the niches, and the anthemion stair railing. Even the semi-circular mullioned windows of the ground floor are reminiscent of Adam's style all through his career. The elegant lightness, the treatment of the large dome, the lanterns all bespeak traditional Adam character. Yet, interestingly, the width of the recessed niches and the broad decorative treatment of the dome were particularly suitable for the grander scale of an opera house.

The set of designs for the opera house consists of the eleven large drawings that comprise Vol. 47, but there are similar and duplicate versions in Vol. 28, Nos. 16–25. Vol. 28, No. 21 corresponds to the drawing illustrated here.

59. NEWBY HALL, YORKSHIRE. Sculpture gallery, *c*1767–72.

To house William Weddell's collection of antique sculpture and casts, Adam designed a gallery to be added to the south side of the house. Characteristically, he conceived of the area not as one large statuary hall but rather as three fairly small spaces. The central domed section, shown in this illustration, is flanked by two square chambers, with small barrel-vaulted passages serving as transitions. Within these spaces, alcoves and niches are also used to vary the wall surface. The walls and ceilings are then treated in conformity with Adam's general tendencies. Neo-classical friezes and bas-relief panels enliven the walls, while both the flat ceilings and central dome are subdivided in the usual Adam manner. These sections of the ceiling, designed in 1767 (Soane Mus., Vol. 11, Nos. 236–37), were executed more or less as designed. Drawings do not exist for the wall elevations, whereas extant designs for a pavement echoing the ceiling schemes either were not executed or have since been covered over (Soane Mus., Vol. 41, Nos. 77–79; dated 1772). The elegant, refined bas-relief decoration in white now exists against a background of two shades of pink.

An inventory of the sculpture in the gallery as early as 25 May 1794 is preserved at the Leeds Public Library, Newby Hall Papers, No. 2801.

60. ARCHERFIELD, EAST LOTHIAN. Design for the drawing room, *c*1790–91. Sir John Soane's Museum, Vol. 27, No. 1.

The elaborate set of designs for Mr. Nisbet's house at Archerfield strikingly demonstrates that Adam's last years were characterized by the elegance that is to be found in his more famous projects of the 1770's. There are both sketches and finished line drawings for five or six different rooms, and all of them are as elegantly detailed as this one. The grotesque pilaster strips, the double guilloche vertical bands, the anthemion frieze, the bas-reliefs, and the elaborate girandoles relate this design to earlier Adam schemes, *e.g.* Byram Hall or Sir Abraham Hume's house in Hill St. (Figs. 55 and 54). The same delicate detail is present. Also present

Compare to contemp. galleries e.g. Dance's Parma design 1763

79

is the most persistent feature of Adam's entire career, the Palladian motif within relieving arch, which he had used from his pre-Grand Tour designs on. In its retention of a Burlingtonian element, as much as in its elegant Neo-classical decoration, the drawing room at Archerfield sums up Adam's style and its development. For the ceiling design, see Fig. 150.

Adam's account book kept during a trip to Scotland in 1791–92 includes payments in 1791 from Mr. Nisbet for balance of 'Bill of Designs' (Register House, Edinburgh, Clerk of Penicuik Papers, No. 4968).

61. HAREWOOD HOUSE, YORKSHIRE.
Music room, decorative detail, c1766–70.

This stucco panel was executed by Joseph Rose and was included in his charge of £35. 5. 0 for 'extra work not in the first Estimate, Viz. Ornamen^td Panels over two doors, & two ditto next Picture frame' (Harewood Archives). The general idea for this panel is shown in Adam's wall elevations (Soane Mus., Vol. 14, No. 118), but there were changes in the arabesque foliage. As executed, the panel consists of a Neo-classical urn topped by a palmette and surrounded by rhythmically curving arabesques. The space is filled by the curling leafage, yet both awkward voids and overcrowding are avoided. Above all, there is a sense of lively elegance and artful composition that contrasts strongly with such thicker and simpler panels as those designed for Hatchlands (Fig. 12). Especially interesting, also, is the way in which this smaller panel is related to the larger grotesque panels in the room (see Fig. 32), with a basic lyre shape employed for the arabesques in both but in each case beautifully adapted to the shape of the panel.

62. SYON HOUSE, MIDDLESEX.
Ante-room, decorative detail, c1761–65.

Detail of the capital, entablature, and top of the walls. In this view one sees the exquisite quality of Adam's decorative detail, as well as its relationship to antiquity. Adam's Neo-classicism does not on the whole consist of outright reproduction of ancient decoration but rather of the imaginative utilization of classical inspiration. This is demonstrated in the Syon ante-room, where Adam combined the Ionic order of the Erechtheum with Roman decoration to create a lively synthesis that is as much Adam as it is antique. Adam's volutes are based

on those of the Erechtheum (Fig. 63), but he has used the Athenian necking pattern not on the necking of his capitals but rather as the frieze above them. For the necking of the Syon order, Adam has introduced a frieze pattern probably derived from Roman *thermae* (Fig. 64). The delicate liveliness that Adam has imparted to his decoration—capitals, entablature, and panels— is also characteristic of his eighteenth-century style. The decorative details are gold against green panels, while the remainder of the wall is greyish cream.

See Fig. 16 for a more general view of the walls of this room.

63. ERECHTHEUM, ATHENS. Detail of Ionic capital, 421–405 B.C. As engraved by J.-D. Le Roy, *Les ruines des plus beaux monuments de la Grèce* (Paris, 1758), Pl. XXXI.
See Fig. 62.

64. ANTIQUE ROMAN CAPITAL AND ENTABLATURE. As engraved by Charles Cameron, *The Baths of the Romans* (London, 1772), Pl. XXXIII.
See Fig. 62.

65. SALTRAM HOUSE, DEVON. Saloon doorway, c1768–71.

Executed as shown on the 1768 room elevations at Saltram (unfinished version at Soane Mus., Vol. 50, No. 68), this elaborate doorway illustrates the subordination of the orders to the decorative significance of the whole design. Instead of using half-columns or even fluted pilasters, Adam has abandoned the conventional use of the classical orders for a display of delicate Neo-classical decoration. The rhythmic double-guilloche side panels are anti-architectonic and highly characteristic of Adam's decorative sense. And the capitals that he has chosen are not of the traditional orders, but rather are a relatively little-known variety, discovered by Adam at Spalato, where they adorned pilasters in the corner of the peristyle (Fig. 66). The anthemion frieze of alternating closed and open forms is also antique, as are the various mouldings. It is typical of Adam's use of ancient sources, however, that they are combined in novel ways and that the motifs themselves are as likely to be unusual varieties as traditional Roman ones. The linear rhythms of the pilaster panels are continued, though accentuated, in the door furniture. Both Adam's concern for such minute details and the liveliness of the composition are hall-marks of his work, as can be seen in Figs. 162 and 163.

66. DIOCLETIAN'S PALACE, SPALATO.
Detail of capital, *circa* A.D.300. As engraved in R. Adam, *Ruins of the Palace of the Emperor Diocletian at Spalatro . . .* (London, 1764), Pl. XLIX.

This relatively obscure antique capital, found by Adam in a corner of the peristyle at Spalato, was used in a number of Adam designs, among them the saloon at Saltram (Fig. 65), the little drawing room at Audley End, and the dining room at Lansdowne House (Fig. 31).

67. CULZEAN CASTLE, AYRSHIRE.
Long drawing room, doorway detail, *c*1778–82.

Although no drawing exists for this decorative detail, it conforms quite closely to the chimney-piece, which was designed in 1778 (Fig. 113; Soane Mus., Vol. 23, No. 113). Both have the same frieze of urns with flowers beneath a series of laurel arches, though on the chimney-piece this procession is interrupted by a decorated tablet. Both also employ paterae on the corner blocks, yet they are different—an oval patera on the doorcase and a circular medallion on the chimney-piece. The details are the same, the pilasters are not. This uniting of the main features of a room without actually duplicating them is a favourite device of Adam's and is as characteristic of his style as are the delicate, elegant decorations that adorn this doorcase.

68. HOME HOUSE, 20 PORTMAN SQ., LONDON. Rear parlour, detail, *c*1775–77.

The lush, yet delicate, quality of Adam decoration in the 1770's is readily evident in this detail of the upper section of the walls in 'Lady Homes Back parlor.' Executed largely as designed (see Fig. 51; Soane Mus., Vol. 14, No. 119), it is a remarkable example of both the beauty of Adam's design and the finesse of the stuccowork. The exquisite and almost lyrical capitals are the most striking feature here; but also noteworthy are the grotesque pilasters with their anthemia and scrolls, the swags and paterae between the capitals, and the frieze of laurel guilloche with heads in the loops. As beautifully restored by the Courtauld Institute of Art, the decoration is in white against a pale and a slightly deeper pink.

69. OSTERLEY PARK, MIDDLESEX.
Etruscan Dressing Room, doorway, 1775–77.

Designed *en suite* with the rest of the room, the doorway continues the 'Etruscan' taste so effectively demonstrated in the dressing room at Osterley. The colouring is the same—terracotta and black decorative details on pale blue-grey panels, with the light blue door matching the dado. The decoration, while similar, is not identical.

The individual panels were designed in accordance with their restricted shapes and thus do not duplicate in miniature the composition on the large expanse of wall. The motifs and character are closely allied to the rest of the room, but the panels demonstrate the concept of theme and variation that was a vital part of Adam's system of decoration. In the same way, the shape and divisions of the doorway relate it to many other Adam examples (the dining room at Osterley, *e.g.*; Fig. 29), even as the colour and decoration mark it as a vital part of the Etruscan Room.

There is no Adam design for the doorway; it was left blank on the wall elevations (Soane Mus., Vol. 14, No. 130; Vol. 27, Nos. 72–73).

70. CROOME COURT, WORCESTERSHIRE. Gallery, detail, 1761–*c*1764.

The antique character of the decoration in the gallery at Croome Court becomes readily apparent in a detail such as this. The panel of griffins confronting an urn amid rinceau foliage is found in various Roman versions, the coffered ceiling was derived from the Basilica of Constantine, and the anthemion frieze is very close to one from the Forum of Trajan (Fig. 71). This anthemion frieze of alternating palmette and lotus, with the former enclosed in a circle, was a popular one with Adam. It also appears for example, in the hall at Syon and on the exterior of Lansdowne House. In his description of this latter design in the *Works* (Vol. II, Part iii, Pl. 3), Adam states that his source was the Temple of Concord in Rome. This ancient frieze no longer survives, but Adam's design is remarkably similar to the early Second Century A.D. frieze from the Forum of Trajan.

Whereas the inspiration for this decoration was antique, the interpretation is typically eighteenth century. This is noticeable in Adam's flattening of the deep-relief coffers into an overall decorative pattern and in the increased flatness and delicacy of the long panel. A parallel example of this Neo-classicizing of more robust Roman decoration is to be seen in the engravings of decorative details in Adam's *Ruins of . . . Spalatro* (1764), as opposed to the decoration actually at Spalato.

The plasterwork was executed by Joseph Rose in 1764 (bill at Croome Estate Office).

See Fig. 20 for a general view of this room.

71. FRIEZE FROM THE FORUM OF TRAJAN, ROME, early second century A.D. Lateran Museum, Rome.

See Fig. 70.

72. FRIEZES FOR GEORGE HOBART'S HOUSE, 33 ST. JAMES'S SQ., LONDON, c1770–72. Sir John Soane's Museum, Vol. 53, p. 14.

Among the volumes of Adam drawings at the Soane Museum is one that is devoted almost exclusively to drawings of friezes for a great many of Adam's projects. As these are not entered in chronological order, this volume must have been compiled from the preparatory drawings at a later date, probably in the 1790's. The page here illustrates five friezes from the house at the south-east corner of Charles St. and St. James's Sq. Their character is typically Adamesque, as is their diversity. They include a variant of the triglyph-and-metope frieze for the dining room, a simple repeat of circled palmettes for the second drawing room, and three friezes with alternating motifs. That for the ante-room features a repeat of two simple forms, whereas the other two friezes combine a simple motif with a pair of opposing forms. The variations possible suggest the breadth of Adam's inventiveness, while the rhythmic flow and linear delicacy show the nature of his style.

73. CUMBERLAND HOUSE, PALL MALL, LONDON. Design for the frieze in the great dining room, 1780. Sir John Soane's Museum, Vol. 49, No. 17.

Dated 29 August 1780. A large-scale detail for the frieze shown on the room elevation (Fig. 56; Soane Mus., Vol. 14, No. 138), this design illustrates the care lavished on minor elements, as well as the elegance of Adam's decorative style. Even the figures on the classical urn have been elongated in keeping with Adam's tendency toward attenuation and delicacy, noticeable also in the sphinxes and foliage.

74. RAPHAEL AND ASSISTANTS. VATICAN *LOGGIE*, ROME, Second decade of the sixteenth century. Detail.

See Fig. 75.

75. OSTERLEY PARK, MIDDLESEX. Dining room, grotesque panel, c1766–68.

Among the best preserved and most accessible of Adam's mature grotesque panels are those in the dining room at Osterley. In their illogical combination of urns, griffins, peltoids, and arabesque foliage in low-relief stuccowork with small inset painted panels, they are highly typical of his work of this type, just as their linear elegance, delicacy, and rhythmic movement are highly characteristic of his mature style. Whereas his earlier designs are thicker and less complex (Castley Ashby, Hatchlands, first scheme for Osterley; Figs. 9, 12, and 26), this example is intricate and involved. Yet its complex ambiguity of components is completely suffused by the flat linear elegance. It thus epitomizes the Neo-classical character at which Adam was aiming. Later examples may be flatter, in even lower relief, yet they are merely elaborations on this theme arrived at in the last half of the 1760's (*cf.*, *e.g.*, the music room at Wynn House or the third drawing room at Cumberland House, Figs. 82 and 57).

Despite the illogical combination of diverse elements, the panel is beautifully composed. There is, for example, the repetition of scrolls and of lyre shapes, the latter seen in the general formations of the middle and upper grouping of arabesques. The heavier scrolls at the bottom are repeated just above them in a lighter vein, these in turn leading to more open scrolls at the top of the middle grouping. Scrolls also appear at the top, but this time reversed. Then, there are three versions of the anthemion, each different. The tightly closed lotus just below the circular painting is altered above that medallion into a flatter, more open one, while at the top of the panel is a completely open, more stylized palmette.

Whereas the panel as a whole clearly expresses an eighteenth-century character, its sources are both antique and Renaissance. The inspiration for such decoration certainly came from ancient grotesques, but Adam's ideas were coloured also by those of the *Cinquecento*. It is the combination of the influences and the manner of presentation that was Adam's contribution. By comparing this illustration with ancient and

Renaissance examples, one can see how Adam transformed his sources. Although the arabesque panels of the Ara Pacis (Fig. 77) were not known to Adam, they are characteristic of the Roman decorations available to him. While obviously related to the Osterley grotesques in the use of foliage scrolls and the general lyre shape in the centre, the Ara Pacis panel is more coherent and organic and in more varied relief. Neither the luxuriant high-relief leafage at the bottom nor the almost impressionistic foliage that barely projects from the background is present in the Adam example. And the whole composition has a logicality that is completely lacking at Osterley. There are objects in the Roman relief that are not part of the foliage—the birds at the top—but they appear appropriate in their setting. The Vatican *loggie* (Fig. 74) and other Italian grotesques of the fifteenth and sixteenth centuries are far more complex than the panel from the Ara Pacis and contain a variety of non-foliate and even non-naturalistic elements —animals, masks, putti, stage sets, inset panels. Yet the Vatican grotesques exhibit a liveliness and freshness that are not at all present in Adam's panels. In their place, Adam has substituted elegance and a classicizing quality that are peculiarly eighteenth century.

The eighteenth-century style of watercolour grotesques also affected Adam's interpretation of his ancient and Renaissance sources. The intermediary between the Ara Pacis and Vatican *loggie* grotesques on the one hand and Adam's on the other is such an example as the copy after Pietro Santi Bartoli shown in Fig. 76. This drawing is even closer to Adam's earliest grotesques (*cf.* Figs. 12 and 9 for Hatchlands and Castle Ashby). The panels in the dining room at Shardeloes (Fig. 13), probably Adam's earliest executed grotesques, illustrate his refinement of these ideas, just as the panel at Osterley represents the mature development of this most significant of Adam decorative innovations.

For two possible contemporary influences or parallels, see Figs. 78 and 79.

See Fig. 28 for Adam's wall elevations and Fig. 29 for a general view of the room.

76. 'PALAZZO DI TITO' (DOMUS AUREA), ROME. Decorative detail. Copy after Pietro Santi Bartoli, probably eighteenth century. Royal Institute of British Architects, Vol. 212B, p. 8.

This drawing, employing the style of delineation characteristic of eighteenth-century watercolour grotesques, is one of a group in a volume given by Charles Inwood. Labelled as purchased at the sale of Adam's effects, it contains a few drawings by Adam and by Thomas Hardwick, in addition to the tracings after Bartoli.

See Fig. 75 for a discussion of the sources of Adam's grotesque decoration. See Figs. 9, 12, and 26 for Adam's early unexecuted grotesques with which this bears closer comparison.

77. ARA PACIS AUGUSTAE, ROME. Foliage panel, 13–9 B.C.

See Fig. 75 (Osterley) and Fig. 13 (Shardeloes).

78. JAMES STUART. Design for the Painted Room at Spencer House, St. James's, London, 1759. British Museum, Print Room, No. 1955-4-6-13.

The date 1759 in a panel above the door marks Stuart's design as the earliest fully Neo-classical decoration in England. It is more advanced than Adam's work of comparable date (the designs for Castle Ashby or Hatchlands; Figs. 9, 10, and 12), while Adam decorations of equal complexity and development are not to be found until about 1762 or 1763 (*e.g.*, the gallery at Syon, Fig. 19). Adam's comments on other Stuart designs of the later 1750's are very disparaging: on 5 September 1758 he wrote his brother James that he had seen some ceilings by Stuart at Spencer House, but 'I dont think I see any thing Surprising in them nor more greek than anothers'; and on 11 December 1758 he described some designs by Stuart for Kedleston which he thought ridiculous (Register House, Edinburgh, Clerk of Penicuik Papers, 4852 and 4854). Even if, despite these remarks, Adam found Stuart's designs in advance of his own, there was probably no direct influence of Stuart on Adam decoration. (For furniture, this is perhaps not true. See E. Harris, *The Furniture of Robert Adam*, London, 1963, pp. 8, 62–63.)

In the Spencer House design, Stuart used an anthemion frieze, capitals, and swags between the capitals that were later employed by Adam, but the rest of the decoration is rather different. While both men enjoyed arabesque pilasters, Adam's are not really close to Stuart's, which seem more directly inspired by Renaissance examples (*cf.* Fig. 74) than Adam's ever do. And

Stuart's grotesque wall decorations are also quite different from Adam's, despite the appearance of 'inset' pictures. The colour, too, is not like Adam's. In this design Stuart used blue, yellow, and purple washes with a good deal of uncoloured space, while the finished room has a dark green background. Stuart's primacy in the introduction of Neo-classicism into England must be acknowledged, but Adam's subsequent development and influence were far more significant.

79. CHARLES-LOUIS CLÉRISSEAU. Hôtel Grimod de la Reynière, Paris. Salon, c1775–77. Drawing by J.-C. Kamsetzer, 1782. University Library, Warsaw, Vol. 173, No. 249.

At some point between the erection of the Hôtel Grimod de la Reynière on the Champs-Elysées about 1768 and the visit to the house by the polish architect Jean-Christian Kamsetzer in 1782 (when this drawing and others were executed), Clérisseau decorated the salon with the grotesque panels shown here. As one of the early examples of Neo-classical grotesque decoration in France, this room and its date have acquired distinct significance. Various writers have proposed different dates, largely in order to substantiate their arguments in the question of English or French primacy. Louis Réau suggested 1769, during the building of the house and just after Clérisseau's return to Paris from Italy; Fiske Kimball advanced 1775 or a little later, after Clérisseau's visit to London in the early part of the 1770's; Charles Bauchal listed 1782 (Réau, *La décoration de l'Hôtel Grimod . . .*, Bull. de la Société de l'Histoire de l'Art Français, 1937, p. 10; Kimball, *The Moor Park Tapestry Suite of Furniture . . .*, Philadelphia Museum Bull., Vol. XXXVI, No. 189, Mar. 1941; Bauchal, *Nouveau dictionnaire biographique et critique des architectes français*, 1887, p. 626). Recently, however, Edward Croft-Murray (*The Hôtel Grimod de la Reynière: The Salon Decorations*, Apollo, LXXVIII, Nov. 1963, 379–81) has uncovered a reference to these decorations in the *Almanach des Artistes* of 1777, where the salon is described as 'nouvellement décoré par M. Clérisseau.' Additional evidence for a dating in the mid-1770's is furnished by Croft-Murray's noting that Lavallée-Poussin, who painted the overdoors and ceiling, only returned to Paris in 1777 after a 15-year stay in Rome. A comparison of the grotesque panels here with other French

examples of the mid-1770's or later (*e.g.*, Bagatelle, 1777; Marie-Antoinette's library, the Méridienne, and the Cabinet Doré at Versailles, 1779–83) also supports a date of c1775–77 for the Hôtel Grimod grotesques.

Despite the essentially French character of the room, the grotesque panels are actually quite similar to Adam's grotesques of the late 1760's, *e.g.* those in the dining room at Osterley (Fig. 75). There are, of course, differences—Adam's white stucco decorations on a coloured ground vs. Clérisseau's apparently flat painted panels with coloured decoration against a white background; the nature of the inset panels; the difference in touch. But the general composition and the components are related. This similarity is perhaps even more striking if one turns one of the panels upside-down. The inset panels, the scrolls, the non-naturalistic motifs all seem to fall into place. The vertical rinceau strips are also akin to those used by Adam in the long gallery at Syon (c1763–68), for example (Fig. 19).

While the context and the spirit of the Hôtel Grimod salon are very French, the grotesque decoration seems related to Adam work of the late 1760's. This is not to say that there is a causal relationship, but the possibility does exist. As Adam's mature grotesques of this period represent a distinct development from those planned for Castle Ashby or Hatchlands (Figs. 9 and 12) through the first executed examples at Shardeloes (Fig. 13), it is unlikely that Clérisseau was a continuing influence on Adam in the 1760's, though there is no doubt of the Frenchman's strong formative influence on him in Italy in 1755–57. If there is an influence, then, it would seem to emanate from the Adam of the mid-to-late-1760's. The problem is, of course, complex, due to the similar source for all Neo-classical grotesques and to the close relationship of Adam and Clérisseau in Italy. Until further documentary evidence is discovered, however, the suggestion must be advanced for Adam's influence, at least in a general way, on Clérisseau's grotesques in the Hôtel Grimod. Clérisseau was in London in the early 1770's and could have seen Osterley or other houses where Adam's mature grotesques are featured. Regardless of their source, however, Clérisseau's grotesques exhibit a definite French character.

80. KENWOOD, HAMPSTEAD, LONDON. Library, decorative detail, 1767–69.

The rhythmic flow of arabesque foliage and

the carefully arranged composition are perhaps the most striking aspects of this example of Adam's mature grotesque decoration. As usual with Adam, there is the variation on a theme, for although the top and bottom portions of the panel are quite similar, they are not identical. The lyre-form is answered by the simpler arabesque scrolls, while the larger and more spread-out palmette at the top echoes but does not repeat the smaller, tighter version at the bottom. Both demonstrate Adam's ability to create a varied whole out of similar parts. Even the actual treatment of the foliage scrolls illustrates this tendency. The bell-flower swag at the top of the panel is very effective in achieving a more interesting panel than would have been the case with only the medallion surrounded by complementary arabesques. The inspiration of antiquity is seen here not only in the medallion and the grotesques but also in the various borders—Greek key, guilloche, and double guilloche. The beautifully executed stuccowork which enriches Adam's conception was by Joseph Rose. For a view of the entire room, see Fig. 33.

81. HAREWOOD HOUSE, YORKSHIRE. Saloon, alcove detail, designed 1767.

The exquisite detailed decoration of the two niches flanking the doorway from the hall was executed almost exactly as designed on Soane Museum, Vol. 11, No. 153. Aside from a spreading out of the design to conform to a semicircular surface, the only noticeable change is in the position of the figure at the top of each panel. The mouldings, too, were reproduced with no alteration. Each of the grotesque panels, like those of the virtually contemporary alcove panels in the library at Kenwood (Fig. 80), demonstrates rhythmic flow amid a carefully composed design. Although perhaps a little crowded, the panels are still characterized by Adam's usual delicacy and restraint. The three panels together also illustrate Adam's finesse at varying his basic design. The two end panels are mirror images of each other, differing only in the pose of the figure at the top. The central panel is very close to these, yet is actually rather different. This is most obvious in the central core of the panels, but it can also be seen in Adam's movement of the thickest swag of foliage from the middle of the central panel to the upper set of scrolls in the flanking panels. The general composition and the

specific motifs are more or less the same; the handling is not. Barry's redecoration of the room during his alterations of 1843–50 has somewhat changed the character of the saloon (now the library), with bookcases replacing screens of columns in the alcoves, but the Adam decoration of the alcove panels remains intact. The present colouring—white decoration on a turquoise ground, with red and brown backgrounds for the mouldings—is not original.

82. WYNN HOUSE, 20 ST. JAMES'S SQ., LONDON. Music room, decorative detail, 1772–c1776.

The increased elegance and delicacy of Adam's decoration in the 1770's is evident in this grotesque panel, keyed to a theme appropriate for a music room. A comparison with the grotesque panels in the dining room at Osterley (Fig. 75) of less than a decade earlier shows this difference quite clearly. For despite the similarities, there is more open space and a generally more delicate touch. The difference is not, of course, as striking as that between the Osterley panel and those planned for Hatchlands (Fig. 12), but one is conscious of Adam's continued development and refinement. Adam's 1773 design for Sir Watkin Williams-Wynn's music room (Soane Mus., Vol. 40, No. 71) also shows the grotesque panels as more crowded than are the executed versions. As realized in the hands of his highly talented stuccoer, Joseph Rose, Adam's design is less congested, but it is still a very complex design of four horizontal levels with central core and flanking drops. There is the familiar combination of a variety of forms, both natural and artificial, yet there is also the elegant flatness and artful composition. The flanking vertical strips also illustrate the delicacy, almost daintiness, seen in the grotesque panel. The present lilac panels with white decoration are based on the coloured rendering noted above. For a general view of the room, see Fig. 39.

83. DERBY HOUSE, 23 (LATER 26) GROSVENOR SQ., LONDON. Great drawing room, door panel, 1774. Sir John Soane's Museum, Vol. 24, No. 264.

Dated 19 August 1774. Closely related to grotesque wall panels were the small door panels, such as those for Lord Stanley's house in Grosvenor Sq., that Adam designed for some of his projects. In this one, a bottom panel for the folding doors of the third (or great) drawing room, can be seen the same motifs and arrangements as in Adam's large wall panels. The classical emblems, the delicate swags, the curling arabesque foliage, and the almost effortless manner in which one part flows into the next are typical. Also characteristic is the way in which Adam repeats his forms, yet varies them. The large arabesque scrolls at the bottom are answered by smaller reversed ones at the top; the small sphinxes are complemented by the larger griffins; the urns and palmettes reappear in different versions; and even the bell-flower swags are repeated in a modified fashion. An engraving of this panel, with the central oval filled with a classical figure, appeared in the *Works* (Vol. II, Part i, Pl. 8).

84. HOME HOUSE, 20 PORTMAN SQ., LONDON. Music room, alcove detail, c1775–77.

In this detail of the alcoves flanking the chimney-piece in Lady Home's music room, we can see the exquisite, delicate decoration that is typical of Adam in the mid-1770's. The character of the decoration and the repetition of the narrow anthemion band in both the half-dome and the entablature tend to tie the whole design together, just as the other parts of the ensemble demonstrate the variety of basically similar patterns. This is seen in the different bands within the half-dome, but it can also be observed in the swag patterns. The swags between the pilaster capitals are related to the swags overlaid on urns above them, but the two are not identical. While the scale of the swag motif on the entablature of the niche is the same as that over the capitals, the actual motif is more closely related to the design between the capitals. All of this variation within set limits is further suffused by the flat, linear elegance that is the keynote of Adam's mature style. For the position of this detail in the whole room, see Fig. 52.

85. HOME HOUSE, 20 PORTMAN SQ., LONDON. Rear parlour, doorway detail, c1775–77.

A comparison of this semi-circular tympanum over the door from the front parlour with the upper portion of the music room alcoves (Fig. 84) reveals how varied Adam designs even of the same date can be. Where this semi-circle has the decoration radiating from the bottom, that in the music room spreads out from the top. The

emphasis on the vertical rays in the back parlour contrasts with the more horizontal emphasis in the other room. The rear parlour overdoor is relatively simple, as opposed to the more minute decoration in the music room niche. Yet, there are similarities as well—the petal motif at the core of the radiating fan and the treatment of the entablature. In both, there are two mouldings in the entablature, a narrow upper band with small-scale repeat and a wide band with a series of evenly spaced basically circular motifs. Both demonstrate the elegance and refinement of Adam's mature style, as well as the fertility of his imagination. Although there are some differences, the rear parlour overdoor was executed more or less as designed (*cf.* Fig. 51).

86. HOME HOUSE, 20 PORTMAN SQ., LONDON. Rear parlour, decorative detail, c1775–77.

The long grotesque drops flanking the chimney-piece in Lady Home's rear parlour are clearly indicative of the delicate refinement of Neo-classical detail that Adam displays in the mid-1770's. The horizontal and oval medallions; the urns and palmettes; and the loops, swags, and scrolls of foliage are all beautifully integrated, as one part leads gracefully into the next. It is this sense of rhythm and continuity, as well as the delicate character of the classical decoration, that marks Adam's most accomplished work. Equally characteristic is the enormous variation on a few basic motifs and combinations, of which this is but one example. That the variation was Adam's and not his craftsmen's can be seen by comparing this detail with the drawing for the room (Fig. 51). Although there are a few differences, the stuccowork and the drawing are amazingly close.

87. HOME HOUSE, 20 PORTMAN SQ., LONDON. Design for one end of the music room, showing the organ, 1775. Sir John Soane's Museum, Vol. 50, No. 33.

Dated 27 January 1775. A large case piece of furniture, the organ designed for Lady Home's music room is closely related to the interior architecture. In keeping with Adam's style of the 1770's, however, it is neither heavy nor architectonic. The attenuated pilasters with delicate capitals; the urns of the entablature; and the garland swags, medallions, and bucrania of the pilaster base all repeat the decoration of the walls. Only the base of the organ and the decoration surrounding the organ pipes are treated differently from the rest of the room (*cf.* Fig. 52), and these are very typical of Adam's mature style. A glance at the flanking sections of this wall reveals how closely integrated into the total composition was the organ, a fact confirmed by a view of the whole room. The addition of the lyre and the trumpet-holding maidens atop the case is typical of Adam's use of themes appropriate to special rooms, but the rest of the decoration announces its classical allegiance even more loudly. See Fig. 88 for an example of Adam's early organ cases, which contrasts sharply with this mature version. If executed, the organ no longer survives.

88. KEDLESTON HALL, DERBYSHIRE. Design for an organ case for the music room, *c*1758–61. Sir John Soane's Museum, Vol. 25, No. 1.

Designed sometime between 11 December 1758, when Adam received the commission for the organ, and 9 April 1761, when Sir Nathaniel Curzon was created Baron Scarsdale, this organ is one of Adam's earliest attempts at furniture (Letter from Robt. to Jas. Adam, 11 Dec. 1758; Register House, Edinburgh, Clerk of Penicuik Papers, No. 4854). Its heavy, architectonic quality and relatively thick and simple decoration are characteristic of Adam's early style of interior architecture. The four caryatids are related to the early chimney-pieces with similar stiles (Figs. 20 and 98), the central wreath and foliage panel recalls one in the design for Castle Ashby (Fig. 10), and the whole character is very much in tune with Adam's work shortly after his return from Italy. The development of his style from the heaviness of the Kedleston organ to a much more delicate, elegant, and complex piece can be seen by comparing it with the organ designed for Cumberland House in 1781 (Fig. 89). The caryatids were replaced by attenuated pilasters and colonnettes, the broad and sparse decoration gave way to intricate and delicate over-all decoration, and the architectonic quality was supplanted by an equally architectural but infinitely more refined format. The simplicity of the urn finials here is in sharp contrast to the delicate complexity of the musical and heraldic trophies atop the Duke of Cumberland's organ. There is another drawing of the Kedleston organ (Soane Mus., Vol. 40, No. 17) almost identical to this, but this design

appears not to have been executed. The present organ is very different.

89. CUMBERLAND HOUSE, PALL MALL, LONDON. Design for an organ case, 1781. Sir John Soane's Museum, Vol. 25, No. 18.

Dated 2 May 1781. Just as the interior decoration for the Duke of Cumberland's town house demonstrates the elegance and delicacy of small-scale decorative detail that are the essence of Adam's most mature style (see Figs. 56 and 57), so this organ case represents this development in case furniture. Its similarity to work of the mid-1770's, though with the delicate, almost brittle qualities accentuated, can be seen by comparing it with the organ designed for Home House (Fig. 87) six years earlier; its difference from Adam's early work is apparent when it is contrasted with the organ conceived for Kedleston (Fig. 88) at least twenty years before. The scale of the parts, the intricacy and complexity of the details, the linear quality all distinguish this later organ case from the Kedleston example. There are human-headed supports in both, but at Kedleston they are large and imposing caryatids while at Cumberland House they are small delicate terms in the upper section. The real counterparts to the Kedleston caryatids, however, are the elongated colonnettes and the pilasters with their elegant grotesque decoration. Bold relief vs. flatness, simplicity vs. intricacy; these are the crucial differences between early and mature Adam work. Whereas no colour is indicated on the Kedleston design, the organ case for Cumberland House was to be coloured in apple green and pale blue with the detailed decoration in 'Etruscan' colours.

90. CROOME COURT, WORCESTERSHIRE. Library bookcase, 1761–65.

The general format of this bookcase was designed as early as November 1761, for it is shown on Adam's 'Section for finishing the Gallery at Croome in the Manner of a Library' (Soane Mus., Vol. 50, No. 10; bill at Croome Estate Office, Worcs.). When this gallery was redesigned as a classical statuary hall in 1763, the library scheme was altered to fit a smaller and virtually square room, with the bookcase design retained. The early design shows the bookcase as executed, with the exception of the central panel of the frieze and the pilaster panels. These details were definitely designed by June

1763, when Adam charged Lord Coventry for 'the ornaments for Mr. Alkin for the Book-cases of the Library.' The bookcases were included in Sefferin Alken's bill for carver's work done at Croome since 1763, which was receipted in full on 4 February 1765 (Croome Estate Office).

Both the heavy architectural quality and the relatively simple decoration are typical of Adam's early work. The motifs are all classical, but they are not handled with the elegance or finesse of Adam's later work. The thickly carved and widely spread out decoration on the entablature panel contrasts sharply with more rhythmically complex panels of similar subjects, and the guilloche pilaster panels lack the tight-ness of more developed Adam decoration. The rapid development of Adam's style of wall furniture, corresponding to the similar mutation in interior decoration in general, can be seen by comparing the Croome bookcase with that at Nostell Priory (Fig. 91). Although only a few years later, the Nostell example is flatter, more delicate, and more intricate. The Ionic pilasters are more elongated, and the relatively loose guilloche has given way to a tight and complex double guilloche. A similar change is also noted in the entablature.

91. NOSTELL PRIORY, YORKSHIRE. Library, c1766–67.

The library at Nostell exemplifies Adam's developed style of bookcase. Although no draw-ing survives for the wall elevations, the room can be dated fairly closely from other drawings and documents. The chimney-piece and ceiling were both designed in 1766, and by the follow-ing year work was definitely under way on William Collins' chimney-piece tablet and Antonio Zucchi's paintings. (The drawings are in Nostel Archives, C3/1/4/148 and 154, with duplicates at the Soane Mus., Vol. 22, No. 222; and Vol. 11, No. 226. For the work in progress in 1767, see letters from Robert Adam to Sir Rowland Winn, 18 Aug. and 15 Sept. 1767; Nostell Archives, C3/1/5/2.) On 30 June 1767, Chippendale charged for making '81 sham books for the doors of the Library' and the very imposing library table shown in the centre of the room. He charged for the lyre-back chairs on 22 January 1768 (Nostell Archives). There is no evidence that the furniture was to Adam's design (probably the reverse was true; see E. Harris, *Furniture of Robert Adam*, p. 28), but

the date of the furniture helps to establish a date for the room.

In contrast to the bookcase for Croome of the early 1760's (Fig. 90), that at Nostell is flatter and both more elegantly and more intricately detailed. The Nostell example is also an integral part of the walls, whereas that at Croome is actually free-standing. The complex and refined double-guilloche pilasters at Nostell make a striking comparison with the simple guilloche pilasters at Croome, and the tightly composed frieze is also very different from the loose, almost straggly panels in the Croome entablature. Another significant variation is in the colour of the wood—dark at Croome, stained light in imitation of maple at Nostell.

92. OSTERLEY PARK, MIDDLESEX. Library, begun c1766.

Closely related to the contemporary library at Nostell Priory (Fig. 91), the library at Osterley also utilizes double-guilloche-decorated Ionic pilasters, but its architectural character is somewhat less pronounced. This is due to the absence of pediments, except on the entrance wall (not shown in this photograph), to the lower and more open dado, and to the white colour which gives the room a lighter effect. The larger space also adds to this lightness. In both rooms there is the small-scale alternating repeat in the bookcase frieze which combines with the double-guilloche decoration to produce the more delicate linear character of Adam work of the later 1760's. The two rooms also demon-strate how effectively Adam varied similar elements to achieve rather different effects. Whereas the individual bookcase units are similar, especially those opposite the window wall at Osterley, the end result is not. The lighter chimney walls, for example, are in sharp contrast to the highly architectural treatment of the same wall at Nostell.

There are dated (1766) drawings for the ceiling and chimney-piece, both of which were executed as designed (Soane Mus., Vol. 11, No. 202; and Vol. 22, No. 209). The wall elevation preserved at Osterley is not dated. Like the other drawings, it was followed fairly closely, but there were two significant changes: a bookcase frieze conforming to that of the walls was substituted for a fluted frieze with acanthus leaves over the pilasters, and the detailed decoration on the chimney-piece (but not the form) was altered to that shown on Soane

Museum, Vol. 22, No. 209. The inset paintings above the bookcases are by Antonio Zucchi, while those above the chimney-pieces have been attributed both to Zucchi and to Cipriani (P. Ward-Jackson, *Osterley Park: A Guide*, London, 1954, pp. 11–12; E. Croft-Murray, *Decorative Painting in England*, typescript of Vol. II).

93. ARCHERFIELD, EAST LOTHIAN. Design for the library, *c*1790–91. Sir John Soane's Museum, Vol. 27, No. 2.

Many of the features that characterized Adam's library designs in the last half of the 1760's, *e.g.* Nostell (Fig. 91) or Osterley (Fig. 92), are still to be seen in this design, which was created only two years or so before Robert's death. The pilaster bookcase frames have become much thinner and more attenuated in keeping with the general tendency of Adam proportions from the 1770's on, but they are still the principal vertical elements. The bookcase entablature, as previously, is related to Adam room frieze designs. The bookcases, like those at Osterley and Nostell, are topped by inset classical paintings, and the room frieze is not unrelated to the frieze at Nostell. The coved ceiling with delicate classical panels is also typical of Adam's mature work. And that most persistent feature of Adam's architecture, the Palladian motif within relieving arch that he inherited from his Burlingtonian predecessors, is still very much in evidence. The whole room illustrates Adam's subsequent refinement of his first developed style. The major difference is in the attenuation and greater delicacy, and this, in essence, is the nature of Adam's development from the late 1760's to the end of his career. There are a number of other sketches and finished line drawings for this room (Soane Mus., Vol. 27, Nos. 3, 4, 17–20, 21, and 25), and these, too, demonstrate Adam's continued attention to detail and the elegance of the total ensemble.

94. ADAM BROTHERS. HOPETOUN HOUSE, WEST LOTHIAN. Red Drawing Room, chimney-piece, *c*1755–56.

Probably the most striking feature of the Red Drawing Room at Hopetoun is the 'Chimney Piece for the Earl of Hopetoun, near ten feet long, and six feet and near ten inches high, with Women, Termes, clothed with drapery; almost Round' that the sculptor Michael Rysbrack noted in his letter to Sir Edward Littleton of

18 November 1756 (published by M. I. Webb, *Michael Rysbrack Sculptor*, London, 1954, **p.** 196). Characteristic of English taste in the mid-eighteenth century (*cf.* Fig. 97), this chimney-piece was but the first of this type used by Adam in the late 1750's and first half of the 1760's (Figs. 98 and 20). Robert's role in the creation of this one is hinted at in two letters written to his sister Jenny from Rome in 1755, in which he mentions sending the Earl of Hopetoun 'a Sketch of his Chimney with some alterations' and then delights at having heard 'how much Hopetoun was pleas'd with the Chimney I sent him' (letters dated 3 May and 9 Aug. 1755; Register House, Edinburgh, Clerk of Penicuik Papers, Nos. 4772 and 4783). There are, however, two undated drawings by Rysbrack that can be related to this work. One (Fig. 95) exhibits very similar terms to those at Hopetoun, but placed frontally rather than diagonally, as executed. Although it also uses a large central tablet breaking the frieze, both the subject of the plaque and the decoration on the frieze are quite different from the Scottish example. The inner mouldings, as well as the cornice, however, are identical. The second drawing (Fig. 96), which is not as close, employs both front- and side-facing console brackets topped by female heads and another unrelated tablet; yet the frieze is that at Hopetoun. The only difference is the reversed position of the candlestick and griffin. The tablet actually used was based partially on a relief by François Duquesnoy (Spada Gallery, Rome, discovered by Webb, *Rysbrack*, p. 135). The putti were copied from the Duquesnoy work, but the reclining woman on the right was added. The questions of Adam's involvement in the design of this piece and of the precise contribution of Rysbrack are made still more complex by the popularity of caryatid chimney-pieces (see Fig. 97) and by the probable appearance of Rysbrack as the carver of the related chimney-piece at Hatchlands before the end of the 1750's (see Fig. 98).

95. MICHAEL RYSBRACK. Design for a chimney-piece, probably for Hopetoun House, *c*1756. Victoria and Albert Museum, No. E.479–1946.
96. MICHAEL RYSBRACK. Design for a chimney-piece, probably for Hopetoun House, *c*1756. Victoria and Albert Museum, No. E.63–1946.

For the relation of these designs to the chimney-piece in the Red Drawing Room at Hopetoun, see Fig. 94.

97. ISAAC WARE. CHESTERFIELD HOUSE, LONDON. Great drawing room, chimney-pice, c1748–50. Now in the Metropolitan Museum of Art, New York (Gift of the Hearst Foundation, Inc., 1956).

The caryatid chimney-piece from Chesterfield House is a fine example, though by no means the only one, of the occurrence of this type before the Hopetoun piece of a half-decade later. Its general similarity to the Hopetoun version (Fig. 94) is obvious, especially in the angled position of the maidens, but there are many differences of detail—full caryatids vs. terms, the inner mouldings, the rich Rococo carving on the frieze as opposed to the much more classical character of the Scottish example. This piece also bears resemblance to Adam's early chimney-pieces in England, *e.g.*, Hatchlands (Fig. 98). For Ware's discussion of caryatid chimney-pieces, see his *Complete Body of Architecture* (London, 1756), Pl. 88. See also, James Parker, *Designed in the Most Elegant Manner, and Wrought in the Best Marbles*, METROPOLITAN MUSEUM OF ART BULLETIN, XXI (Feb. 1963), 202–13.

98. HATCHLANDS, SURREY. Great dining room, chimney-piece, c1759.

The principal room of Adam's first major project in England, the dining room (now drawing room) at Hatchlands, has as its chimney-piece the kind with caryatid stiles that the Adam brothers had used in the Red Drawing Room at Hopetoun (Fig. 94) a few years before. This type of chimney-piece, which was not uncommon in England in the second quarter of the eighteenth century (see Fig. 97), was to be used by Adam in some of his early projects, though less frequently after 1765. The Hatchlands example is related to its predecessor at Hopetoun in general form and mouldings and in the division of frieze and central plaque, but full caryatids have been used in place of the canted terms in Scotland. The frieze motifs and the tablet are basically classical, though in the frieze this is not so obvious as it is at Hopetoun. Like the Hopetoun chimney-piece, that at Hatchlands was probably carved by Rysbrack. M. I. Webb feels that it is 'so exceedingly like Rysbrack's work that there can be little doubt

that he did' the Hatchlands piece, and it is also significant that the monument to Admiral Boscawen, the patron at Hatchlands, was designed by Adam and carved by Rysbrack (*Michael Rysbrack Sculptor*, London, 1954, p. 183; the monument, dated 1763, is in St. Michael Penkevil, Cornwall). Whereas for Hopetoun the extant drawings are by Rysbrack, the Hatchlands designs are Adam's (Soane Mus., Vol. 22, Nos. 11 and 12). Dated 1759, they were executed as designed, with, however, certain changes. The caryatids were made stouter and their drapery was altered, the frieze decoration was added, and a different tablet was substituted. The original idea of a battle between tritons and sea-monsters, however, would perhaps have been more appropriate for the home of an admiral.

99. SHARDELOES, BUCKINGHAM-SHIRE. Design for the drawing room chimney-piece, 1761. Sir John Soane's Museum, Vol. 22, No. 32.

100. SHARDELOES, BUCKINGHAM-SHIRE. Drawing room, chimney-piece, 1761–c1764.

Designed by Adam in 1761, this was executed sometime before 1765, when Benjamin and Thomas Carter submitted their bill to William Drake. Included on it was a charge of £513. 13. 10½d. for this 'Collumn Chimney Peice,' with £75. 13. 6 of the total itemized for 'Carving a Tablet Composed of a Basket of flowers & two peices of Freeze with Festoons of Laurel leaves and Drops with Six flowers, two Antique Capitals all richly Carved and polish'd' (Buckingham County Record Office, Aylesbury, Shardeloes MSS). As can be seen by comparing the existing piece with Adam's drawing for it, the Carters followed the original conception very closely. The only changes were a slight modification of the Ionic volutes, amplification of the basket of fruit design, and the fluting of the columns. This type of chimney-piece had been used by the Adam brothers in Scotland *e.g.*, drawing room at Arniston) and was quite popular with Robert in his first seven or eight years in England, for seventeen can be dated before 1765. Of these, all but two use colonnettes rather than pilasters, whereas after 1765 pilasters are much more common (see Figs. 106 and 114), another indication of Adam's increasing tendency toward flatness.

101. SHARDELOES, BUCKINGHAM-
SHIRE. Dining room, chimney-piece, 1761–
c1764.

Designed in 1761, this chimney-piece in the dining room (or large parlour) at Shardeloes was carved by Benjamin and Thomas Carter, who described it on their bill of 1765 as 'The Double Truss Chimney.' For this, the most expensive item on the bill, they charged £218. 13. 0½d., of which £96. 14. 0 was for 'Carving the Ornaments Consisting of a Tablet of Boys & two peices of freeze with Laurel leaves six side of Scrooler with large rafled flowers and two peices of Ornaments on Trusses & folliage, all richly Carved & polish'd' (Buckingham County Record Office, Aylesbury, Shardeloes MSS). The background of the frieze is a dark red; the rest of the piece is white. As executed, the chimney-piece follows Adam's drawings (Soane Mus., Vol. 22, Nos. 28–30) in general format, though there were changes in the frieze and the height of the outside truss. The overmantel shown on the drawings was not executed. Despite the classical detailing, this type of chimney-piece had been used in the Adam brothers' Scottish work (e.g., Dumfries House, Fig. 3). Robert employed this double truss design only four times in England (all before 1765; see, e.g., Fig. 18), but single trusses, facing either to the front or side, are quite common, both before and after 1765 (see, e.g., Figs. 11, 102, and 104). In this design, unlike the dining room chimney-piece at Syon (Fig. 18), Adam began the truss immediately below the mantel shelf. The Shardeloes example also illustrates the use of a continuous frieze broken by a central tablet, as opposed to the central tablet flanked by symmetrical frieze motifs, as at Coventry House (Fig. 102).

102. COVENTRY HOUSE, 29 (NOW 106) PICCADILLY, LONDON. Lady Coventry's dressing room, chimney-piece, 1766–67.

This elaborate chimney-piece with side-facing trusses and much detailed decoration was designed by Adam in 1766 and completed by the following year, when John Devall charged £136 for executing it (Croome Estate Office, Worcs.). His bill includes a minute description, which conforms not only to the piece but also to Adam's drawing (Soane Mus., Vol. 22, No. 70). The chimney-piece, executed exactly as designed except for a change in the central oval plaque, shows the increasing refinement and delicacy of Adam's work of the mid- and late-1760's. This is especially noticeable if contrasted with the basically similar dining room chimney-piece at Shardeloes (Fig. 101). Though both are filled with classical motifs, the antique elements are more numerous and more refined in the later example. The many finely carved small-scale mouldings, the crossed torch and quiver, the rhythmically flowing rinceau of the amorini-altar frieze motifs, the shape of the central tablet, and the delicate guilloche band filled with palmettes attest to this. The chimney-piece with side-facing trusses was frequently used by Adam. At least thirty-eight examples can be found all through his career, with the largest number dating between 1761 and 1772. Coventry House is now the St. James's Club, and this chimney-piece is preserved in the main hall.

103. HAREWOOD HOUSE, YORKSHIRE. Design for a chimney-piece for the dining room, 1766. Sir John Soane's Museum, Vol. 22, No. 181.

Although the drawing is labelled for Gawthorpe, the name of the house was changed to Harewood during construction, and all designs from 1767 on bear the new name, rather than the old one, as here. The bracket-supported mantel shelf seen in this design was among Adam's most common chimney-piece treatments. Employed by the Adam brothers in Scotland (Yellow Drawing Room at Hopetoun), it appears on almost a hundred of Robert's designs between 1759 and 1791 (see, e.g., Figs. 9, 35, and 36). As is characteristic of his work in the mid-1760's, there is here a certain amount of delicate small-scale detail, as in the guilloche inner border. This motif was also used on the chimney-piece at Coventry House, of the same year, shown in Fig. 102, but the total effect of the two pieces is not at all the same. A comparison of these two illustrates how Adam mixed and combined elements in order to produce an amazing variety of designs. The presence of a guilloche border and the treatment of the frieze as two symmetrical motifs flanking a central tablet are the major similarities, but within this framework, there are more differences than affinities. Even the guilloche patterns have different centres, while the Harewood example has, in addition, an inner fluted moulding that is missing in the Coventry House chimney. The actual symmetrical frieze motifs and the tablet subjects are unrelated, and one employs trusses below a corner block while the other has short brackets directly beneath the mantel shelf. As the dining room was drastically altered during Barry's remodelling at Harewood in the 1840's with Adam's gallery chimney-piece installed in place of the original dining room one, it is not certain if this piece was executed.

104. NO. 38 BERKELEY SQ., LONDON.
Design for a chimney-piece for the bed chamber, 1769. Sir John Soane's Museum, Vol. 22, No. 216.

For Robert Child, his client at Osterley, Adam also furnished designs for the redecoration of a town house in Berkeley Square. Included was this chimney-piece design with side-facing trusses. Unlike the trusses in Lady Coventry's dressing room (Fig. 102), these have female heads between the truss and mantel shelf, a treatment also used elsewhere by Adam. While both of these chimney-pieces feature friezes with a central tablet flanked by symmetrical motifs, the carefully composed arrangement of five individual elements here replaces the altar-amorini-rinceau frieze motif at Coventry House. Again, both chimney-piece tablets have oval subject plaques but with the remainder of the tablet in each treated quite differently. Although this design for Child's chimney-piece leaves the plaque blank, a less finished version (Soane Mus., Vol. 22, No. 217) includes a lively scene. Again, as so often with Adam, we see immense variety within relatively few basic formats.

105. NOSTELL PRIORY, YORKSHIRE.
Design for a chimney-piece for the saloon, 1772. Sir John Soane's Museum, Vol. 22, No. 226.

Although pilasters tend to be employed more frequently than colonnettes in Adam chimney-pieces after the mid-1760's, there are a number of later designs that feature the more three-dimensional colonnettes. Among these is the saloon chimney-piece at Nostell, which was executed exactly as designed. Here Adam combined fluted colonnette stiles with capitals of his own design and a continuous unbroken frieze of alternating urns and stylized palmettes. The delicacy of the frieze and of the capitals is typical of Adam's style in the 1770's. These capitals also demonstrate Adam's willingness to invent new designs in a classical vein or to adapt known antique models to suit his purposes and taste. While related to the capital from the

peristyle at Spalato (Fig. 66) that he sometimes used, those at Nostell employ delicate leafage scrolls, plants, and bell-flowers in place of the flutes above the row of acanthus leaves. The paterae on the corners, the small lion masks in the cornice, the dentils, and the specific details of the frieze complete the Adamesque character —an elegantly refined essay on classical themes. For a substantially different treatment of relatively similar components, see Fig. 106.

106. WYNN HOUSE, 20 ST. JAMES'S SQ., LONDON.
Design for a chimney-piece for Lady Williams-Wynn's dressing room, 1772. Sir John Soane's Museum, Vol. 23, No. 13.

Dated 27 August 1772. Flat pilasters with a decorative panel in place of flutes, delicate small-scale decoration, and myriad classical motifs are the principal elements of this chimney-piece, a fine and typical example of Adam's work in the 1770's. Its similarities to and differences from the contemporary chimney-piece designed for the saloon at Nostell (Fig. 105) show the variety of Adam's mature designs. Pilasters contrast with colonnettes. A central tablet amid a frieze of elongated hexagons with tiny oval medallion centres is opposed to an unbroken frieze of relatively larger-scale motifs. And a narrow lower frieze receives the attention given to an elaborate cornice on the other design. Yet both have Adamesque versions of classical capitals, and both are variations on a similar basic conception of a chimney-piece. Interestingly, the chimney-piece that was actually executed in Lady Williams-Wynn's dressing room is somewhat of a cross between these two extremes. The stiles became fluted half-colonnettes, the capitals were altered to a rather more typical version of the Ionic order, and the frieze was changed to a more restrained swag motif. The corner medallions were executed as designed, and the concepts of a central tablet and of a narrow lower frieze were retained, though substantially modified. All of this was foreshadowed in the pencil sketches shown on the blank right half of the drawing illustrated here. It is further explained in John Hinchliff's bill for chimney-pieces which bears dates from 1773 to 10 May 1776 (National Library of Wales, Aberystwyth, Wynnstay MSS, Box 115/17):

'A Statuary Marble Inlaid Chimney Peice for Lady Wynnes Dressing Room, was Estim-

ated for a Pillaster one at ... £128. 0. 0
'Extra to the Above being a Column Chimney Peice ... ... £22. 0. 0.'

There is a pen sketch by Adam (Soane Mus., Vol. 14, No. 204) that conforms very closely to the first version shown on this drawing, indicating how closely the draftsmen followed the architect's conceptions. Antonio Zucchi appears to have been responsible for some of the drawings for this particular piece, as his bill to Sir Watkin Williams-Wynn includes a charge of £8. 0. 0 for 'Paintings in Distemper for the Chimney piece of Lady Wynn's Dressing room' (National Library of Wales, Aberystwyth, Wynnstay MSS, Box 115/17). This may possibly have been the drawing of the central tablet for the guidance of the carver, as this is the one section of the executed chimney-piece that is not shown on the sketch or the chimney-piece rendering, but it may also have included the corner medallions. For a similar use of Zucchi, see Fig. 107.

107. WYNN HOUSE, 20 ST. JAMES'S SQ., LONDON. First drawing room, chimney-piece, 1772–c1774.

This chimney-piece represents a new source of inspiration for Adam in the early 1770's and later—the designs published in Piranesi's *Diverse maniere d'adornare i cammini* of 1769. While the total compositions of Piranesi's illustrated chimney-pieces were too complex for Adam's uses, various parts were not only grist for his mill, but a totally new conception to add to his repertoire. A comparison of this piece with Fig. 108 (*Diverse maniere*, Pl. 9A) reveals at a glance the relationship. Wide stiles with subject panels, classical nymphs playing instruments, and a long subject frieze are common to both, as is the actual division of the various parts of the chimney-pieces. Adam's is much flatter and more delicate, as one would expect of him, but the similarity is unmistakable. The Adam drawing (Soane Mus., Vol. 23, No. 10), though very close to the executed version, is even more akin to the Piranesi design, for the nymphs are playing the same instruments and their costumes are still closer to those on the Italian original. Although Adam has raised his maidens on pedestals and in the actual chimney-piece altered the costumes somewhat and changed the instrument of the left-hand nymph, the stiles are very similar. The frieze has a different subject, but another of Piranesi's designs

(*Diverse maniere*, Pl. 8A) is closer to Adam's without being a specific source. Piranesi's eagles with heavy guttae below them were classicized into elegant paterae and a fluted band with delicate decoration. The whole is typically Adam in its refined and elegant classicism, but the inspiration is Piranesi.

The Adam drawing is dated 1 October 1772. Some time after that but before 8 June 1775, Antonio Zucchi made drawings of the classical subject details for the use of the sculptor, and these drawings probably represent the link between the Adam rendering and the executed piece. The drawings do not survive, but Zucchi's bill to Sir Watkin Williams-Wynn describes them as follows:

'Drawing of a Bas relief representing Aurora going before the Sun & the different Hours to be executed in marble in first drawing room £6. 0. 0
'Two figures for the jambs of the said Chimney ... ... £2. 0. 0.'
(National Library of Wales, Aberystwyth, Wynnstay MSS, Box 115/17).

108. GIOVANNI BATTISTA PIRANESI. Design for a chimney-piece. From *Diverse maniere d'adornare i cammini* ... (1769), Pl. 9A.

See Fig. 107.

109. NORTHUMBERLAND HOUSE, CHARING CROSS, LONDON. Design for a chimney-piece and overmantel for the Glass Drawing Room, 1773. Sir John Soane's Museum, Vol. 22, No. 55.

In place of the architectual overmantels that he had used in the first few years in London (cf. Fig. 18, Syon dining room), Adam in his later, more mature work often employed delicately detailed linear mirrors above his chimney-pieces. Characteristic of this tendency is the chimney-glass shown here, which was executed with only minor changes. (It is now installed in the Victoria and Albert Museum, Northumberland House having been demolished in 1874.) The linear quality of the design is accentuated by the extreme elongation and elegance, as in the female terms, dancing maidens on pedestals, and sphinxes, and by the delicate, almost fragile nature of the whole design. Similarly linear and non-architectonic is the chimney-piece included here, which may or may not have been executed. (The chimney-piece itself no long survives.) Instead of the traditional separation of stiles and friezes, Adam has combined the two by means of the inner L-shaped panels with delicate circles and grotesque drops. Classical motifs abound here and in the central tablet, all within a basically flat surface intended to be created of scagliola inset in a white marble ground. Quite close to the chimney-piece in the Countess' dressing room at Derby House (Soane Mus., Vol. 23, No. 51; *Works*, Vol. II, Part i, Pl. 6), this one appears possibly to have been superseded in the revised designs of 1774. Adam's bill for drawings from 9 June 1773 to 4 August 1774 (Alnwick Castle Archives, U. I. 46) includes the following references to the chimney-piece and chimney-glass: 9 June 1773—one-half of the chimney side, probably corresponding to Soane Mus., Vol. 39, No. 6 (and to the end wall illustrated in Fig. 42); 26 June 1773—chimney-glass; 29 June 1773—chimney-piece, full-size and coloured (£5. 5. 0); 15 July 1773—another drawing of this, but with alterations; 15 March 1774—another design of both chimney-piece and mirror (£8. 8. 0); 21 March 1774—still another design of the chimney-piece alone (£3. 3. 0); 26 March 1774 —a larger-scale drawing of the chimney-piece; 11 April 1774—a drawing of the chimney-glass, full-size (£2. 2. 0); and 10 May 1774—further alterations to the glass over the chimney.

110. HOME HOUSE, 20 PORTMAN SQ., LONDON. Front parlour, chimney-piece and overmantel, 1775–77.

Designed in 1775, this white marble chimney-piece and its flat and linear overmantel were executed as designed (Soane Mus., Vol. 23, No. 63) with only slight modification of two of the horizontal bands in the overmantel and elimination of the elaborate circular medallion planned for the centre of that space. The flatness of the overmantel is in sharp contrast to Adam's early, more architectural features of this kind (*cf.* Fig. 18, Syon dining room) but is characteristic of his style in the 1770's. The delicate capitals above attenuated pilasters whose shafts have become merely flat panels with exquisite decorative patterns are joined by an anthemion frieze that is related to the pilaster panels but does not simply repeat them. The other details are equally classical and restrained, and the whole composition is extremely flat, almost two-dimensional. In contrast, the chimney-piece is somewhat plainer with very little minute decoration of the kind found in the over-

mantel; yet it is quite similar in general character. The elongated stands in the centre of the stiles and the circled urns above them correspond to the pilasters of the overmantel, and both are topped by heads. In the overmantel, these heads are placed within circles above the square capitals, whereas on the chimney-piece, the heads are set within squares atop the circled urns. The rectangular central tablet of the mantel is answered by the oval medallion at the top; the flutes of the chimney-piece are parallels to the two frieze bands of the overmantel. By these subtle means, Adam has created a two-part composition that is neither repetitive nor jarring. Rather, it demonstrates the idea of variation on a theme that is such an integral part of the Adam style.

111. HOME HOUSE, 20 PORTMAN SQ., LONDON. Etruscan Room, chimney-piece 1775–77.

Although the drawing for this chimney-piece is labelled for the third drawing room, it was executed in the Countess of Home's bed chamber and corresponds in colouring to the 'Etruscan' decoration of that room. The terra-cotta and black scagliola decoration on the white marble is the main indication that this was to be part of an Etruscan Room; in all other respects it is closely related to Adam's new chimney-piece designs of the 1770's. The wide stiles with central panel and narrow flanking strips are the most typical feature of this new breed of chimney-pieces, but the delicate and rhythmic detailing and such specific elements as the addorsed sphinxes at the base with a central column of decoration rising up between them are also part of this new trend. The existing chimney-piece follows Adam's finished drawing (Soane Mus., Vol. 23, No. 69) quite closely, the only significant change being the conversion of square subject panels on the corner blocks into circular medallions within squares. In addition to this drawing, there are two sketches (Soane Mus., Vol. 23, Nos. 189 and 226) that reveal other steps in the creation of the final piece. Both of these preliminary sketches call for a central subject tablet in the centre of the frieze, which is itself essentially the same as executed; and the lower frieze band is shown as a small-scale decorative repeat, rather than the fluted band actually used. While there are slight differences in the stiles and in other aspects of the decorative details, the idea as a whole is already close to the eventual product. Adam's ability to produce a quite different result out of very similar elements and even similar 'Etruscan' colouring can be seen by comparing this chimney-piece with Fig. 112, a design for Cumberland House.

112. CUMBERLAND HOUSE, PALL MALL, LONDON. Design for a chimney-piece for the great dining room, 1780. Sir John Soane's Museum, Vol. 23, No. 148.

On this chimney-piece in 'Etruscan' colouring for the Duke of Cumberland's great dining room, Adam lavished a good deal of care. In addition to this finished rendering and two sketches, there are large-scale details of the frieze and stiles. The most interesting sketch is Soane Museum, Vol. 23, No. 185, for it shows two alternate possibilities for the stiles and corner blocks. The two designs are fairly similar, but the left-hand version has a wider central panel and slightly different filling and uses a circular medallion to bridge the transition from the stile to the corner block. This scheme was worked out for both sides of the chimney-piece in the other sheet (Soane Mus., Vol. 24, No. 145). The right-hand stile of the first sketch was followed in the finished rendering illustrated here, as were the frieze and central tablet, for which no alternatives are shown. A detail of the fluted frieze with delicate flowering urns in the flutes and of the guilloche lower frieze band is represented in Soane Mus., Vol. 23, No. 252, while No. 253 is a large drawing of the stiles.

A comparison of this design with a chimney-piece at Home House of five years earlier (Fig. 111) reveals Adam's facility for producing widely variant essays on similar themes. Both employ 'Etruscan' colours; and both utilize the wide tripartite stiles, wide and narrow friezes, and complex detailed decoration characteristic of Adam's work after 1770. At Home House, the whole end sections project out, whereas at Cumberland House only part of the end areas project, though in addition the centre of the frieze is also advanced. A continuous frieze of fairly widely-spaced motifs is contrasted with a smaller-scale repeat broken by a central rectangular panel. Circular corner medallions at Home House give way to ovals in the later design. The bases of the Cumberland House stiles are plain; its counterparts' are not. In place of a few larger motifs within the central panel of the stiles, the newer design has a drop

of small-scale objects. Where the narrow flanking strips at the Duke of Cumberland's are filled with a continuous bell-flower pattern, the earlier chimney-piece has wider and more varied strips. The tops of the stiles are similar, yet different. The total ensembles are amazingly alike in spirit, surprisingly varied in detail.

113. CULZEAN CASTLE, AYRSHIRE. Long drawing room, chimney-piece, designed 1778.

By using the same frieze of laurel arches encompassing urns with flowers as he had employed for the room frieze and the doorway (Fig. 67), Adam related this chimney-piece to the total ensemble of the long (or second) drawing room at Culzean. The corner blocks, too, are akin to those on the doorway, but circles with classical emblems have been used in place of ovals with stylized flowers. The side pieces, on the other hand, are quite different. Those flanking the door are plain pilasters with delicate, stylized Corinthian capitals, while the chimney-piece stiles are pilasters in the form of decorative panels, topped by highly unusual capitals that are composed of classical elements but are totally divorced from the usual antique orders. The combination of four horizontal levels featuring reeds, swags, addorsed sphinxes, and acanthus leaves very effectively demonstrates Adam's freedom in creating Neo-classical designs based on diverse antique sources. The wide and complex stiles are also characteristic of Adam's later chimney-pieces, and the use of unorthodox capitals similarly is not untypical of these post-1770 designs. Rhythmical and classical, the chimney-piece illustrates traditional Adam qualities as well as his innovations of the 1770's. It was executed in very close conformity to the drawing (Soane Mus., Vol. 23, No. 113), which is dated 1778.

114. NEWLISTON, WEST LOTHIAN. Bedroom, chimney-piece, c1789–92.

The bedroom chimney-piece in Thomas Hogg's house at Newliston includes the pilaster stiles frequently encountered earlier, as well as the delicate capitals and the shafts transformed into panels of bell-flower drops likewise typical of Adam's work. A central tablet with classical motifs, flanked by urns and garland swags, and fragile plants on the corner blocks complete the pattern. The attenuation and finesse seen here also demonstrate the continuity of Adam's development. While there are late examples that are more restrained, even they share many of the characteristics of the 1770's and early 1780's; and chimney-pieces as elaborate as this one are not at all uncommon in the last years of Adam's life. The drawing for this chimney-piece is not preserved, but other drawings for Newliston are dated as early as December 1789 (Soane Mus., Vol. 32, Nos. 67–76). Adam visited the house on 23 August 1791, and payments to him for surveying are recorded on 17 October and 21 November of that year (Register House, Edinburgh, Clerk of Penicuik Papers, No. 4968).

115. THISTLEWORTH HOUSE, MIDDLESEX. Design for the drawing room ceiling, 1759. Sir John Soane's Museum, Vol. 11, No. 2.

Adam's first executed interior in England was the drawing room added to General Bland's house in Isleworth, of which this is the design for the coved ceiling. It is on the whole more Neo-classical than the wall elevation (Fig. 11), though the heavy nature of the decoration is characteristic of both. The inner flat of the ceiling features such classical motifs as anthemia, urns, and figures, but in the thicker style of delineation found in the early works. Already, however, we see Adam's tendency to sub-divide his areas and to integrate them. The grotesques of the outer coved area, together with the classical subject medallions, urns, griffins, and rinceau foliage, are even more evocative of the influence of his just-completed Grand Tour and the materials out of which his more mature style was to be welded. By 1759 the elements of this style were thus already apparent, waiting only to be flattened, refined, made more elegant, and subjected to control and restraint.

116. NO. 16 LOWER GROSVENOR ST., LONDON. Design for the drawing room ceiling, 1761. Sir John Soane's Museum, Vol. 11, No. 64.

One of the earliest coloured drawings to issue from Adam's office, this design for the Earl of Hertford's town house employs colours that are basically untypical of the Adam style—grey, orange, a golden green, turquoise, and white. The heavier, thicker detail, however, is characteristic of Adam's early drawings; and this, as well as the general conception, relates it to such early schemes as General Bland's drawing

room at Thistleworth (Fig. 115) and a ceiling at Hatchlands (Soane Mus., Vol. 11, No. 7), both dated 1759. Like the central flat of the Thistleworth ceiling, this scheme has a wide oval band with a rosette in the centre and foliage sprays on the two long axes. In both ceilings, too, there are rectangular plaques filling out the rectangle, but in Lord Hertford's ceiling they are in the corners amid foliage while at Thistleworth, the plaques merely occupy the ends of the rectangle. The division of the oval band into alternating blocks of rinceau-lyres and flutes is also found in the Hatchlands ceiling, along with diagonally placed corner blocks, but the eight-part division at Hatchlands has become twelve-part here. This twelve-part division is not repeated, but the octagonal arrangement is a very common Adam treatment. As early as 1761, Adam demonstrated his skill at varying components and motifs in order to produce a host of related yet different designs. The ceiling design illustrated here does not survive in the house, which still retains some Adam decoration.

117. HATCHLANDS, SURREY. Design for the drawing room ceiling, 1759. Sir John Soane's Museum, Vol. 11, No. 3.
118. HATCHLANDS, SURREY. Drawing room, ceiling detail, 1759–61.

Although this particular version was unusual, both the octagonal division of a ceiling and the idea of a central motif with radiating members were quite popular with Adam. Here, however, Adam was experimenting with a design that he used only in the drawing room (now the library) at Hatchlands, but not thereafter. The heavy, rather thick decoration is characteristic of his early work, though in the executed ceiling this quality has already been refined. The central rosette and the foliage scrolls around the edges are related to such other early schemes as Thistleworth and Lord Hertford's house in Lower Grosvenor St. (Figs. 115 and 116). Many of the other details are less typical, with some of the specific motifs—the naval emblems, dolphins, and trident—being chosen as tributes to Adam's client, Admiral Boscawen. For the design of the four diagonal panels, Adam turned to a source that he frequently used in his early career, the Villa Pamphili. The particular model can be seen in Fig. 119, a drawing owned by Adam that illustrates the panel of a dome at the seventeenth-century Italian site. As usual, he altered his prototype substantially, changing the tree to a decorative panel topped by a winged head and the swag at the bottom to military trophies, but the conception of the figures atop the classical medallion and the treatment of their arms and legs is the same in both. In the end, the medallions were left blank. The executed version also shows the increased crispness, elongation, and elegance that were to be characteristic of Adam's subsequent development.

119. VILLA PAMPHILI (NOW DORIA-PAMPHILI), ROME, c1644–52. Drawing of a panel of a dome. Sir John Soane's Museum, 'Miscellaneous Sketches and Drawings by Robert Adam and Others,' No. 46.

For Adam's use of this source, see Figs. 117 and 118.

120. SHARDELOES, BUCKINGHAM-SHIRE. Hall, ceiling, 1761–63.

Designed in 1761, this ceiling was executed by Joseph Rose, who included it in his bill for stuccowork between 10 October 1761 and 19 February 1763 (Buckingham County Record Office, Aylesbury, Shardeloes MSS). Adam's drawing, dated October 1761 (Soane Mus., Vol. 11, No. 63), was followed very closely. The basic format is related to certain Burlingtonian ceilings (e.g., the White Drawing Room at Houghton, c1726–34), though Adam's version is flatter and more classical. Two months after the Shardeloes design, Adam again used this scheme (Syon, ante-room), though with completely different decorative details. In both ceilings, but especially in the Shardeloes example, the individual members are fairly thick. The increased lightness and delicacy within less than two years can be seen by comparing this ceiling with that executed in the Tapestry Room at Croome Court (Fig. 121), though even that is relatively bold as opposed to mature Adam examples (Figs. 137 and 142, e.g.). While the less-involved format and the relief present in the Shardeloes ceiling are characteristic of Adam's early period, the design itself points the way to such refined, elegant, and complex creations as the centre section of the drawing room ceiling at Northumberland House (Fig. 137).

121. CROOME COURT, WORCESTER-SHIRE. Tapestry Room, ceiling, c1763. As

re-installed in the Metropolitan Museum of Art, New York (Gift of the Kress Foundation, 1958–59).

Although designed for the library in January 1763, this ceiling was executed in the Tapestry Room. Adam charged £10. 10. 0 for his design (Croome Estate Office, Worcs.; Soane Mus., Vol. 11, No. 37), which was carried out by Joseph Rose with virtually no change. As was common with Adam, he treated the main portion of the ceiling as a square, then filled in the remainder with auxiliary panels. In this case, the end sections feature delicate rinceau foliage that is related to the decoration in the segments between the central octagon and its encompassing circle. The lightness of these forms is in contrast to the somewhat heavier members of the central panel, which therefore tend to dominate the composition, as they should. In various ways, the Croome ceiling recalls earlier Adam designs, but the lighter quality here immediately marks this as a slightly later example. While the central octagonal motif is related to the hall ceiling at Shardeloes of sixteen months earlier (Fig. 120) and the corner loops resemble those in the Shardeloes dining room (Fig. 122), the differences are more striking than the similarities.

122. SHARDELOES, BUCKINGHAM-SHIRE. Dining room, ceiling, 1761–63.
123. OSTERLEY PARK, MIDDLESEX. Dining room, ceiling, c1766–68.

This is one of the very few examples of a design that Adam re-used in another house. Usually, he combined parts from various designs into a substantially different composition or produced a new creation whose spirit and perhaps details recall other works without really duplicating them at all. But in a surprisingly scant number of cases, virtually exact duplicates can be found. About five years after he designed the dining room ceiling at Shardeloes, Adam repeated that ceiling for the dining room at Osterley. There are certain minor differences, and the Osterley version is somewhat richer and more lush; but both ceilings employ the same basic composition and virtually identical details. As now existing, the principal distinction is in colouring, though there is no documentary evidence for Adam's choice of colour. The Shardeloes design (Soane Mus., Vol. 11, No. 69), executed exactly as drawn, is not coloured, and no drawing survives for the

Osterley ceiling. Before the remodelling of c1960, that at Shardeloes was in tan on a blue-green ground, whereas the Osterley version has blue-grey outer and inner backgrounds, pink colour in the middle ring and around the corner medallions, and white decoration. Also very similar to these is the unexecuted design for the Green Drawing Room at Harewood (Soane Mus., Vol. 11, Nos. 163 and 164; dated 1765).

124. SYON HOUSE, MIDDLESEX.
Entrance hall, ceiling, c1761.

Designed in October 1761 (Soane Mus., Vol. 11, Nos. 12 and 13), the hall ceiling at Syon is typical of Adam's heavier early manner. The depth of the relief is in sharp contrast to all the tendencies of his more developed style, and it is even very pronounced in comparison with such basically masculine entrance halls as those at Osterley or Newby (Figs. 27 and 35). The simplicity, too, is opposed to the much more complex designs of his typical style. Although the relief is much greater here, there is a certain similarity to the contemporary hall ceiling at Shardeloes (Fig. 120), which also features a heavy fluted concave border with acanthus leaves at the angles. Despite the reminiscence of Adam's predecessors in the emphasis on projecting elements, the character of the decoration in the Syon ceiling recalls Italy and Adam's Grand Tour. This is especially true of the border around the ceiling, which is remarkably close to a specific Roman frieze, originally in the Forum of Trajan (Fig. 71).

For a marked contrast with this ceiling, compare the ceiling of the long gallery at Syon (Fig. 15). For a view of one end of this room, see Fig. 14.

125. SYON HOUSE, MIDDLESEX.
Drawing room, ceiling detail, 1762–64.

Both the design and execution of this ceiling are very well documented. In 1761, Adam decided on a coved ceiling and created his first design, which called for medallions and swags in the cove and three octagonal motifs amid scrolls in the central flat (Soane Mus., Vol. 11, No. 21). This scheme of decoration with its broad and relatively heavy detailing was replaced by December of that year by a composition resembling the executed version, but with certain differences (Soane Mus., Vol. 11, No. 19). This was simplified in the final design, a

detail of which is dated 1762 (Soane Mus., Vol. 11, No. 20). Work began on the room fairly shortly, for on 4 November 1763 the Earl of Northumberland, in discussing the progress on the drawing room, wrote Adam that he was pleased 'that Mr. Rose will get the Cieling of that Room complete before the Frost comes on, so that it may have time to be gilt early in the Spring, by which Time I hope the Painting's will be ready to be fixed up' (Alnwick Castle Library, XCIV, 44–45). As to the paintings, Lord Northumberland had more to say in this same letter. Commenting on some confusion about the price, he stated that his idea was based on 'what Cipriani himself told me when I showed him the Two Paintings one with a Single the other with double Figures, which were done as Specimens, and which I am certain he then offered to paint for the whole Room at Two Guineas each picture & to finish them in the best Manner.' The small Cipriani paintings, which are on paper, are set in a myriad of octagons and diamonds with gilded mouldings, giving the whole ceiling an almost jewelled effect. It is an effect, however, that Adam chose not to repeat, for this particular idea is quite unusual in the Adam *oeuvre*, despite the typical Adam character of many of the individual details.

126. AUDLEY END, ESSEX. Design for a ceiling for the little drawing room, 1763. Scrap Book at Audley End, p. 110.

Signed and dated 1763. Labelled 'Design of a Ceiling in the Stile of the paintings of the Ancients,' this unexecuted drawing is as dependent on an antique model as any design Adam ever created. The source was a ceiling in the Baths (or Palace) of Augustus (Fig. 127), and Adam followed it quite closely. While he changed the border, added baskets of foliage and an octagonal border around the central medallion, and altered certain other details, the resemblance is very striking. The general composition was one that Adam often used, and both the details and the handling are typical of his work in the early 1760's. This is especially seen in the foliage and the corner elements; but the anthemion band, the side panels, and the medallions are also characteristic. The medallions, for example, are quite comparable to those in the drawing room ceiling at Syon (Fig. 125) of the same date.

Adam charged Sir John Griffin Griffin

£15. 15. 0 for this drawing, which he included in his bill, under date of August 1763. Here, too, he described the design as 'in the Taste of the Paintings of the Ancients' (Essex Record Office, Chelmsford, Braybrooke Papers, D/DBy A365).

127. BATHS (OR PALACE) OF AUGUSTUS, ROME. From Charles Cameron, *The Baths of the Romans* (1772), Pl. 57.
For Adam's use of this antique source, see Fig. 126.

128. 'CIELING OF A ROOM AT Mrs MONTAGU'S HOUSE IN HILL STREET,' LONDON, 1766. Sir John Soane's Museum, Vol. 11, No. 200.
129. HILL ST., LONDON. Carpet for Mrs. Montagu, c1766. Sir John Soane's Museum, Vol. 17, No. 166.
Typical of the close relationship that Adam often created between the ceiling and carpet of a room are these designs for a room in Mrs. Montagu's Hill St. house. Here, as was so often the case, the designs are complementary rather than simply imitative. The general composition is quite close, but the actual details differ substantially. Both have a central circle treated as a valerium with decoration arranged in concentric circles around the centre; both have circular or oval motifs in the four corners; and both have a wide border surrounding the main square area. Whereas the central motifs are differentiated only by colour, the rest of the compositions differ in specific treatment. The complex small-scale decoration of the outer border of the ceiling is countered by a simple swag border on the carpet. In place of the circular paterae in the corners of the ceiling, Adam has planned oval subject panels in the corresponding sections of the carpet. The decorative bands, the detailed decorative motifs, and the colouring are not at all the same. It is this subtle kind of relationship that demonstrates Adam's facility for integrating the parts of a room into a whole.

In addition to the abundant classical motifs, Adam has here included touches of *Chinoiserie*, which are very unusual in his work, though this taste was noted in the early Scottish career of the Adam brothers (see Fig. 5). Here, oriental subjects have been introduced into the medallions of the ceiling and the corner ovals of the carpet, and some peltoid shields have been converted into Chinese bells. It is as lighthearted a use of things Chinese as was true of the fancies of James and Robert Adam in the early 1750's, but these exotic touches seem especially unusual in the Neo-classical context of these two designs.

Adam's craftsmen were at work on this room in the summer and autumn of 1766, for on 11 October he wrote Mrs. Montagu that 'I hope this Month we shall nearly finish Your Room in Hill Street, The Gilders are at Work, and I am doing all I can to push them on . . . ' (Printed in Bolton, *Arch. of R. & J. Adam*, II, 319). In addition to the drawings illustrated here, the Adam collection at the Soane Museum also includes a sketch for this carpet (Vol. 54, Part i, No. 12), a variant design for the carpet (Vol. 17, No. 167), and a chimney-piece design (Vol. 22, No. 218).

130. MERSHAM-LE-HATCH, KENT. Drawing room, ceiling detail, designed 1766.
Executed as designed on Soane Museum, Vol. 11, No. 182, this ceiling illustrates the delicate and rhythmic small-scale decoration that is typical of Adam's work in the mid- and late-1760's. The complex treatment of the central motif, the tendency to fill most of the area with light curvilinear foliage, and the general flatness all contrast sharply with designs of the early 1760's, as, for example, the hall ceiling at Shardeloes of 1761–63 (Fig. 120). The relatively thick and simpler forms of that design include corner motifs that are very similar to those at the corner of the central area at Mersham, but one is broad and self-contained while the other is the delicate central sector of an elegantly curving rinceau. The double guilloche borders of the two ceilings exhibit differences of the same order. Even in comparison with the 1763 Tapestry Room ceiling at Croome Court (Fig. 121), the Mersham ceiling is markedly more intricate and conveys a much more strongly two-dimensional decorative effect. The substantial amounts of blank space at Croome contrast with the profusion of decoration at Mersham, and the rinceau bands are not nearly so tight. In colour, too, the Mersham ceiling is more complex and delicate. While that at Croome is an overall bluish-white, the other ceiling features white and golden brown decoration on pale grey-green and beige backgrounds. The plasterwork at Mersham was the work of Joseph Rose, to whom payments are

recorded in Sir Edward Knatchbull's book of 'House Building and Furnishing Account, 1762 to 1784' (Kent County Record Office, Maidstone).

131. HAREWOOD HOUSE, YORKSHIRE.
Saloon, ceiling detail, 1767–c1770.

Joseph Rose charged £158. 0. 0 for the ceiling and cove of this room, which he executed in conformity with Adam's design of 1767 (Soane Mus., Vol. 11, No. 152; Rose's bill, 24 Jan. 1766–10 Mar. 1770, is at Harewood). The decoration is an exquisite example of Rose's skill but also of the faithfulness with which he carried out Adam's conceptions. The crisp elegance of the execution goes hand-in-hand with the delicate two-dimensional rhythm of the design. From the guilloche and Greek key borders to the urns, anthemia, medallions, and arabesques we can see the fortunate combination of an imaginative designer and a brilliant stuccoer. The room, which was converted into a library by Charles Barry, still retains a good deal of the Adam decoration, of which the ceiling is a very fine example. It is presently painted with white decoration on pink, tan, turquoise, and red, though these seem not to have been the original colours. For details of the alcoves flanking the door, see Fig. 81.

132. HAREWOOD HOUSE, YORKSHIRE.
Design for the ceiling of the gentleman's dressing room, 1767. Sir John Soane's Museum, Vol. 11, No. 148.

133. HAREWOOD HOUSE, YORKSHIRE.
Alternate design for the ceiling of the gentleman's dressing room, 1767. Sir John Soane's Museum, Vol. 11, No. 149.

Two very different treatments were envisioned by Adam for the circular (or octagonal) gentleman's dressing room in the principal apartments at Harewood. For this room to the south of the Old Library and to the east of the entrance hall (beyond the back stairs), Adam offered a choice of two styles of decoration—the more elaborate and brightly coloured version 'proposed to be Painted in the Style of the Ancients' (Fig. 132) and the delicate but less crowded composition utilizing low-relief stouccowork (Fig. 133). In addition to the ceilings illustrated here, Adam also submitted wall elevations to match. Soane Museum, Vol. 14, No. 121, and Vol. 50, No. 87 both correspond to the elaborately painted proposal (Fig. 132); Soane Museum, Vol. 14,

No. 120 is the counterpart to Fig. 133. Although the general treatment of the walls and general configuration of the ceiling designs are similar, the alternatives are on the whole quite different. Despite the presence of similar central motifs and the medallions in the outer band, one is more struck by the crowded and vivacious composition on the one hand and the emptier, more restrained presentation on the other. Though both are equally classical, the effects are amazingly diverse. Part of this is due to the nature of the decoration, but colour also plays an important role in the distinction. The gay, multi-coloured decoration on a white background in Fig. 132 is in sharp contrast to the greyish-white decoration on pink, grey-green, and blue grounds. Although the room has been destroyed and converted into a corridor, it was executed, Joseph Rose charging £125 for the stuccowork (bill, 24 Jan. 1766–10 Mar. 1770, at Harewood). This charge would suggest that the stucco version was chosen, but a description of the room in the early nineteenth century calls it 'richly ornamented with an antique marriage, the rape of Proserpine, a group of the Muses, Jupiter, Juno and Neptune, Petition by a Roman Emperor by Milo, and four paintings of boys playing by Zucchi' (John Jewell, *The Tourist's Companion*, Leeds, 1819, p. 36; quoted by Bolton, *Arch. of R. & J. Adam*, I, 177).

134. LANSDOWNE (SHELBURNE) HOUSE, BERKELEY SQ., LONDON.
Design for the drawing room ceiling, 1767. Sir John Soane's Museum, Vol. 11, No. 83.

135. LANSDOWNE (SHELBURNE) HOUSE, BERKELEY SQ., LONDON.
Drawing room ceiling, 1767–73. As re-installed in the Philadelphia Museum of Art.

Although the drawing illustrated in Fig. 134 is dated 1767, there is some confusion about the actual beginning of this scheme, for a year earlier (August 1766) Adam had included the following items on his bill to the Earl of Shelburne:

'To a design of a section of 4 sides of the Drawing Room coloured in the stile of the Ancients £16. 16. 0
To a design of a painted ceiling for ditto Room in the same stile ... ... £12. 12. 0'
(Printed in Bolton, *Arch. of R. & J. Adam*, II, 340).

The conclusion, too, is somewhat shrouded.

Whereas the family moved into the house in August 1768 (Letter from Lord Shelburne to his wife, 11 August 1768; Wm. L. Clements Library, University of Michigan, Shelburne Papers), the bills for painting in this room are dated 1771 and 1773. On 6 February 1771 Cipriani submitted his account which listed £100 for 'the five Pinting in the Ceiling,' while Zucchi's bill 'pour les peintures faites dans la Maison en Berkly Square de My Lord Shelburne pour en plafond peint en ornements' is dated 2 April 1773 (Printed in F. Kimball, *Lansdowne House Redivivus*, PHILADELPHIA MUSEUM BULLETIN, Vol. XXXIX, Nov. 1943). Cipriani's five inset paitings are, as is often the case, quite different from the suggestions on the Adam drawing, but Zucchi's grotesque decoration faithfully follows the Adam designs. The entire ceiling, in fact, was executed as designed, with the exception of the inset paintings and a few minor changes. There also appear to have been differences in colouring, although the ceiling at present has been darkened and dulled by age. The Adam drawing calls for a light green background to the end sections with green and gold arabesques and various coloured flowers in darker circles within cream diamonds. The background of the rest of the ceiling is uncoloured, with decoration in green, gold, brown, and blue. The mouldings were to be gilded.

Both in its arrangement and in its decoration, this is a typical Adam ceiling, especially, of course, of the period just before the 1770's. Adam's frequent device of emphasizing a square area in the centre of the ceiling, with flanking end pieces, is seen here, as is the basic X-shape central format. The insertion of circular and semi-circular classical subject panels amid a profusion of delicate Neo-classical forms is also characteristic. Medallions, griffins, urns, arabesque foliage, and paterae are introduced into the decoration in a rhythmic and elegant manner, though the complexity and variety of the parts are overshadowed by a flat, unifying force. While the general similarity to many Adam ceilings of the late 1760's and early 1770's is readily apparent, the variation is even more fascinating. For example, the end sections of Fig. 136 (Eglington House, 1769) are closely related to the Lansdowne House ceiling, and the use of the five inset paintings and a general X-shape scheme in the central area also recalls the earlier ceiling. Yet, the actual ceilings differ

substantially in both detail and dominant emphasis. Or compare Fig. 137 (Northumberland House, 1770), whose central square with circular and semi-circular painted inserts and diagonal decorative motifs is not at all unrelated to the central section of the Lansdowne House example. But, again, the flanking end sections differ radically from those seen here, and the actual details result in a different creation. While Fig. 138 (Chandos House, 1771) likewise illustrates the basic X-shape format within a tripartite arrangement, it, too, is by no means to be confused with the Lansdowne House design.

136. 'CIELING FOR THE GREAT ROOM FRONTING PICCADILLY FOR THE EARL OF EGLINGTON,' 79 PICCADILLY (AT STRATTON ST.), LONDON, 1769. Sir John Soane's Museum, Vol. 11, No. 263.

The elaborate ceiling that Adam designed for the principal room of Eglington House represents the elegant refinement but also the freshness and variety of Adam's work at the end of the 1760's. While this complex creation of overall delicate decoration conforms to the basic concept of many Adam ceilings of this period, it also demonstrates its designer's ability to adapt his formulae and to produce an almost infinite variety of designs which evince a family resemblance. Aside from the addition of a segmental panel to accommodate the bow-window on Stratton St., the rest of this design has a relatively common division into a square central section and oblong flanking pieces (cf. Figs. 134, 137, 138, 149, and 150). The central X-motif with a circular inset painting in the middle and often with semi-circular panels at the four sides of the central area is also not infrequently employed by Adam (cf. Figs. 134, 137, 138, and 142), but the placing of this composition within a circle is more unusual. In a similar way, although the end sections with their alternation of diamonds and filling of arabesque scrolls are quite close to those in Fig. 134 (Lansdowne House, drawing room, 1767), the differences are not insignificant— introduction of tiny diamonds between the large ones and more varied lozenge fillings at Eglington House, as opposed to the simpler repeat at Lansdowne House. By these kinds of variations, Adam produced scores of designs that evoke the same spirit and include many related elements but are actually not at all the same.

Despite the elaborate detail of this ceiling design, it adheres very closely to Adam's sketch (Soane Mus., Vol. 8, No. 149). Even the colour was not left to the whim of the draftsman, for the colour notations on the sketch were followed in the rendering illustrated here. Although executed, the ceiling no longer survives.

137. NORTHUMBERLAND HOUSE, CHARING CROSS, LONDON. Design for the drawing room ceiling, 1770. Sir John Soane's Museum, Vol. 11, No. 33.

Executed as designed in June 1770, this ceiling was another of Adam's brilliantly coloured and delicately detailed tripartite ceilings. It was destroyed with the demolition of the house in 1874, but its colouring can be seen from a watercolour drawing of the room and from this design. A pale green background was enlivened by red, blue, pink, and gold. The composition and details demonstrate Adam's system of variation, not only in comparison with other works, but even in various parts of the same one. In this case, the design of the central area has also served as the basis for the end sections but without reducing the whole design to a series of absolute repeats. The basic idea of a circular and octagonal motif with four rectangular projections has been converted into an oval with square projections, while the semi-circles in the middle of the sides have become quandrants in the corners. The middle panel of the end sections is, in turn, flanked by semi-circles that are related to those of the major area. In the same way, the entire design of the Northumberland House ceiling is related to other Adam ceilings. The X-plan central section is similar to that in the drawing room at Lansdowne House of 1767 (Fig. 134), but it has here been wedded to the central octagon with projections, as in the hall at Shardeloes (Fig. 120). The end sections are quite different. Other comparisons reveal the same type of relationships, as, for example, drawing room ceilings at Eglington House (Fig. 136) and Chandos House (Fig. 138). While all three are tripartite compositions with X-shapes in the middle section, there are substantial differences in both the central panels and end sections. All are characteristic of Adam's work around 1770; their variety is equally characteristic.

138. CHANDOS HOUSE, CHANDOS ST., LONDON. Design for the ceiling of the first drawing room, 1771. Sir John Soane's Museum, Vol. 13, No. 55.

With the exception of the urn-amid-rinceau semi-circular panels around the edges of the central area which were left blank, this ceiling for the Duke of Chandos' town house was executed as designed. It survives in excellent condition in the only major Adam house in London that is still a private residence. In addition to the finished rendering, there is also an extant sketch (Soane Mus., Vol. 8, No. 20), which was followed very closely by the draftsman of this drawing. Like a number of other ceilings of this period in Adam's career, this one utilizes both a tripartite arrangement and an X-shaped format for the central panel (cf., e.g., Figs. 134, 136, and 137). Yet it is also quite different in treatment and detail from them. Even more illustrative of Adam's ability to create substantially different designs out of similar components, arrangements, and motifs is the relationship between this design and the gallery ceiling at Harewood of two years earlier (Figs. 139 and 140). At Harewood there is the repeat of a basic pattern along the entire length of the ceiling, as opposed to the simple three-part ceiling at Chandos House, but the basic pattern at Harewood is actually quite close to this ceiling. As at Chandos House, the principal motif consists of an X-shape with curved sides, semi-circular panels in the spaces formed by the curves, and Greek crosses at the corners. On the other hand, the centres of the X's are not the same (circle vs. octagon), the particular classical decorations vary, and thin borders at Chandos House replace the aureoles and rectangles between the crosses. Despite all of these variations, and others, the two designs are a fascinating example of Adam's re-use of certain ideas in totally different contexts. By itself, the Chandos House ceiling is also a fine example of Adam's sense of composition and of the elegant and refined Neo-classical manner that he had achieved by the late 1760's and early 1770's.

139. HAREWOOD HOUSE, YORKSHIRE. Gallery, ceiling detail, c1769–70.

Adam's first designs for the gallery ceiling at Harewood are dated 1765, during which year he produced two different proposals, one for an overall small-scale repeat and the other for three equal sections with the central motif being a variant of the end ones (Soane Mus., Vol. 11, Nos. 169 and 168, respectively). Four years later he created the design that was executed (Soane Mus., Vol. 11, No. 170; dated 1769). An extant sketch (Soane Mus., Vol. 8, No. 144) shows Adam at a stage prior to the finished rendering, for despite the close similarity between the two drawings, the sketch employs a rather fat oval in place of the more elongated aureole shape used between the crosses on both the rendering and the ceiling. This finished drawing was carried out virtually unchanged, except for the inset classical paintings, which almost never correspond to the stock indications on an Adam drawing. There is today a difference in colour, but the present paint may not be based on the original colours. On the drawing, the light green background serves as a foil for the pink X-shapes, the yellow crosses, the inset paintings, and the white decoration. Today the background is beige, with the X-shapes in light blue, the crosses in light green, and the decoration in white and gold. The exquisite stuccowork is by Joseph Rose, who charged £335 for 'The great Gallery' in his bill for work between 24 January 1766 and 10 March 1770 (Harewood Archives). Although the £335 included all plasterwork in the room, the ceiling would have accounted for the vast majority of it. Various late eighteenth- and early nineteenth-century visitors assign the inset paintings to Biagio Rebecca (e.g., *Tour to the Western Highlands*, 1788; and John Jewell, *The Tourist's Companion*, 1822; see Bolton, *Arch. of R. & J. Adam*, I, 175).

For a discussion of Adam's re-use of the central motif of this ceiling as the basis for a very different type of ceiling, see Fig. 138 (Chandos House, first drawing room, 1771). For a view of the whole gallery at Harewood, see Fig. 140.

140. HAREWOOD HOUSE, YORKSHIRE. Gallery, c1765–77.

For a detail of the gallery ceiling and a more extensive discussion of its design and execution, see Fig. 139.

The gallery as executed is completely different from Adam's first conception of it. As shown in an undated drawing (inscribed for Gawthorpe House), this room was to have been a statuary-ornamented gallery along the lines of the gallery at Croome (Fig. 20) or the dining rooms at Syon or Lansdowne House (Figs. 18

and 31). That drawing may date as early as 1765, when Adam's first (unexecuted) ceiling designs were produced (Soane Mus., Vol. 11, Nos. 168 and 169), but in any case it was no later than 1767, when it was decided to change the name of the house from Gawthorpe to Harewood. Although none of the fireplace wall was retained, the Palladian motifs and the pelmetted windows were used, but with some difference in the pelmets. The executed ceiling was designed in 1769, but the final design for the chimney-piece was not created until 1777 (Soane Mus., Vol. 22, Nos. 201–204). As late as 1776, Adam was still toying with a very different piece (Soane Mus., Vol. 22, No. 200). The caryatid chimney-piece that was executed is now in the dining room, having been moved there by Barry, who substituted two new chimney-pieces for Adam's one original piece. In his redecoration of the 1840's, Barry also altered the Palladian motifs, introducing brackets and piers in place of Adam's columns. Despite these changes, the Harewood gallery is a highly impressive room, due primarily to its proportions, ceiling, and pelmets.

141. DESIGN FOR A CEILING FOR MRS. FITZROY'S CIRCULAR DRESSING ROOM, NEAR SOUTHAMPTON, 1774. Sir John Soane's Museum, Vol. 52, No. 137.

Despite the sketchy quality, this drawing illustrates the complex linear elegance of Adam's mature work of the mid-1770's. The sketchiness, itself, actually adds to the liveliness and sparkle, as well as to the delicacy. The series of concentric rings of decoration is fairly common in Adam ceilings (cf. Figs. 128, 132, 145, and 149), but here they are interconnected by arching lines that form the faint outline of an eight-pointed star. The almost lyrical complexity thus created is suffused with flatness, elegance, and an ultra-refined classicism that are the hallmarks of the mature Adam manner. This sketch with its colour notations was the guide followed by the draftsman in executing the finished rendering and its office copy (Soane Mus., Vol. 12, No. 156). These designs were apparently part of alterations and decorations that included other ceilings, two room elevations, and plans (Soane Mus., Vol. 3, No. 109; Vol. 5, No. 66; Vol. 12, Nos. 157–58; Vol. 27, Nos. 29–30; Vol. 50, No. 89; and Vol. 45, Nos. 9–11). It is not known whether or not these were executed.

142. BOLTON HOUSE, 26 SOUTH-AMPTON ROW (LATER IN RUSSELL SQ.), LONDON. Design for the ceiling of the Duchess of Bolton's dressing room, 1770. Sir John Soane's Museum, Vol. 12, No. 35.

Although a square ceiling with one semi-circular bay, this ceiling is very close to the central section of a number of Adam ceilings of the years around 1770. The central octagon with circular centre and squarish projections is quite similar to the centre of the drawing room ceiling at Northumberland House of the same year (Fig. 137), though the semi-circles at the sides have become quadrants in the corners, as in the side panels at Northumberland House itself. Interestingly, however, this central octagonal motif has been set in a pronounced X-shape with curved sides, which was used with a different central feature in the first drawing room at Chandos House the following year (Fig. 138). The wide border here can be related to still other ceilings, the drawing rooms at Lansdowne (Figs. 134 and 135) and Eglington (Fig. 136) Houses, where the diamond repeat is used in the end sections of tripartite ceilings. As in the other examples, there are noticeable differences between these three, especially seen in the curved sides of the diamond shapes at Bolton House in contrast to the straight edges in the other two.

Despite the classical character of all of these various ceilings, it is not always possible to connect individual examples with related antique prototypes. In the case of the Bolton House ceiling, however, there is such a model, albeit Early Christian rather than Imperial Roman—the crypt of Lucina in the Cemetery of St. Calixtus, just outside Rome, of *circa* A.D.220. (Fig. 143). The details are, of course, very different, but the basic composition is quite close. While this particular vault may not have been Adam's exact source, a similar one must surely have been his inspiration.

The finished rendering illustrated here was based on Adam's sketch, dated June 1770 (Soane Mus., Vol. 8, No. 29), which it follows very closely. Bolton House was largely destroyed when it was incorporated into later buildings on Russell Square.

143. CEMETERY OF ST. CALIXTUS, NEAR ROME. Vault in the crypt of Lucina, *circa* A.D.220.

For Adam's use of this type of Early Christian ceiling, but without the Judeo-Christian symbolism of Daniel in the lion's den, see Fig. 142.

144. HOME HOUSE, 20 PORTMAN SQ., LONDON. Rear drawing room, ceiling detail, 1775–77.

The elegant small-scale decorative treatment of Adam ceilings of the mid-1770's is evident in this detail from the Countess of Home's rear drawing room. From the delicate roundels with flowers and putti in the outer border to the components of the quadrant fan, the keynote is delicacy. The detail shown here is most of the end section of a tripartite scheme, which has in addition a subsidiary sector beyond a screen of columns. As executed, the ceiling follows very closely the Adam design of 25 March 1775 (Soane Mus., Vol. 12, No. 167). The colours shown on the drawing are a pale green background, with lilac, a medium green, and a few touches of pink, together with blue backgrounds to the roundels.

145. WORMLEYBURY, HERTFORD-SHIRE. Dining room, ceiling detail, 1777–79.

For the dining room of Sir Abraham Hume's country house, Adam produced on 27 September 1777 an elegant and refined design that is quite typical of his work at that time. The drawing (Soane Mus., Vol. 14, No. 22) was followed exactly, although the original colours no longer exist. The present white ceiling replaces the white decoration on a pale green background and a greyish-blue panel background, which conform to the treatment of the walls as designed (Soane Mus., Vol. 50, No. 23) and as partially extant today (see Fig. 53). In planning the ceiling, Adam chose to divide it into a central square and two relatively narrow end sections, one of which can be seen at the bottom of this illustration. The guilloche band just above the end panel completely enframes the central section, which is treated as a series of concentric rings, with delicate decoration on the rings and in the corner projections. The flatness of the composition is readily apparent here, as is the delicacy of the classical elements. The format is related to other Adam ceilings (*e.g.*, Fig. 149), but the details and colouring are, of course, quite different. For the carpet design for this room, see Fig. 153.

146. DRURY LANE THEATRE, LONDON. Design for the ceiling, 1776. Sir John Soane's Museum, Vol. 14, No. 16.

In 1775–76 Adam refronted the Drury Lane Theatre and altered and redecorated the interior. As part of this work, he produced two different designs for the ceiling. One of these, the unexecuted version, is illustrated here. Filled with characteristic Adam motifs and arrangements, it is a subdivided ceiling that revolves around a central panel with a classical subject medallion. Among the motifs employed in the various panels are long subject plaques, ovals, valerium fans, octagons with rosettes, and patterns of subdivided panels composed of nine adjacent octagons. The controlled variation in panel size and content reflects Adam's sense of unity amid variety, and the refined Neo-classical character of the decoration is also typical of Adam's domestic work, especially the houses decorated in this same decade of the 1770's. The executed design (Soane Mus., Vol. 14, No. 17) is illustrated in the *Works*, Vol. II, Part v, Pl. 7. The theatre—with Adam's decorations—was demolished in 1791.

147. REGISTER HOUSE, EDINBURGH. Detail of interior of the dome, c1771–85.

Although the decoration of the dome as eventually executed was shown on Adam's cross-section published in January 1775 (actually signed 1771; *Works*, Vol. I, Part iv, Pl. 7), it had not been completed by 23 December 1784, when the following was listed among the work scheduled to be done the following year: 'To finish the Ceiling of the Dome agreeable to a design given by Mr. Adam' (Register House, Edinburgh, 'Sederunt Book, Register House Trustees,' I, 88–89). The plasterwork in the dome was the work of Thomas Clayton of Edinburgh, whose contract was approved on 12 March 1785 (*Ibid.*, I, 92–93). As finally completed, the decoration follows very closely the illustration in the *Works*. The only significant changes were the altering of the rib decoration from bell-flowers to double guilloche scrolls, the shortening of the bottom band of decoration, and the reducing of the size of the medallions in the large panel. The principal result of this was the creation of more open space in this section of the dome than was originally planned. The dome decoration is very typical of Adam's interior work, mainly of course domestic, during the 1770's and 1780's. The

stairhall dome of Home House (Fig. 49; 1775–77), for example, is similar in its division of decorative bands and in certain aspects of the decoration, though there are naturally differences in the detailing, as well as in scale. Probably this variation in size between a relatively small and a large dome accounts for a good part of the difference between the generally smaller-scale detail of the Home House dome and the somewhat less minutely detailed ceiling at the Register House. Still, the delicacy and elegance of Adam's mature manner is as evident in the public building as it is in the private residence. The colours now present are a beige background to the top panel and the large lower panel; blue grounds to the elongated hexagons, the medallions, the ribs, and the bottom band; and red on the two bands of flutes and the rib decoration. The detailed decoration is white.

148. WEALD HALL, ESSEX. Design for the eating room ceiling, 1778. Sir John Soane's Museum, Vol. 14, No. 46.

As part of his alterations to Christopher Tower's house in Essex in 1778–79, Adam created a new eating room, whose ceiling was executed as illustrated in this drawing. Even the inset central painting basically followed the Adam drawing, an exception to the usual Adam custom. The only even vaguely noticeable changes are in the four classical bas-reliefs in the outer band and the four classical medallions above them. The exquisite small-scale detailing and the general delicacy are especially characteristic of Adam's work in the 1770's, while the basic composition is a variation on a fairly popular Adam scheme. The elongated oval treatment is the feature that most distinguishes this ceiling from such contemporary examples as the dining room ceiling at Wormleybury, designed the previous year (Fig. 145). Whereas the oval format of the Weald Hall ceiling occupies the entire rectangular ceiling, at Wormleybury narrow end panels flank a circular central space. But both include a central inset painting surrounded by a minutely subdivided band with swags beyond it. And both have an outer band with sphinxes and rectangular panels, as well as corner motifs. There are many differences in detail, which are themselves fascinating examples of Adam's skill and imagination, but the general similarity within two different basic frameworks is especially indicative of the nature of his thematic variations.

149. CUMBERLAND HOUSE, PALL MALL, LONDON. Design for the great dining room ceiling, 1780. Sir John Soane's Museum, Vol. 14, No. 79.

Dated 3 August 1780. Although the Duke of Cumberland's Pall Mall house has been demolished, certain of the rooms decorated by Adam can be substantially reconstructed from the Adam drawings. This is especially true of the great dining room, whose ceiling (illustrated here), walls, chimney-piece, carpet, frieze, and pelmets are preserved in existing drawings (see Figs. 56, 73, and 112). The room was decorated in the 'Etruscan' taste, as is reflected in the colouring; and the designs are, of course, quite typical of the elegant, delicate Adam decoration of the 1770's and early 1780's. The ceiling design, for example, is related in both format and detail to a number of other ceilings of the period (cf. Figs. 141 and 145). The Cumberland House version is rather long, but after the end sections beyond the columnar screens have been examined separately, the remainder is not at all unlike the dining room ceiling at Wormleybury of 1777–79 (Fig. 145). While the actual detailed motifs are somewhat different, the basic conceptions are quite close, even to the narrow panels that flank the central square. A central circular inset painting, a small-scale many-sectioned surrounding band, swags, an outer band broken at the corners, and repeated circles in the flanking panels are to be found in both. While some individual motifs are the same, most of the details and colours are different.

The Cumberland House colours are also indicated on a sketch (Soane Mus., Vol. 5, No. 33), that conforms fairly closely in design to the rendering illustrated, though there are differences in detail. The major variations between the two drawings are the choices offered on the sketch for the inner and outer bands of the central panel and the central motif of the whole ceiling and the end section. Interestingly, some of the rejected alternatives were incorporated in the carpet design (Soane Mus., Vol. 17, No. 207), which beautifully complements the ceiling, as is so often the case with Adam.

150. ARCHERFIELD, EAST LOTHIAN. Design for the drawing room ceiling, c1790–91. Sir John Soane's Museum, Vol. 27, No. 23.

Among the substantial number of projects in the last years of Robert Adam's life was Mr. Nisbet's house at Archerfield, for which Adam made a great many designs. Such drawings as those for the drawing room illustrated here and in Fig. 60 demonstrate the elaboration of Adam's late work, as well as the similarity to his projects of the 1760's, 1770's, and early 1780's. The coved ceiling here, for example, is a type that he used in his earliest project, General Bland's house at Isleworth (Fig. 115), and at various other times throughout the next thirty years. The swags of the cove, panels of griffins confronting an urn, boy-in-rinceau plaques, guilloche, peltoids, and long subject panels are all common Adam motifs. Similarly, the general format of the central section with its inner and outer circular bands joined by loops is also characteristic, as in the great dining room ceiling for Cumberland House (Fig. 149). Adam's ability to combine similar elements and motifs into an immense variety of different designs is evident in this comparison, as it had been during his entire career. The Neo-classical elegance of the Adam style persisted to the end.

151. KEDLESTON HALL, DERBYSHIRE. Design for a carpet, c1758–61. Sir John Soane's Museum, Vol. 17, No. 164.

Inscribed for 'Sir Nathaniel Curzon Baronet,' this design dates sometime between Adam's first commission for Kedleston in December 1758 and his client's elevation to Baron Scarsdale on 9 April 1761 (see letter from Robert to James Adam, 11 Dec. 1758, Register House, Edinburgh, Clerk of Penicuik Papers, No. 4854). The style and especially the thick and relatively simple forms also testify to the early date. Compare, for example, the ceilings for General Bland and the Earl of Hertford (Figs. 115 and 116). Similarly, the central oval with simulated coffering and a wide outer band is quite close to the central motif of the dining room ceiling at Hatchlands, though the diamond with concave sides replaces the large leaf employed in the centre of the Hatchlands composition. Many of the other motifs—loops, grape-and-leaf vine, cornucopiae, circled rosettes—are also found in early Adam designs. This large drawing was based on a small sketch (Soane Mus., Vol. 54, Part i, No. 37), which was somewhat altered in detail. It is not known if this carpet was executed, but it does not exist at Kedleston today.

152. SYON HOUSE, MIDDLESEX. Design for the ante-room pavement, *c*1761. Sir John Soane's Museum, Vol. 18, No. 60.

This colourful design for the scagliola pavement is but one of many examples of Adam's correlation of ceiling and floor. Although this is more common with carpets, it is also found in pavements, as at Osterley or Newby (Figs. 27 and 35), as well as here. Like the ceiling, the pavement design consists of a central octagon with four rectangular projections and irregular corner panels, supplemented by three panels at one end. But the floor is not a duplicate of the ceiling, for the detail of each panel differs from its counterpart above. Instead of a ring of double loops around the central flower, the pavement employs a ring of elongated octagons. Where the ceiling uses griffin-and-urn panels, the floor offers a pattern of octagons and diamonds. The a-b-a arrangement of the three end panels is found in both, though the actual motifs are variations on each other, not copies. Colour is even more a distinguishing feature, for the simple, subdued ceiling is answered by a brilliantly coloured floor. This drawing was executed as designed, though the colours were altered slightly to the present gold, red, blue, and green.

153. WORMLEYBURY, HERTFORD-SHIRE. Design for the dining room carpet, 1778. Sir John Soane's Museum, Vol. 17, No. 197.

Although Adam often designed carpets to mirror the ceilings of his rooms, he did not always do so. Here, for example, both feature central squares with relatively narrow end sections divided into seven small elements (*cf.* Fig. 145), but there the similarity ceases. Yet all of the forms of the carpet design are typical of his work, and the general format of the central section is related to a number of Adam ceiling (*cf.* Fig. 120) and floor designs. The ante-room pavement at Syon (Fig. 152; *c*1761), like the Wormleybury carpet, has a central octagon with rectangular projections and irregular corners. Both use circular central motifs with floral centres, and in both the corners are occupied by an encircled single object. Though the details vary substantially, the band decorations in both employ such common Adam motifs as guilloche, double guilloche, Vitruvian scroll, and Greek key. The character of the rendering and the colouring are the most striking differences, but the similarity is perhaps more interesting than the difference.

Whereas the design of the Wormleybury carpet does not reflect the ceiling, the colouring is closer, for both use the pale green background also prescribed for the walls. Still, light violet panel and border grounds replace the bluish-grey of the ceiling and walls, while other colours not present in the rest of the room enliven the carpet—pink and red rosettes, green and yellow swags and wreaths with mauve flowers, yellow urns and valerium, the latter edged with green. There exists a pencil sketch (Soane Mus., Vol. 5, No. 31, reverse) that is very close to the rendering, and its colour notations were followed by the draftsman. It is not known if this design was executed, the present carpet being an Aubusson of an entirely different design.

154. COVENTRY HOUSE, 29 (NOW 106) PICCADILLY, LONDON. Sketch design for a carpet, *c*1767. Sir John Soane's Museum, Vol. 8, No. 106.

155. COVENTRY HOUSE, 29 (NOW 106) PICCADILLY, LONDON. Office copy of a rendering for a carpet, offering alternate colour schemes, *c*1767. Sir John Soane's Museum, Vol. 17, No. 169.

156. *Right:* COVENTRY HOUSE, 29 (NOW 106) PICCADILLY, LONDON. Pencil design for a carpet. *Left:* SYON HOUSE, MIDDLESEX. Pencil design for the gallery carpet, with small- and large-scale details. *c*1767. Sir John Soane's Museum, Vol. 8, No. 105.

157. COVENTRY HOUSE, 29 (NOW 106) PICCADILLY, LONDON. Large-scale detail of design for a carpet, *c*1767 (detail). Sir John Soane's Museum, Vol. 5, No. 78.

158. *Left:* COVENTRY HOUSE, 29 (NOW 106) PICCADILLY, LONDON. Large-scale detail of design for a carpet. *Right:* SYON HOUSE, MIDDLESEX. Large-scale detail of design for the gallery carpet. *c*1767. Sir John Soane's Museum, Vol. 49, No. 53.

Although none of these five drawings is dated, they appear to represent five steps in the designing of a carpet for the Great Room at Coventry House, the drawings for which are listed under July 1767 in one of Adam's bills to the Earl of Coventry (Croome Estate Office, Worcs.). Two of the drawings (Figs. 156 and

158) include sections for a different design altogether, the gallery carpet at Syon, and these will be considered below.

The five drawings or segments connected with the Coventry House carpet present an almost unparalleled picture of the workings of the Adam office. Taken together, they illustrate beautifully the roles of Adam and his draftsmen and the process of the creation of a design. Beginning with a quick charcoal sketch by Adam with colour notations (Fig. 154), we move to the more detailed pencil drawing (Fig. 156), whose right half illustrates the overall effect of Adam's basic design. It is more carefully and completely delineated, but nothing has been added that was not indicated on the Adam sketch. Fig. 155 is a coloured rendering of part of the carpet, with some of the colours filled in. Its design conforms to the Adam sketch, while the colouring of the left half follows the notations given by Adam—light green background; brownish red circle background; red, blue, and large pink flowers; smaller bands and fillings in orange, yellow, red, and dark green. The right half of Fig. 155 offers an alternate colour scheme of a warm beige background; a more chocolate brown circle background; yellow and large fuchsia flowers; and small bands and fillings of lavender, pale green, and pink. In the outer border, blue-green filling replaces the brown of the first version. The rest is not coloured on the right version, though the left employs pale green with orange bands and flowers. Fig. 157 and the left half of Fig. 158 are large-scale details, probably for the weaver. They are similar in design and colour, though there are differences in both. On the whole, however, the colouring of both corresponds to the right half of Fig. 155, except that the border of Fig. 157 follows the background colouring of the main part of Fig. 155's left half, while the border in Fig. 158 conforms to the border colour of Fig. 155's right half. This variation is explained by a note at the bottom of Fig. 157, which reads: 'Mr Adam had not time to fix the Colours of the Border But thinks that need not Stop the Estimate from being made. When that is fixt if the drawing is returned to Mr Adam he will Settle the other Parts of the Colouring.' On Adam's charcoal sketch (Fig. 154), the border is the only part for which no colours are given. It therefore becomes apparent that despite the skill of the draftsmen, it was Adam's hand and imagination that created the designs. The draftsmen were office assistants closely dependent on the inspiration and creation of Robert himself.

If executed, the carpet unfortunately no longer exists at Coventry House. The detail drawings and the inscription suggest that the design may well have been woven, and it may correspond to one of the carpets listed on a bill from Thomas Moore to the Earl of Coventry, perhaps the 'fine Persia Carpet to your own plan,' for which he charged £112. 1. 0 on 29 October 1768 (Croome Estate Office).

The designs for the gallery carpet at Syon (on Figs. 156 and 158) are part of a series that includes two other drawings, a sheet with two variant designs and a very large scale detail (Soane Mus., Vol. 17, No. 172, and Vol. 18, No. 57, respectively). Again, neither of these is dated, but the Syon carpet scheme can similarly be assigned to c1767, as the Duke of Northumberland's Memorandum Book of Work at Syon, which bears only one dated entry, that of 13 October 1767, lists the gallery carpet among works to be carried out shortly (Alnwick Castle Archives, U. I. 59). While also an overall design and vaguely similar in part to the Coventry House carpet, it is, of course, quite different. Adam's source for the Syon design was a Roman mosaic pavement of a type found in the Second and Third Centuries A.D. (e.g., in Ostia, in a house under Sta. Sabina in Rome, and in the Palace of Septimius Severus on the Palatine. For these, see M. E. Blake in MEMOIRS OF THE AMERICAN ACADEMY IN ROME, Vol. XIII, 1936, Pl. X, Fig. 2; and Vol. XVII, 1940, Pl. XII, Fig. 3, and p. 84). It is not known if either of the versions illustrated in this group of designs was executed, but if so the carpet no longer exists at Syon.

159. WYNN HOUSE, 20 ST. JAMES'S SQ., LONDON. Stair railing, c1772–74.

On 9 July 1774, William Kinman charged Sir Watkin Williams-Wynn £200 for this elegant stair railing for his London town house (Natl. Library of Wales, Aberystwyth, Wynnstay MSS, Box 115/17). As delicate and refined in the Neo-classical taste as anything Adam designed, this balustrade demonstrates the care that Adam lavished on the decorative accessories of his commissions. The procession of elongated baluster urns filled with anthemia elegantly and gracefully leads one up the staircase, accompanied by such other Neo-classical motifs as bell-flowers and low urns. The style is, of course, quite characteristic of Adam's mature manner of the 1770's, and the execution is typical of the finesse and perfection that Adam generally demanded of the craftsmen whom he employed. Even in details such as stair railings, Adam demonstrated his skill and imagination in the creation of a great variety of related but basically different designs. The stair railing at Home House of c1775–77 (Fig. 48) has the same basic composition of a series of vertical classical forms, but the details are not at all the same. Terms or pedestal forms replaced Sir Watkin's urns, and many of the other motifs are different, though the general treatment and the spirit show the strong kinship as well as the variety that one expects of Adam.

160. CROOME COURT, WORCESTER-SHIRE. Design for a grate and fender for the gallery, 1765. Sir John Soane's Museum, Vol. 17, No. 121.

The earliest securely dated example of a fire grate by Adam, this piece and its fender correspond to Adam's charge of £5. 5. 0 in June 1765 for the design of a grate and fender for the gallery, together with drawings at large (Crrome Estate Office, Worcs.). This design may in turn be the basis for the grate, fender, etc., that were included in Hartley & Cooper's bill of 16 June 1766 for smith's work for the Earl of Coventry 'By Order of Robert Adam Esqr,' for which they charged £55. 4. 4 (Croome Estate Office). Both the grate and fender were still in use at Croome as late as the early twentieth century (illustrated in Bolton, *Arch. of R. & J. Adam*, I, 182), though they are no longer present there now. As executed, Adam's designs were followed very closely, with the exception of the back plate, which was plain. Characteristic of the Adam style, not only in decorative adjuncts but in walls and ceiling as well, are the various classical bands of the fender and the horizontal and vertical bands of the grate itself. Similarly, the urn finials and the other details can also be found in Adam's other work. By these means, as well as by the general character, Adam integrated the various parts of his ensemble into a highly effective and unified decorative composition.

161. WYNN HOUSE, 20 ST. JAMES'S SQ., LONDON. Design of candelabrum, 1773. Sir John Soane's Museum, Vol. 25, No. 126.

Dated 9 March 1773. Among the Adam projects that included furnishings and minor decorative objects was Sir Watkin Williams-Wynn's London town house, for which Adam designed ink stands, watch cases, silver dishes and tureens, candlesticks and candelabra, as well as the interior decorations that are encountered in the vast majority of his commissions. An example of the attention that Adam lavished on the minor decorative objects for this client is the elegant double-branched candelabrum illustrated in this drawing. The linear rhythm of the curved supports, of the candle arms, and of the decoration is characteristic of Adam's mature style, as are the myriad classical motifs—ram's heads, boy-in-rinceau, swags, anthemion, circled rosettes, guilloche, and the like. Just as in his ceilings and walls, Adam has combined a variety of classical forms into a suave and elegant composition indicative of the tastes of the last half of the eighteenth century.

Although there were a few changes, this design was apparently executed in 1774 by John Carter, as a set of four candelabra bearing his hall-mark and conforming quite closely to the Adam design have been preserved in the collection of Lloyd's of London (see R. Rowe, *Adam Silver*, 1965, Pls. 12 and 13).

162. DESIGN FOR DOOR FURNITURE, POSSIBLY FOR OSTERLEY PARK, MIDDLESEX, c1770. Sir John Soane's Museum, Vol. 25, No. 49.

This exquisitely detailed and rhythmically classical design for escutcheon and door knob is neither dated nor identified as to client, but it is quite close to an illustration in the *Works in Architecture* and to existing door furniture in the Tapestry Room at Osterley. While there are minor differences between this design and one included in the *Works*, Vol. II, Part iv, Pl. 8 (dated 1770), the conceptions are so nearly exact as to justify a date of about 1770 for this design. Again, there are a few slight variations between this design and the Osterley door knob and plate (Fig. 163), but the virtual identity is very striking. The style and character of the design, with its classical motifs and delicately curving foliage, is typical of Adam work in the 1770's and evocative of Adam's concern for the most minute aspects of interior decoration.

163. OSTERLEY PARK, MIDDLESEX. Tapestry Room, detail of door furniture and panel, mid-1770's.

The refinement and perfection of the decoration in Adam houses is seldom better illustrated than in this detail of wood carving and ormolu casting. The crispness of the carved guilloche border with rosette centres and the beaded bands flanking it is equalled, if not surpassed, by the exquisitely cast and chased door furniture. The latter, especially, features the lively linear rhythm and sense of delicate Neo-classical design that is at the heart of the Adam style. The door furniture is very close to the design illustrated in Fig. 162, but even if that drawing was not the specific model for Adam's craftsman, the virtual identity of the two proclaims the dominant role of Adam and the faithful and highly accomplished execution of his craftsmen.

For a view of the room and documentation for the date, see Fig. 44.

164. KEDLESTON HALL, DERBYSHIRE. Saloon, wall sconce, c1761–70.

Adam originally planned rectangular niches containing either statues or large urns for the spaces between the alcoves and doorways of the saloon (Soane Mus., Vol. 40, Nos. 3 and 19), but in the end he substituted candelabra with classical plaques, one of which is illustrated here. This change was proably fortunate, as these decorative features add liveliness and colour to the room. The stucco reliefs with white figures on a dark red ground are characteristic of Adam's Neo-classical subject panels in bas-relief or grisaille, though they exhibit a vitality that is not always present in such pieces. Set in a gilded enframement of swags, bow-knot, paterae, and wreaths, they serve as a foil to the five candle arms curving gracefully above them. The quality of the work is commensurate with Adam's strict demands, but the relative heaviness of the gilded bronze elements contrasts with the more delicate and rhythmic metalwork of the 1770's, as in the door furniture at Osterley (Fig. 163).

165. DERBY HOUSE, 23 (LATER 26) GROSVENOR SQ., LONDON. Design for a curtain cornice in the great drawing room, 1774. Sir John Soane's Museum, Vol. 17, No. 111.

Dated 13 September 1774. Among the more minor decorative details with which Adam concerned himself were curtain cornices. For Derby House alone there are at least seven, including the one illustrated here. In all of these, the valance is treated as a continuous repeat of small-scale motifs common in the Adam repertoire, such as the palmette-topped urns on foliage scrolls used here. The palmette motif reappears in the acroterion, while the urn in a substantially altered form is a prominent feature of the superstructure. An elegant, refined classicism is the keynote, as in so much of Adam's work of the 1770's. And while specific details of the cornice are not repetitions of the motifs in the rest of the room (Fig. 41), the spirit and general character go hand-in-hand.

166. DESIGN FOR A TOWER IN THE GOTHIC STYLE, 1753. Blair Adam Collection, No. 99.

167. DESIGN FOR A HOUSE IN THE GOTHIC STYLE, 1753. Blair Adam Collection, No. 102.

These two drawings illustrate Adam's taste in the 1740's and early 1750's for the fanciful, unauthentic version of the Gothic style fashionable in England at the time. Fig. 166, a tower in the form of a tall, narrow octagon with flying buttresses, finical detailing, and an open crown cupola on the order of St. Giles, Edinburgh, is as insubstantial as it is delightful. The house in Fig. 167 combines the symmetrical façade and staccato rhythm of Palladian architecture (which was also interesting Adam at the time) with such flights of Gothic fancy as buttresses, pointed arches, tracery, crockets, a cupola in the form of a ciborium with a flying peak, and Gothicized Palladian windows. The whole design, but especially this last feature, indicates how unarchaeological was his approach to the architecture of the Middle Ages and already how strongly imbued he was with the principles and details of Burlingtonian Palladianism.

168. ALNWICK CASTLE, NORTHUMBERLAND. Design for the library, c1769 or slightly later. Sir John Soane's Museum, Vol. 24, No. 214.

This design illustrates the fanciful type of Gothic that had appealed to Adam in the years before his Grand Tour and that recurred to mind when he was subsequently asked to design interiors in the 'Gothick' mode. The delicate complex vaulting, the Tudor arches, the attenuated buttresses, the profusion of crockets and other small-scale decorations are typical of this whimsical, unarchaeological Gothic. And the lightness and delicacy seen here are as characteristic of Adam's Gothicisms as they are of his more common Neo-classical manner. The small-scale repeats, as in the chimney-piece cornice or the decoration above it, are also related to his non-medieval tendencies. The exact date of this design is not certain, but in 1769 Adam designed a Gothic chimney-piece for the library at Alnwick (Soane Mus., Vol. 22, No. 54), though it is very different from the one shown here. Alnwick was completely re-done in the nineteenth century, thus sweeping away almost all of Adam's Gothic decorations.

169. STRAWBERRY HILL, MIDDLE-SEX. Design for a ceiling, 1766. Sir John Soane's Museum, Vol. 11, No. 234.
170. STRAWBERRY HILL, MIDDLE-SEX. Design for a chimney-piece, 1767. Sir John Soane's Museum, Vol. 22, No. 229.

Aside from a cottage in the rustic style that he designed in 1768 (Wilmarth Lewis Collection, Farmington, Conn., U.S.A.), the room for which these were intended was the only work that Adam did for Horace Walpole. Despite his well-known criticisms of Adam in the 1770's and 1780's (e.g., letters to Wm. Mason, 29 July and 17 Sept. 1773; 16 July 1778; and 14 Feb. 1782, in *The Letters of Horace Walpole*, ed. Toynbee, VIII, 313 and 336; X, 282; XII, 166), Walpole complimented Adam on a number of occasions (e.g., letters to Countess of Upper Ossory, 21 June 1773, and to Wm. Mason, 29 Feb 1776, in *Letters*, VIII, 291–92; IX, 333) and even employed him at Strawberry Hill. Adam's use of Gothic was, of course, dictated by Walpole, who furnished his architect with suitable models. An undated letter from client to architect supplies this information: 'Mr. Walpole has sent Mr. Adam the two books, and hopes at his leisure he will think of the ceiling and chimney-piece. The ceiling is to be taken from the plate 165 of St. Paul's, the circular window/The chimney from the shrine of Edward the Confessor at Westminster' (Printed in THE BUILDER, 6 Jan. 1866, p. 6).

The ceiling (Fig. 169) reveal its Gothic source in its general wheel shape, the lancets, quatrefoils, and cusps; but the delicacy and complex linear rhythm are also characteristic of Adam's classical designs. The colouring, too, is rather typical of Adam, much more so than of medieval stained glass. Adam proposed yellow and brown main tracery and white minor tracery with inner lancets and smaller quatrefoils of light blue, larger lancets of pink, large quatrefoils of green,

and purple half-quatrefoils around the perimeter.

In the chimney-piece (Fig. 170), Adam's Neo-classicisms are much more apparent. The three-cusped opening, the capitals, and some of the mouldings are the only obviously unclassical features. Adam did use Edward the Confessor's shrine for inspiration, but he classicized much of what he borrowed. The powerful and angular twisted columns were softened and made more antique, the circles and even guilloche were domesticated into a typical Adam pattern, and the diamond shapes were transformed into a frieze pattern not at all unlike such characteristic Adam friezes as that in the Red Drawing Room at Harewood. The bell-flowers above the capitals and on the shafts and some of the mouldings are familiar Adam details. The whole process is in a sense analogous to Adam's adaptation of antique sources, for one sees, as always, the refining hand of Adam making of his inspiration something more delicate, elegant, and characteristically eighteenth-century. Actually, Adam's first design for the Strawberry Hill chimney-piece (Soane Mus., Vol. 22, No. 228; 1766) is considerably closer to St. Edward's shrine. In general, it is basically similar to the 1767 design illustrated here, but both the inner border and the frieze are more directly related to the tomb in Westminster Abbey. This is especially evident in the frieze, which follows that of the shrine with only slight modification. On the whole, however, even the first scheme reflects the elegant refinement of Adam. There are two large-scale partly coloured details for the design in Fig. 170 (Soane Mus., Vol. 18, Nos. 59 and 61), showing the fine quality of Adam's designs in the Gothic style.

Both of these designs were executed and are still extant in the Beauclerk Room at Strawberry Hill.

171. HULNE ABBEY, NORTHUMBER-LAND. Window and entablature detail, c1778.
172. HULNE ABBEY, NORTHUMBER-LAND. Chimney-piece, c1778.

Despite the loss of Adam's more elaborate and extensive Gothic decorations at Alnwick Castle, Hulne Abbey on the Alnwick estate still retains its Neo-medieval decoration. These features are probably part of the designs listed under 10 June 1778 in Adam's bill to the Duke of Northumberland, when he charged £17. 17. 0 for a section of the four sides and a ceiling for 'a

Room in the Gothick Stile' (Alnwick Castle Archives, U. I. 46). Both elements recall the light, fanciful Gothic employed for the library at Alnwick, *c*1769 or a little later (Fig. 168), a Gothic style that is characterized at the same time by the linear delicacy of Adam's Neo-classical manner. The delicacy is especially evident in the tracery of the window reveal, but it is also seen in the small-scale repeat of the frieze and series of arches beneath it (Fig. 171). This row of arches and the ogee arch with crockets and finial are also used in the chimney-piece (Fig. 172). The profusion of lancets on the chimney-piece is reminiscent of another of Adam's Gothic designs, the ceiling for Strawberry Hill (Fig. 169). The chimney-piece frieze at Hulne Abbey illustrates Adam's ingenuity at incorporating the emblems of his patron in his designs. The crescents used here, and in the room freize, are Northumberland insignia, while the ducal coronet and the *H* between inverted *D*'s are tributes to Hugh, Duke of Northumberland. As presently existing, the stucco decoration is white and the chimney-piece cream against yellow walls.

173. J.-M. MOREAU LE JEUNE. Fête at Louveciennes, 1771. Cabinet des Dessins, Musée du Louvre, Paris.

This watercolour illustrates the interior of Mme. du Barry's pavilion at Louveciennes, designed for her in 1770 by C. -N. Ledoux and built in the following year. The celebration depicted by Moreau was the official inauguration of the pavilion, which is an excellent example of fully-developed Neo-classicism in France. As such, it makes a striking comparison with Adam. While both the Louveciennes pavilion and an Adam interior of the late 1760's or early 1770's (*e.g.*, Kenwood or Wynn House, Figs. 33 or 39) represent characteristic and assured Neo-classicism, they are not really alike. The large ceiling painting, pronounced coffers, colossal pilasters, simple rectangular mirrors, and relatively high-relief stucco panels are quite at variance with that which one would find in Adam work of the same date. The spirit—elegant, refined, and classical—is the same, as are some of the details, but the total effect is different.

INDEX

(italic figures refer to Notes to Plates, bold figures to Plates)

1.   OSTERLEY PARK, MIDDLESEX. Design for a chimney-board for the Etruscan Dressing Room, 1777 (*Sir John Soane's Museum*).

2. WILLIAM ADAM. ARNISTON, MIDLOTHIAN. Hall, begun c1726.

3. ADAM BROTHERS. DUMFRIES HOUSE, AYRSHIRE. Drawing room, *c*1754–59.

4.   ADAM BROTHERS. HOPETOUN HOUSE, WEST LOTHIAN. Yellow Drawing Room, ceiling detail, begun *c*1752

5. ADAM BROTHERS. HOPETOUN HOUSE, WEST LOTHIAN. Red Drawing Room, ceiling, *c*1754–60.

6. ADAM BROTHERS. ARNISTON, MIDLOTHIAN. Drawing room, ceiling, begun *c*1754.

7. ADAM BROTHERS. ARNISTON, MIDLOTHIAN. Drawing room, ceiling detail, begun c1754.

8. Reconstruction based on Roman baths, *c*1755–57 (*Sir John Soane's Museum*).

Sketch of a Section for the Earl of Northamptons Hall

at Castle Ashby

4 June 1759

9.   CASTLE ASHBY, NORTHAMPTONSHIRE. Sketch design for the hall, 1759 (*Sir John Soane's Museum*).

10. CASTLE ASHBY, NORTHAMPTONSHIRE. Design for the hall, 1759 (*Sir John Soane's Museum*).

11. THISTLEWORTH HOUSE, MIDDLESEX. Design for the drawing room, 1758 (*Sir John Soane's Museum*).

12.   HATCHLANDS, SURREY. Design for the great dining room, 1759 (*Sir John Soane's Museum*).

13. SHARDELOES, BUCKINGHAMSHIRE. Dining room, *c*1761–64.

14.   SYON HOUSE, MIDDLESEX. Entrance hall, begun *c*1761.

15. Syon House, Middlesex. Long gallery, *c*1763–68.

16. SYON HOUSE, MIDDLESEX. Ante-room, *c*1761–65.

17. TROPHY OF OCTAVIANUS AUGUSTUS (Trophy of Marius). Roman Imperial
sculpture (G. B. Piranesi, *Trofèi di Ottaviano Augusto*).

L

18. SYON HOUSE, MIDDLESEX. Dining room, *c*1761–69.

19. SYON HOUSE, MIDDLESEX. Long gallery, detail, *c*1763–68.

20. CROOME COURT, WORCESTERSHIRE. Gallery, 1761–*c*1766.

21.   KEDLESTON HALL, DERBYSHIRE. Hall, *c*1761–70.

22.　Kedleston Hall, Derbyshire. Drawing room, begun 1760.

23. KEDLESTON HALL, DERBYSHIRE. Dining room, begun 1760.

24. KEDLESTON HALL, DERBYSHIRE. Saloon, begun *c*1761.

25. SYON HOUSE, MIDDLESEX. Design for the circular closet off the long gallery, 1764
(*Sir John Soane's Museum*).

Section through Osterly House from West to East

26.   OSTERLEY PARK, MIDDLESEX. Cross-section of the first scheme, 1761 (*Drawing at Osterley*).

27. OSTERLEY PARK, MIDDLESEX. Hall, designed 1767–68.

28.   OSTERLEY PARK, MIDDLESEX. Design for the dining room, *c*1766–68 (*Sir John Soane's Museum*).

29. OSTERLEY PARK, MIDDLESEX. Dining room, *c*1766–68.

30. LANSDOWNE (SHELBURNE) HOUSE, BERKELEY SQ., LONDON. Design for the ante-room, detail, 1766 (*Sir John Soane's Museum*).

31.   LANSDOWNE (SHELBURNE) HOUSE, BERKELEY SQ., LONDON. Dining room, 1766–68 (*As re-installed in the Metropolitan Museum of Art, New York, Rogers Fund*, 1932).

32.   HAREWOOD HOUSE, YORKSHIRE. Music room, c1765–71.

33. KENWOOD, HAMPSTEAD, LONDON. Library, 1767–69.

34.   KEDLESTON HALL, DERBYSHIRE. Design for the painted breakfast room, 1768 (*Sir John Soane's Museum*

35.   NEWBY HALL, YORKSHIRE. Entrance hall, *c*1769–72.

36. OSTERLEY PARK, MIDDLESEX. Drawing room, begun late 1760's—completed by 1773.

37.   PALMYRA, TEMPLE OF THE SUN. Soffit, early first century A.D. (R. Wood, *Ruins of Palmyra*).

38.   Wynn House, 20 St. James's Sq., London. Stairhall, c1772–74.

39.   WYNN HOUSE, 20 ST. JAMES'S SQ., LONDON. Music room, 1772–c1776.

40.　LLOYD'S COFFEE HOUSE, LONDON. Design for the interior, 1772 (*Sir John Soane's Museum*).

DERBY HOUSE, 23 (later 26) GROSVENOR SQ., LONDON. Great drawing room, *c*1773 (R. & J. Adam, *Works in Architecture*).

42.   NORTHUMBERLAND HOUSE, CHARING CROSS, LONDON. Design for the Glass Drawing Room, *c*1773 (*Sir John
Soane's Museum*).

43.   NORTHUMBERLAND HOUSE, CHARING CROSS, LONDON. Detail of the Glass Drawing Room, *c*1773–75 (*Victoria and Albert Museum*).

44.   OSTERLEY PARK, MIDDLESEX. Tapestry Room, c1772–76.

. HOME HOUSE, 20 PORTMAN SQ., LONDON. Design for the Etruscan Bedroom, c1775 (*Sir John Soane's Museum*).

46.   OSTERLEY PARK, MIDDLESEX. Etruscan Dressing Room, 1775–77.

47. GIOVANNI BATTISTA PIRANESI. Design for a chimney-piece and wall (*Diverse maniere d'adornare i cammini . . .* , 1769).

48. HOME HOUSE, 20 PORTMAN SQ., LONDON. Stairhall, 1775–77.

49. HOME HOUSE, 20 PORTMAN SQ., LONDON. Stairhall, 1775–77.

50.   HOME HOUSE, 20 PORTMAN SQ., LONDON. Design for the stairhall, *c*1775 (*Sir John Soane's Museum*).

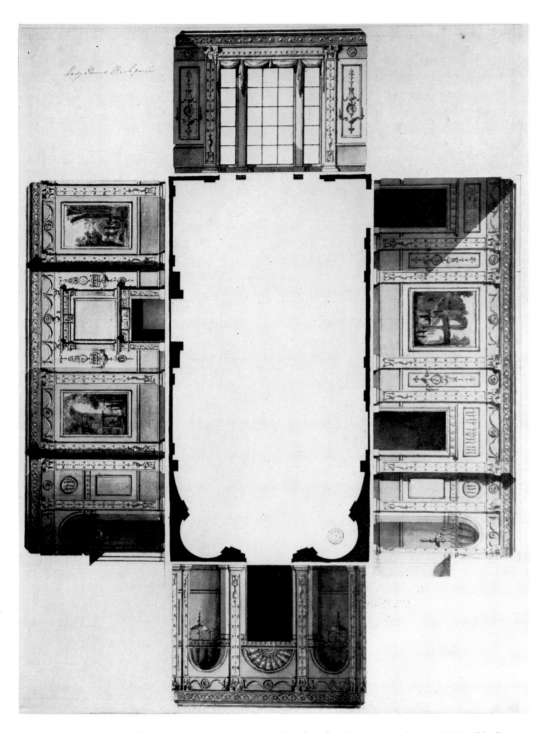

51.   HOME HOUSE, 20 PORTMAN SQ., LONDON. Design for the rear parlour, c1775 (*Sir John Soane's Museum*).

52. HOME HOUSE, 20 PORTMAN SQ., LONDON. Music room, *c*1775–77.

53.   WORMLEYBURY, HERTFORDSHIRE. Dining room, 1777–79.

54.   No. 17 Hill St., London. Design for the great drawing room, detail, 1779 (*Sir John Soane's Museum*)

55. BYRAM HALL, YORKSHIRE. Design for the drawing room, detail, *c*1780 (*Sir John Soane's Museum*).

56. CUMBERLAND HOUSE, PALL MALL, LONDON. Design for the great dining room, 1780 (*Sir John Soar Museum*).

Drawing Room for the Duke of Cumberland

7. CUMBERLAND HOUSE, PALL MALL, LONDON. Design for the third drawing room, *c*1780 (*Sir John Soane's Museum*).

58.   DESIGN FOR AN OPERA HOUSE, HAYMARKET, LONDON, *c*1789 (*Sir John Soane's Museum*).

59. NEWBY HALL, YORKSHIRE. Sculpture gallery, c1767–72.

60. ARCHERFIELD, EAST LOTHIAN. Design for the drawing room, *c*1790–91 (*Sir John Soane's Museum*).

61. HAREWOOD HOUSE, YORKSHIRE. Music room, decorative detail, c1766–70.

62. SYON HOUSE, MIDDLESEX. Ante-room, decorative detail, *c*1761–65.

63. Erechtheum, Athens. Detail of Ionic capital, 421–405 B.C. (J.-D. Le Roy, *Les ruines . . . de la Grèce*).

64. Antique Roman Capital and Entablature (Charles Cameron, *The Baths of the Romans*).

65. SALTRAM HOUSE, DEVON. Saloon doorway, *c*1768–71.

Plate XLIX

Pannels of the Arched Cieling of the Temple of Æsculapius

Capital and Pilaster in the Angle of the Peristylium

66. DIOCLETIAN'S PALACE, SPALATO. Detail of capital, *circa* A.D.300 (R. Adam, *Ruins of . . . Spalatro*).

67.   CULZEAN CASTLE, AYRSHIRE. Long drawing room, doorway detail, c1778–82.

68.   HOME HOUSE, 20 PORTMAN SQ., LONDON. Rear parlour, detail, c1775–77.

69. OSTERLEY PARK, MIDDLESEX. Etruscan Dressing Room, doorway, 1775–77.

70. CROOME COURT, WORCESTERSHIRE. Gallery, detail, 1761–c1764.

71. FORUM OF TRAJAN, ROME. Frieze, early second century A.D. (*Lateran Museum, Rome*).

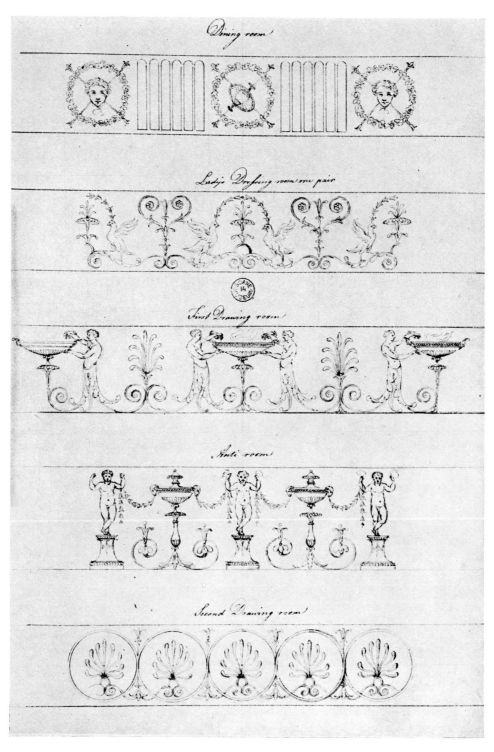

72.   GEORGE HOBART'S HOUSE, 33 ST. JAMES'S SQ., LONDON. Designs for friezes, *c*1770–72
(*Sir John Soane's Museum*).

Frieze for the Great Dining room at Cumberland House.   *Adelphi 29. August 1780.*

3   CUMBERLAND HOUSE, PALL MALL, LONDON. Design for the frieze in the great dining room, 1780 (*Sir John Soane's Museum*).

74. RAPHAEL AND ASSISTANTS. VATICAN *LOGGIE*, ROME. Detail,
second decade of the sixteenth century.

75. OSTERLEY PARK, MIDDLESEX. Dining room, grotesque panel, c1766–68.

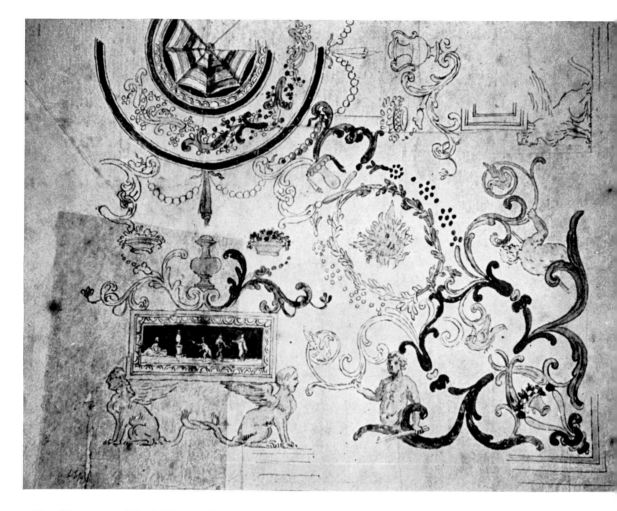

76. 'PALAZZO DI TITO' (DOMUS AUREA), ROME. Decorative detail. Copy after Pietro Santi Bartoli, probably eighteenth century (*Royal Institute of British Architects*).

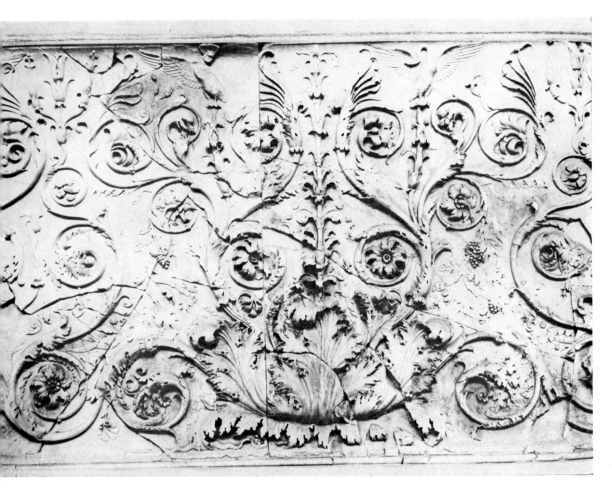

77. ARA PACIS AUGUSTAE, ROME. Foliage panel, 13–9 B.C.

78. JAMES STUART. SPENCER HOUSE, ST. JAMES'S, LONDON. Design for the Painted Room, 1759 (*British Museum*).

Decoration du Salon du côté de la Poele

79. CHARLES–LOUIS CLÉRISSEAU. HÔTEL GRIMOD DE LA REYNIÈRE, PARIS. Salon, *c*1769–82. Drawing by J.-C. Kamsetzer, 1782 (*University Library, Warsaw*).

80. Kenwood, Hampstead, London. Library, decorative detail, 1767–69.

81. HAREWOOD HOUSE, YORKSHIRE. Saloon, alcove detail, designed 1767.

82.　Wynn House, 20 St. James's Sq., London. Music room, decorative detail, 1772–*c*1776.

83.   DERBY HOUSE, 23 (later 26) GROSVENOR SQ., LONDON. Great drawing
room, design for door panel, 1774 (*Sir John Soane's Museum*).

84.   HOME HOUSE, 20 PORTMAN SQ., LONDON. Music room, alcove detail, c1775–77.

85.   HOME HOUSE, 20 PORTMAN SQ., LONDON. Rear parlour, doorway detail, *c*1775–77.

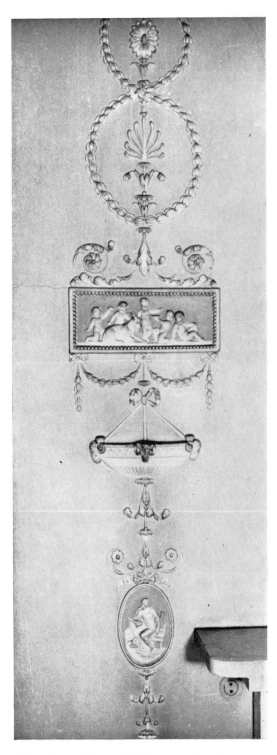

86. HOME HOUSE, 20 PORTMAN SQ., LONDON.
Rear parlour, decorative detail, c1775–77.

87.   HOME HOUSE, 20 PORTMAN SQ., LONDON. Design for one end of the music room, showing the organ, 1775
(*Sir John Soane's Museum*).

88. KEDLESTON HALL, DERBYSHIRE. Design for an organ case for the music room, *c*1758–61 (*Sir John Soane's Museum*).

Design of an Organ Case for His Royal Highness The Duke of Cumberland.

89. CUMBERLAND HOUSE, PALL MALL, LONDON. Design for an organ case, 1781 (*Sir John Soane's Museum*).

90. CROOME COURT, WORCESTERSHIRE. Library, bookcase, 1761–65.

91. NOSTELL PRIORY, YORKSHIRE. Library, c1766–67.

92.   OSTERLEY PARK, MIDDLESEX. Library, begun *c*1766.

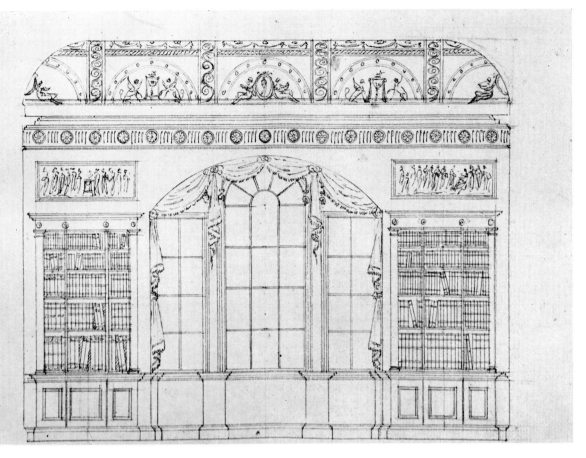

93.   ARCHERFIELD, EAST LOTHIAN. Design for the library, *c*1790–91 (*Sir John Soane's Museum*).

94.   ADAM BROTHERS. HOPETOUN HOUSE, WEST LOTHIAN. Red Drawing Room, chimney-piece, *c*1755–56.

95. MICHAEL RYSBRACK. DESIGN FOR A CHIMNEY-PIECE, probably for Hopetoun
House, c1756 (*Victoria and Albert Museum*).

96. MICHAEL RYSBRACK. DESIGN FOR A CHIMNEY-PIECE, probably for Hopetoun
House, c1756 (*Victoria and Albert Museum*).

97.   Isaac Ware. Chesterfield House, London. Great drawing room, chimney-piece, *c*1748–50 (*Metropolitan Museum of Art, New York, Gift of the Hearst Foundation, 1956*).

98.   HATCHLANDS, SURREY. Great dining room, chimney-piece, *c*1759.

Chimney Piece for the Drawing Room at Shardiloes

99.   SHARDELOES, BUCKINGHAMSHIRE. Design for the drawing room chimney-piece, 1761 (*Sir John Soane's Museum*).

100.   SHARDELOES, BUCKINGHAMSHIRE. Drawing room, chimney-piece, 1761–c1764.

101.   SHARDELOES, BUCKINGHAMSHIRE. Dining room, chimney-piece, 1761–c1764.

102.   COVENTRY HOUSE, 29 (now 106) PICCADILLY, LONDON. Lady Coventry's dressing room,
chimney-piece, 1766–67.

Design of a Chimney Piece for the Dining Room at Gawthorp.

103. HAREWOOD HOUSE, YORKSHIRE. Design for a chimney-piece for the dining room, 1766 (*Sir John Soane Museum*).

Chimney Piece for the Bed Chamber at Rob.t Child Esq.r in Berkly Square

104.   No. 38 BERKELEY SQ., LONDON. Design for a chimney-piece for the bed chamber, 1769 (*Sir John Soane's Museum*).

Chimney Piece for the Salon at Nostel

1772.

105. NOSTELL PRIORY, YORKSHIRE. Design for a chimney-piece for the saloon, 1772 (*Sir John Soane's Museum*).

Chimney Piece for Lady Williams Wynn's Dressing room

106. Wynn House, 20 St. James's Sq., London. Design for a chimney-piece for Lady Williams-Wynn's dressing room, 1772 (*Sir John Soane's Museum*).

107. WYNN HOUSE, 20 ST. JAMES'S SQ., LONDON. First drawing room, chimney-piece, 1772–c1774.

108.   GIOVANNI BATTISTA PIRANESI. Design for a chimney-piece (*Diverse maniere d'adornare i cammini* . . .
1769).

109. NORTHUMBERLAND HOUSE, CHARING CROSS, LONDON. Design for a chimney-piece and overmantel for the Glass Drawing Room, 1773 (*Sir John Soane's Museum.*)

110.   HOME HOUSE, 20 PORTMAN SQ., LONDON. Front parlour, chimney-piece and overmantel, 1775–77.

111. HOME HOUSE, 20 PORTMAN SQ., LONDON. Etruscan Room, chimney-piece, 1775–77.

112.   CUMBERLAND HOUSE, PALL MALL, LONDON. Design for a chimney-piece for the great dining room, 1780
(*Sir John Soane's Museum*).

113.   CULZEAN CASTLE, AYRSHIRE. Long drawing room, chimney-piece, designed 1778.

114. NEWLISTON, WEST LOTHIAN. Bedroom, chimney-piece, *c*1789–92.

115.   THISTLEWORTH HOUSE, MIDDLESEX. Design for the drawing room ceiling, 1759 (*Sir John Soane's Museum*).

Ceiling for the Earl of Hertford's Drawing room in Grosvenor Street

16. NO. 16 LOWER GROSVENOR ST., LONDON. Design for the drawing room ceiling, 1761 (*Sir John Soane's Museum*).

117. HATCHLANDS, SURREY. Design for the drawing room ceiling, 1759 (*Sir John Soane's Museum*).

118. HATCHLANDS, SURREY. Drawing room, ceiling detail, 1759–61.

119. VILLA PAMPHILI (now DORIA-PAMPHILI), ROME, c1644–52. Drawing of a panel of a dome (*Sir John Soane's Museum*).

120.   SHARDELOES, BUCKINGHAMSHIRE. Hall, ceiling, 1761–63.

121.   CROOME COURT, WORCESTERSHIRE. Tapestry Room, ceiling, *c*1763 (*As re-installed in the Metropolitan Museum of Art, New York, Gift of the Kress Foundation, 1958–59*).

122.   SHARDELOES, BUCKINGHAMSHIRE. Dining room, ceiling, 1761–63.

123. OSTERLEY PARK, MIDDLESEX. Dining room, ceiling, c1766–68.

124. SYON HOUSE, MIDDLESEX. Entrance hall, ceiling, c1761.

125. SYON HOUSE, MIDDLESEX. Drawing room, ceiling detail, 1762–64.

126.   AUDLEY END, ESSEX. Design for a ceiling for the little drawing room, 1763 (*Audley End*).

Plate LVII.　　　　　　　　　　　　　　　Planche LVII.

Ceiling at the Palace of **AUGUSTUS**.　　　Plafond du Palais d'**AUGUSTE**.

127. BATHS (or PALACE) OF AUGUSTUS, ROME (Charles Cameron, *The Baths of the Romans*).

Ceiling of a room at Mrs Montagus House in Hill Street

128. MRS. MONTAGU'S HOUSE, HILL ST., LONDON. Design for a ceiling, 1766 (*Sir John Soane's Museum*).

129.   Mrs. Montagu's House, Hill St., London. Design for a carpet, *c*1766 (*Sir John Soane's Museum*).

130.   MERSHAM-LE-HATCH, KENT. Drawing room, ceiling detail, designed 1766.

131. HAREWOOD HOUSE, YORKSHIRE. Saloon, ceiling detail, 1767–c1770.

132. HAREWOOD HOUSE, YORKSHIRE. Design for the ceiling of the gentleman's dressing room, 1767 (*Sir John Soane's Museum*).

133.   HAREWOOD HOUSE, YORKSHIRE. Alternate design for the ceiling of the gentleman's dressing room, 1767 (*Sir John Soane's Museum*).

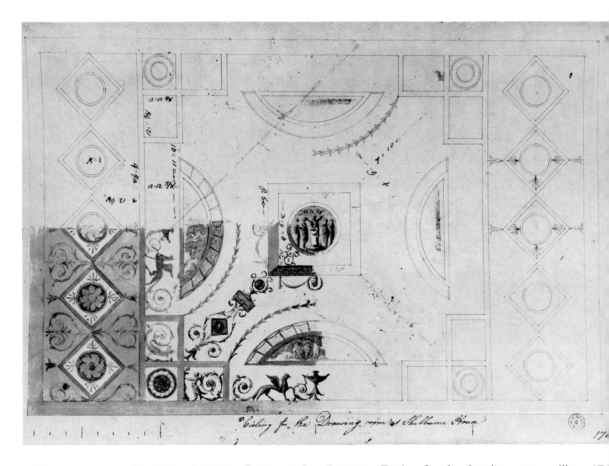

134.   LANSDOWNE (SHELBURNE) HOUSE, BERKELEY SQ., LONDON. Design for the drawing room ceiling, 176
(*Sir John Soane's Museum*).

135.   LANSDOWNE (SHELBURNE) HOUSE, BERKELEY SQ., LONDON. Drawing room, ceiling, 1767–73 (*As re-installed in the Philadelphia Museum of Art*).

136.   Eglington House, 79 Piccadilly, London. Desing for a ceiling for the great room, 1769 (*Sir Joh*
Soane's Museum).

137. NORTHUMBERLAND HOUSE, CHARING CROSS, LONDON. Design for the drawing room ceiling, 1770 (*Sir John Soane's Museum*).

Ceiling of the 1.st Drawing room at Chandos House

138.   CHANDOS HOUSE, CHANDOS ST., LONDON. Design for the ceiling of the first drawing room, 1771 (*Sir John Soane's Museum*).

139. HAREWOOD HOUSE, YORKSHIRE. Gallery, ceiling detail, *c*1769–70.

140. HAREWOOD HOUSE, YORKSHIRE. Gallery, *c*1765–77.

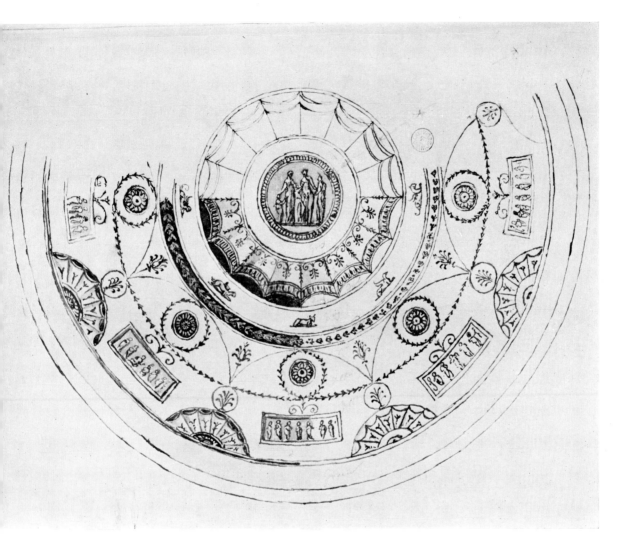

141.   Mrs. Fitzroy's Circular Dressing Room, Near Southampton. Design for a ceiling, 1774 (*Sir John Soane's Museum*).

142. BOLTON HOUSE, 26 SOUTHAMPTON ROW (later in RUSSELL SQ.), LONDON. Design for the ceiling of the Duchess of Bolton's dressing room, 1770 (*Sir John Soane's Museum*).

143.   CEMETERY OF ST. CALIXTUS, NEAR ROME. Vault in the crypt of Lucina, *circa* A.D.220.

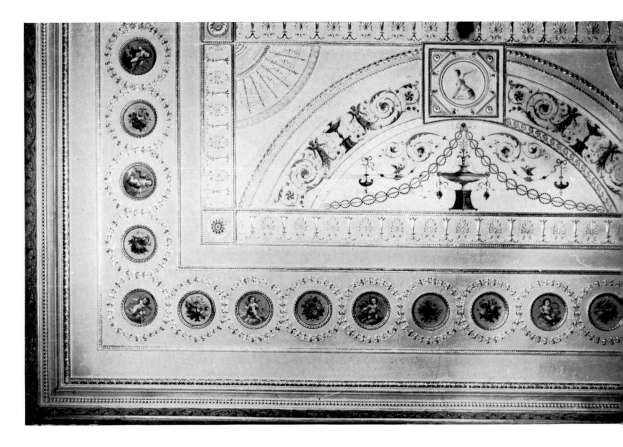

144.   HOME HOUSE, 20 PORTMAN SQ., LONDON. Rear drawing room, ceiling detail, 1775–77.

145. WORMLEYBURY, HERTFORDSHIRE. Dining room, ceiling detail, 1777–79.

146. DRURY LANE THEATRE, LONDON. Design for the ceiling, 1776 (*Sir John Soane's Museum*).

147.   REGISTER HOUSE, EDINBURGH. Detail of interior of the dome, *c*1771–85.

148. WEALD HALL, ESSEX. Design for the eating room ceiling, 1778 (*Sir John Soane's Museum*).

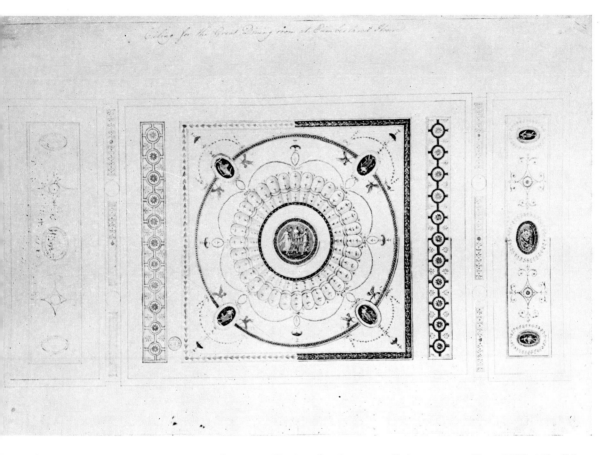

49. CUMBERLAND HOUSE, PALL MALL, LONDON. Design for the great dining room ceiling, 1780 (*Sir John Soane's Museum*).

150.   ARCHERFIELD, EAST LOTHIAN. Design for the drawing room ceiling, c1790–91 (*Sir John Soane's Museum*).

Carpet for Sir Nathaniel Curzon Baronet

151.   KEDLESTON HALL, DERBYSHIRE. Design for a carpet, *c*1758–61 (*Sir John Soane's Museum*).

152.   SYON HOUSE, MIDDLESEX. Design for the Ante-room pavement, *c*1761 (*Sir John Soane's Museum*).

153. WORMLEYBURY, HERTFORDSHIRE. Design for the dining room carpet, 1778 (*Sir John Soane's Museum*).

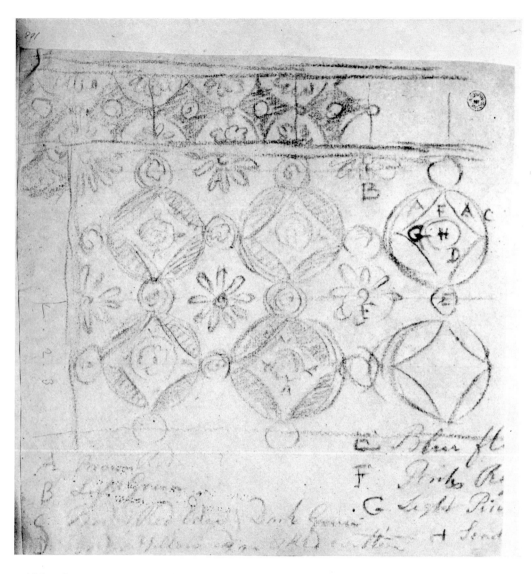

154.   COVENTRY HOUSE, 29 (now 106) PICCADILLY, LONDON. Sketch design for a carpet, *c*1767
(*Sir John Soane's Museum*).

Carpet for The Earl of Coventry

155.   COVENTRY HOUSE, 29 (now 106) PICCADILLY, LONDON. Office copy of a rendering for a carpet, offering
alternate colour schemes, c1767 (*Sir John Soane's Museum*).

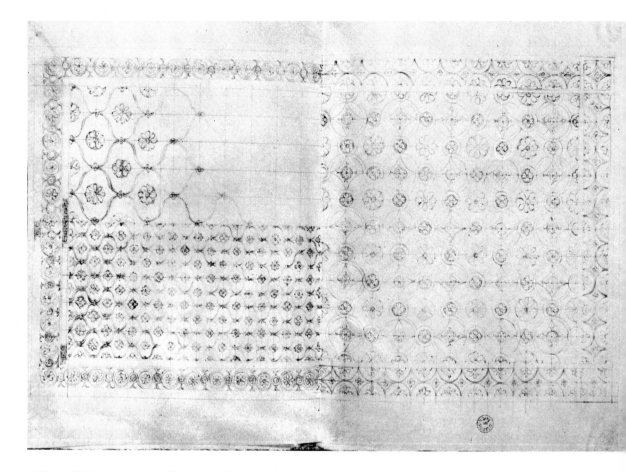

156. *Right:* COVENTRY HOUSE, 29 (now 106) PICACDILLY, LONDON. Pencil design for a carpet. *Left:* SYON HOUSE, MIDDLESEX. Pencil design for the gallery carpet, with small- and large-scale details, *c*1767 (*Sir John Soane's Museum*).

157.   COVENTRY HOUSE, 29 (now 106) PICCADILLY, LONDON. Large-scale detail of design for a carpet, *c*1767
(detail) (*Sir John Soane's Museum*).

158. *Left:* COVENTRY HOUSE, 29 (now 106) PICCADILLY, LONDON. Large-scale detail of design for a carpet.
Right: SYON HOUSE, MIDDLESEX. Large-scale detail of design for the gallery carpet, *c*1767 (*Sir John Soane's Museum*).

159. WYNN HOUSE, 20 ST. JAMES'S SQ., LONDON. Stair railing, *c*1772–74.

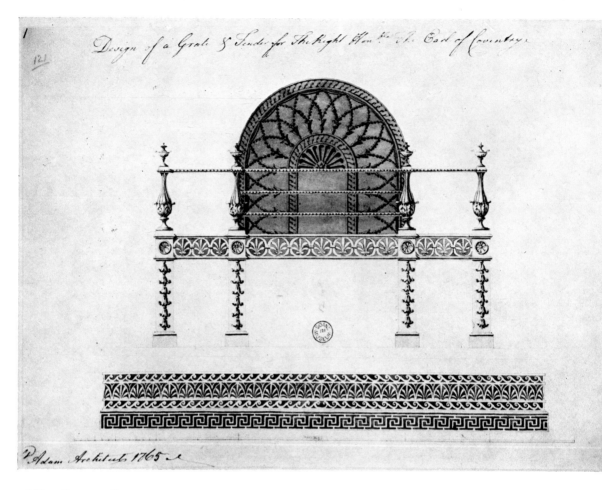

160.   CROOME COURT, WORCESTERSHIRE. Design of a grate and fender for the gallery, 1765 (*Sir John Soane's Museum*).

161. WYNN HOUSE, 20 ST. JAMES'S SQ., LONDON. Design of a candelabrum, 1773 (*Sir John Soane's Museum*).

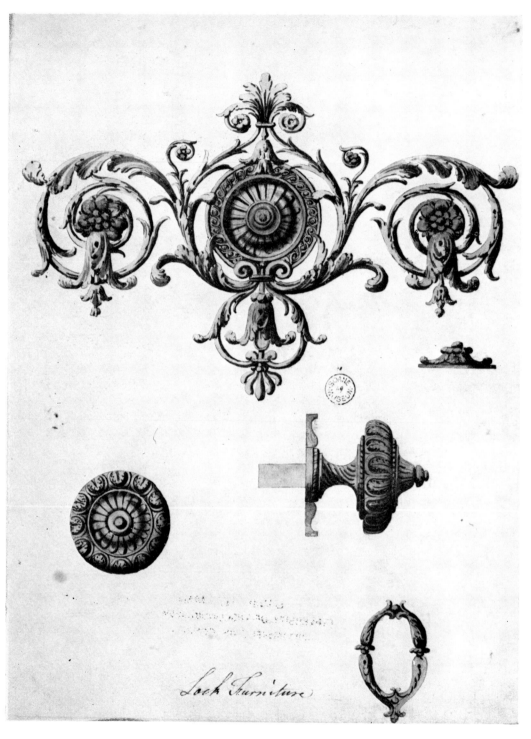

162. DESIGN FOR DOOR FURNITURE, possibly for Osterley Park, Middlesex, *c*1770 (*Sir John Soane's Museum*).

163.   OSTERLEY PARK, MIDDLESEX. Tapestry Room, detail of door furniture and panel,
mid-1770's

164. KEDLESTON HALL, DERBYSHIRE. Saloon, wall sconce, c1761–70.

Curtain Cornice for the Great Drawing Room at Lord Stanley's in Grosvenor Square Adelphi September 15th 1774

165. DERBY HOUSE, 23 (later 26) GROSVENOR SQ., LONDON. Design for a curtain cornice in the great drawing room, 1774 (*Sir John Soane's Museum*).

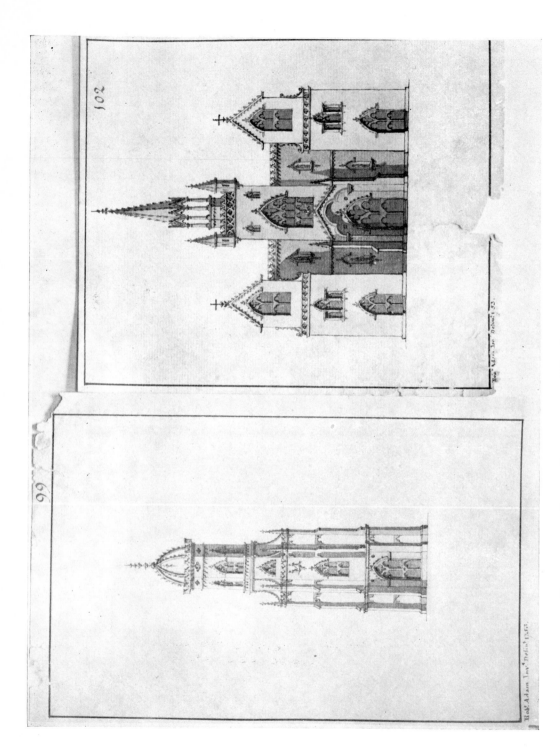

166.   DESIGN FOR A TOWER IN THE GOTHIC STYLE,
1753 (*Blair Adam Collection*).

167.   DESIGN FOR A HOUSE IN THE GOTHIC STYLE, 1753
(*Blair Adam Collection*).

168. ALNWICK CASTLE, NORTHUMBERLAND. Design for the library, *c*1769 or slightly later (*Sir John Soane's Museum*).

Ceiling for the Honorable Horace Walpole Esq.

Scale of ——————————————————————— *feet*   1766

169.   STRAWBERRY HILL, MIDDLESEX. Design for a ceiling, 1766 (*Sir John Soane's Museum*).

Defigne of a Chimney Piece for the Honorable Horace Walpole

170.   STRAWBERRY HILL, MIDDLESEX. Design for a chimney-piece, 1767 (*Sir John Soane's Museum*).

171.   HULNE ABBEY, NORTHUMBERLAND. Window and entablature detail, *c*1778.

172. Hulne Abbey, Northumberland, Chimney-piece, *c*1778.

173.   J.-M. MOREAU LE JEUNE. FÊTE AT LOUVECIENNES, 1771 (*Louvre, Paris*).